More praise for *The Investor's Anthology*

"Investors should learn the lessons of history well. Human behavior—as it fluctuates in auction market dynamics—has not, and will not, change. Henry David Thoreau put it this way in 1854: 'Every generation laughs at the old fashioned, but follows religiously the new.' Reading this carefully selected collection of thoughtful works will help prevent errors of the past from creeping into the future."

Arthur Zeikel
President
Merrill Lynch Asset Management

"This is a remarkable collection of short, clear, and incisive commentaries on both the art and the practical realities of investments. There is food for thought in each of the small offerings in this wonderful banquet laid out for those who would understand the world of investments."

Jay O. Light
Professor of Business Administration
Harvard University

"A cornucopia of investment perspectives that will delight the appetite and challenge the mind of any investor."

Gary P. Brinson
President and Managing Partner
Brinson Partners, Inc.

"For the past 35 years, Charley Ellis has been the most consistently thoughtful and provocative observer of the markets that I have known. He makes you think."

Richard H. Jenrette
Senior Advisor
Donaldson, Lufkin & Jenrette, Inc.

The Investor's Anthology

The Investor's Anthology

Original Ideas from the Industry's Greatest Minds

Charles D. Ellis
with James R. Vertin

John Wiley & Sons, Inc.

New York • Chichester • Weinheim • Brisbane • Singapore • Toronto

Copyright © 1997 by Charles D. Ellis with James R. Vertin.
Published by John Wiley & Sons, Inc.

Library of Congress Cataloging-in-Publication Data:

Ellis, Charles D.
    The investor's anthology :   original ideas from the industry's
greatest minds /   Charles D. Ellis with James R. Vertin.
       p.   cm.
    Includes index.
    ISBN 0-471-17605-2 (alk. paper)
    1. Investments—United States. 2. Stock exchanges. I. Vertin,
James R. II. Title.
HG4910.E463   1997
332.6—dc20   96-46166

For Allan Munro and Rodger Smith,
David Fox and Peter Garrison

With great admiration and affectionate appreciation
of our many years as partners building Greenwich Associates.

Preface

Welcome! This book is your invitation into the "global village" of investment management, where you will join those who are already initiated as adventurers in the exploration of investment concepts, ideas, and techniques. The articles contained in this anthology are from such masters of the game as Ben Graham, Warren Buffett, John Maynard Keynes, Bob Kirby, Roy Neuberger, Claude Rosenberg, Dave Babson, Sidney Homer, Phil Fisher, and T. Rowe Price.

While constantly competing with each other in pursuit of good investment results for their clients, you will find the members of this community are bound together by their continual commitment to learning; their long history of sharing ideas and information; their informal "first-name" ways of getting together in personal meetings and over the telephone; their interest in teaching through books and articles, through academic and professional courses, and the Chartered Financial Analyst program of the AIMR (which has certified nearly 30,000 professionals and has even more enrolled in the strenuous, three-year course of study and examinations leading to the CFA charter); and their sustaining commitment to high, professional standards in a community that is socially very democratic, while professionally an uncompromising meritocracy.

One of the truly great free markets in the world is the free market for ideas that work. The pursuit of investment wisdom and good investment results—linked through advanced information technology—makes the community of investors one of the most vigorous and effective parts of the Information Age. Far from perfect, we exemplify Piet Hein's amusing description of The Path to Wisdom: "To err and err and err again—but less."

Our wish is that you, too, will enjoy the great personalities and minds that are brought together here—for they are the natural leaders of this great community that has meant so very much to us.

CHARLES D. ELLIS
JAMES R. VERTIN

Greenwich, Connecticut
Portola Valley, California
January 1997

Contents

━━━━━

Part Two   Advice, Opinions, and Commentary

Part Three   Visions and Amusements

Part Four   Innovative Ideas and Proven Paradigms

Part Five   Speculation, Crashes, and Financial Turmoil

Part Six Forecast, Analysis, and Performance Measurement

Part Seven Tips, Rules, and Commandments

Contents
By Author, in Alphabetical Order

The Investor's Anthology

Part One

Concepts and Market History

The Market and Prices

ADAM SMITH

"Value" was a concept that challenged early economists almost to distraction. How could something of such obvious necessity and great usefulness as water, for example, be "worth" next to nothing in terms of either its cost as a commodity or its purchasing power? Adam Smith elegantly explained this phenomenon—and, indirectly, introduced us to the fact that "value" and "price" need not be synonymous—more than 200 years ago.

. . .

The word *value*, it is to be observed, has two different meanings, and sometimes expresses the utility of some particular object, and sometimes the power of purchasing other goods that the possession of that objective conveys. The one may be called *value in use*, the other, *value in exchange*. The things that have the greatest value in use have frequently little or no value in exchange; and, on the contrary, those which have the greatest value in exchange have frequently little or no value in use. Nothing is more useful than water: but it will purchase scarce anything; scarce anything can be had in exchange for it. A diamond, on the contrary, has scarce any value in use; but a very great quantity of other goods may frequently be had in exchange for it.

Reprinted from the *World Journal Tribune*, October 30, 1996, pp. 4–6.

Growth Companies vs. Growth Stocks

PETER L. BERNSTEIN

Peter Bernstein has contributed an impressive share of the accumulated wisdom in investment management. A generation ago, he was teaching investors how to separate growth *companies* from growth *stocks*—a distinction we now know to be crucial in separating the leaders from the followers.

· · ·

The magic words *growth company* are high praise in the business world today. It is perfectly proper for the spotlight to focus on those companies that are either making a significant contribution to, or benefiting greatly from, the vigorous growth patterns of our modern economy. But in order to avoid dangerous oversimplifications and in order to apply the term *growth company* only where it has some useful meaning, the following considerations should be borne in mind:

1. Growth is a dynamic concept. The growth company can never be a passive beneficiary of economic change. Rather it must be an active agent at the technological or geographical frontiers of our society. Thus, it is not enough to be in, say, the chemical or electronic industries; a firm cannot become a growth company "by association." There may be more elements of growth— i.e., market creation—in a company like General Motors than in many chemical or electronic companies.

2. It is a mistake to believe that superior earning power is to be found only among growth companies, but it is a very decisive test for all such firms. Creativity and ambition in product development and merchandising alone are not enough; the

ability to make money out of creativity is certainly at least as important.

3. The enchantment that some growth companies convey to the stock market lends a premium to their common stocks that is not always justified by the statistical background. An investor may do well with such stocks, but there is good reason to believe that he can do even better by giving the financial results— such as those shown by measures of increase-in-earnings power—a completely cold-blooded and objective analysis. No amount of study in this area can minimize the importance of trying to buy at a fair price; buying at any price and hoping that the future will take care of itself is a good shortcut to disappointing results.

Indeed, perhaps the most important conclusion of this analysis is that the term *growth stock* is meaningless; a growth stock can be identified only with hindsight—it is simply a stock that went way up. But the concept of *growth company* can be used to identify the most creative, most imaginative management groups; and if, in addition, their stocks are valued at a reasonable ratio to their increase-in-earnings power over a period of time, the odds are favorable for appreciation in the future.

The Crowd: A Study of the Popular Mind

GUSTAVE LeBON

"A Crowd," explained Gustave LeBon, "is like a savage; it is not prepared to admit that anything can come between its desire and the realization of that desire." Here he explains the "Law of Mental Unity of Crowds" and notes that the existence of a Crowd does "not always involve the simultaneous presence of a number of individuals on one spot."

. . .

In its ordinary sense the word *crowd* means a gathering of individuals of whatever nationality, profession, or sex, and whatever be the chances that have brought them together. From the psychological point of view the expression *crowd* assumes quite a different signification. Under certain given circumstances, and only under those circumstances, an agglomeration of men presents new characteristics very different from those of the individuals composing it. The sentiments and ideas of all the persons in the gathering take one and the same direction, and their conscious personality vanishes. A collective mind is formed, doubtless transitory, but presenting very clearly defined characteristics. The gathering has thus become what, in the absence of a better expression, I will call an *organised crowd*, or, if the term is considered preferable, a *psychological crowd*. It forms a single being and is subjected to the *law of the mental unity of crowds*.

It is evident that it is not by the mere fact of a number of individuals finding themselves accidentally side by side that they acquire the character of an organized crowd. A thousand individuals accidentally gathered in a public place without any determined object in no way con-

From Gustave LeBon, *The Crowd: A Study of the Popular Mind* (London: Unwin Hyman Limited, 1977; originally published 1895), 23–34.

stitute a crowd from the psychological point of view. To acquire the special characteristics of such a crowd, the influence is necessary of certain predisposing causes of which we shall have to determine the nature.

The disappearance of conscious personality and the turning of feelings and thoughts in a different direction, which are the primary characteristics of a crowd about to become organised, do not always involve the simultaneous presence of a number of individuals on one spot. Thousands of isolated individuals may acquire at certain moments, and under the influence of certain violent emotions—such, for example, as a great national event—the characteristics of a psychological crowd. It will be sufficient in that case that a mere chance should bring them together for their acts to at once assume the characteristics peculiar to the acts of a crowd. At certain moments half a dozen men might constitute a psychological crowd, which may not happen in the case of hundreds of men gathered together by accident. On the other hand, an entire nation, though there may be no visible agglomeration, may become a crowd under the action of certain influences. . . .

It being impossible to study here all the successive degrees of organisation of crowds, we shall concern ourselves more especially with such crowds as have attained to the phase of complete organisation. In this way we shall see what crowds may become, but not what they invariably are. It is only in this advanced phase of organisation that certain new and special characteristics are superimposed on the unvarying and dominant character of the race; then takes place that turning already alluded to of all the feelings and thoughts of the collectivity in an identical direction. It is only under such circumstances, too, that what I have called above the *psychological law of the mental unity of crowds comes into play*. . . .

The most striking peculiarity presented by a psychological crowd is the following: Whoever be the individuals that compose it, however like or unlike be their mode of life, their occupations, their character, or their intelligence, the fact that they have been transformed into a crowd puts them in possession of a sort of collective mind that makes them feel, think, and act in a manner quite different from that in which each individual of them would feel, think, and act were he in a state of isolation. There are certain ideas and feelings that do not come into being, or do not transform themselves into acts, except in the case of individuals forming a crowd. The psychological crowd is a provisional being formed of heterogeneous elements, which for a moment are combined, exactly as the cells that constitute a living body form by their reunion a new being that displays characteristics very different from those possessed by each of the cells singly. . . .

It is easy to prove how much the individual forming part of a crowd differs from the isolated individual, but it is less easy to discover the causes of this difference.

To obtain at any rate a glimpse of them it is necessary in the first place to call to mind the truth established by modern psychology, that unconscious phenomena play an altogether preponderating part not only in organic life, but also in the operations of the intelligence. The conscious life of the mind is of small importance in comparison with its unconscious life. The most subtle analyst, the most acute observer, is scarcely successful in discovering more than a very small number of the unconscious motives that determine his conduct. Our conscious acts are the outcome of an unconscious substratum created in the mind in the main by hereditary influences. This substratum consists of the innumerable common characteristics handed down from generation to generation, which constitute the genius of a race. Behind the avowed causes of our acts there undoubtedly lie secret causes that we do not avow, but behind these secret causes there are many others more secret still that we ourselves ignore. The greater part of our daily actions are the result of hidden motives that escape our observation.

It is more especially with respect to those unconscious elements that constitute the genius of a race that all the individuals belonging to it resemble each other, while it is principally in respect to the conscious elements of their character—the fruit of education, and yet more of exceptional hereditary conditions—that they differ from each other. Men the most unlike in the matter of their intelligence possess instincts, passions, and feelings that are very similar. In the case of everything that belongs to the realm of sentiment—religion, politics, morality, the affections and antipathies, etc.—the most eminent men seldom surpass the standard of the most ordinary individuals. From the intellectual point of view an abyss may exist between a great mathematician and his bootmaker, but from the point of view of character, the difference is most often slight or nonexistent.

It is precisely these general qualities of character, governed by forces of which we are unconscious, and possessed by the majority of the normal individuals of a race in much the same degree—it is precisely these qualities, I say, that in crowds, become common property. In the collective mind the intellectual aptitudes of the individuals, and in consequence their individuality, are weakened. The heterogeneous is swamped by the homogeneous, and the unconscious qualities obtain the upper hand.

This very fact that crowds possess in common ordinary qualities explains why they can never accomplish acts demanding a high degree of intelligence. The decisions affecting matters of general interest come to by an assembly of men of distinction, but specialists in different walks of life, are not sensibly superior to the decisions that would be adopted by a gathering of imbeciles. The truth is, they can only bring to bear in common on the work in hand those mediocre qualities which are the birthright of every average individual. In crowds it is stupidity and not mother wit that is accumulated. It is not all the world, as is so often repeated, that has more wit than Voltaire, but assuredly Voltaire that has more wit than all the world, if by "all the world" crowds are to be understood. . . .

Different causes determine the appearance of these characteristics peculiar to crowds, and not possessed by isolated individuals. The first is that the individual forming part of a crowd acquires, solely from numerical considerations, a sentiment of invincible power that allows him to yield to instincts that, had he been alone, he would perforce have kept under restraint. He will be the less disposed to check himself from the consideration that, a crowd being anonymous, and in consequence irresponsible, the sentiment of responsibility that always controls individuals disappears entirely.

The second cause, which is contagion, also intervenes to determine the manifestation in crowds of their special characteristics, and at the same time the trend they are to take. Contagion is a phenomenon of which it is easy to establish the presence, but that it is not easy to explain.

It must be classed among those phenomena of a hypnotic order, which we shall shortly study. In a crowd every sentiment and act is contagious, and contagious to such a degree that an individual readily sacrifices his personal interest to the collective interest. This is an aptitude very contrary to his nature, and of which a man is scarcely capable, except when he makes part of a crowd.

A third cause, and by far the most important, determines in the individuals of a crowd special characteristics that are quite contrary at times to those presented by the isolated individual. I allude to the suggestibility of which, moreover, the contagion mentioned above is neither more nor less than an effect. . . . The conscious personality has entirely vanished; will and discernment are lost. All feelings and thoughts are bent in the direction determined by the crowd itself.

Such is approximately the state of the individual forming part of a psychological crowd. He is no longer conscious of his acts. In his case, as in the case of the hypnotised subject, at the same time that certain faculties are destroyed, others may be brought to a high degree of exaltation. Under the influence of a suggestion, he will undertake the accomplishment of certain acts with irresistible impetuosity. This impetuosity is the more irresistible in the case of crowds than in that of the hypnotised subject, from the fact that, the suggestion being the same for all the individuals of the crowd, it gains in strength by reciprocity. The individualities in the crowd who might possess a personality sufficiently strong to resist the suggestion are too few in number to struggle against the current. At the utmost, they may be able to attempt a diversion by means of different suggestions. It is in this way, for instance, that a happy expression, an image opportunely evoked, has occasionally deterred crowds from the most bloodthirsty acts.

We see, then, that the disappearance of the conscious personality, the predominance of the unconscious personality, the turning by means of suggestion and contagion of feelings and ideas in an identical direction, the tendency immediately to transform the suggested ideas into acts; these, we see, are the principal characteristics of the individual forming part of a crowd. He is no longer himself, but has become an automaton who has ceased to be guided by his will.

Moreover, by the mere fact that he forms part of an organised crowd, a man descends several rungs in the ladder of civilisation. Isolated, he may be a cultivated individual; in a crowd, he is a barbarian—that is, a creature acting by instinct. He possesses the spontaneity, the violence, the ferocity, and also the enthusiasm and heroism of primitive beings, whom he further tends to resemble by the facility with which he allows himself to be impressed by words and images—which would be entirely without action on each of the isolated individuals composing the crowd—and to be induced to commit acts contrary to his most obvious interests and his best-known habits. An individual in a crowd is a grain of sand amid other grains of sand, which the wind stirs up at will.

It is for these reasons that juries are seen to deliver verdicts of which each individual juror would disapprove, that parliamentary assemblies adopt laws and measures of which each of their members would disapprove in his own person. Taken separately, the men of the French Revolutionary Convention were enlightened citizens of peaceful habits. United in a crowd, they did not hesitate to give their adhesion to the most savage proposals, to guillotine individuals most clearly innocent, and, contrary to their interests, to renounce their inviolability and to decimate themselves.

It is not only by his acts that the individual in a crowd differs essentially from himself. Even before he has entirely lost his independence, his ideas and feelings have undergone a transformation, and the transformation is so profound as to change the miser into a spendthrift, the sceptic into a believer, the honest man into a criminal, and the coward into a hero. The renunciation of all its privileges that the French nobility voted in a moment of enthusiasm during the celebrated night of August 4, 1789, would certainly never have been consented to by any of its members taken singly.

The conclusion to be drawn from what precedes is that the crowd is always intellectually inferior to the isolated individual, but that, from the point of view of feelings and of the acts these feelings provoke, the crowd may, according to circumstances, be better or worse than the individual. All depends on the nature of the suggestion to which the crowd is exposed. This is the point that has been completely misunderstood by writers, who have only studied crowds from the criminal point of view. Doubtless a crowd is often criminal, but also it is often heroic. It is crowds rather than isolated individuals that may be induced to run the risk of death to secure the triumph of a creed or an idea, that may be fired with enthusiasm for glory and honour, that are led on—almost without bread and without arms, as in the age of the Crusades—to deliver the tomb of Christ from the infidel, or, as in '93, to defend the fatherland. Such heroism is without doubt somewhat unconscious, but it is of such heroism that history is made. Were peoples only to be credited with the great actions performed in cold blood, the annals of the world would register but few of them.

An Informal History of Interest Rates

SIDNEY HOMER

Did you know that a wife, if pledged for a loan in Babylonia, could be seized by a creditor, or that doors were valuable collateral? Sidney Homer provides summary highlights from his book *A History of Interest Rates* in this easy overview. Those attracted to the full book will be well rewarded.

. . .

Babylonia

In ancient Babylonia, credit was widely used and its terms were closely regulated by the government. The famous Code of Hammurabi, circa 1,800 B.C., established legal maxima for interest on all loans: 20 percent for loans of silver—by weight, there was no coinage—and 33$^1/_3$ percent for loans of grain. Crop failure caused by storm or drought served to cancel interest due on a land loan for that year. A higher-than-legal rate collected by subterfuge served to cancel the debt.

Any property, real or personal, could be pledged—wife, concubine, children, land, houses, utensils, doors. (Wood was very scarce and house doors were valuable.) If the debtor defaulted, the creditor could seize the property hypothecated. If he seized the wife, he must treat her well and return her at the end of three years in as good condition as when she was received. Women's property rights were protected by the Code; the husband alone could not dispose of joint property without the wife's consent. Property could not be sold outside the family except for debt.

Greece

In Attica at the beginning of the sixth century B.C., there was a credit crisis. Farmers were heavily in debt and often could not keep more than a sixth part of their produce. They threatened rebellion. At this point the poet and wise man, Solon, was called upon to assume supreme legislative power for a limited period and revise the laws. His reforms were radical and for the most part they endured. He scaled down many debts, abolished personal slavery for debt, removed all restrictions on rates of interest or other credit terms, devalued the drachma by one-quarter, reapportioned political power according to property and granted citizenship to skilled immigrants. Later on, democracy was established in Athens and Athens soon outdistanced all Greek cities in trade and finance, as in arts and culture.

The Athenians took every precaution to maintain the integrity of their currency, the silver "owls," while most Greek cities engaged in unscrupulous alloying of their coins. Athenian owls, made of silver from rich Athenian mines, became the most acceptable currency throughout the Mediterranean world for 600 years, long after Athens lost her political power. They became a valuable item of export.

In her golden age, Athens became a leading trade center and Athenians invested extensively at home and abroad. Bottomry loans at 20 to 30 percent were popular to finance foreign trade; in these the lender took the risk of disaster at sea and he often went along as a passenger. Speculation in commodities was unpopular as was investment in land. There were private bankers who at times underwrote loans to Greek city-states. The credit standing of the bankers was often better than that of the cities. One city pledged her public colonnades, defaulted, and lost their use. "Of all kinds of capital," said Demosthenes, "the most productive is Confidence and if you don't know that, you don't know anything." Demosthenes charged his clients interest at 12 percent per annum if they delayed paying his legal fees. Even Socrates, the philosopher, had a banker friend to whom he entrusted his investment problems.

In the classical period in Attica ownership of real estate was designated by sunken marking stones called *horoi*, which marked the boundaries. Many of these horoi have been found and studied. The visible half was often engraved, giving notice that the property was encumbered, some said for how much, to whom and at what rate of interest. In the fifth century B.C., these rates were usually 8 to 12 percent but by the late third century B.C., some loans in Athens were quoted as low as 6 percent.

Rome

The Romans were a nation of farmers and soldiers. They left manufacture, commerce, and banking largely to foreigners, mostly to Greeks. Cato said, "How much worse the money lender was considered by our forefathers than the thief." Nevertheless, Cato himself invested in mercantile loans, probably secretly. In the first century B.C., the legal limit on interest was 12 percent. Nevertheless the noble senator Marcus Junius Brutus loaned money to the city of Salamis at 48 percent interest. Cicero, when he heard of the transaction, was shocked and reprimanded Brutus.

Julius Caesar was a daring borrower and financed an important part of his political rise on credit. When he finally ended his wars in complete victory and returned to Rome, he was confronted with three domestic problems: the rapid rise in the cost of living in Italy, the large number of unemployed citizens in Rome, and the deterioration of the Italian soil due to centuries of overly intensive farming. His assassination left these problems for Augustus, his successor.

Roman interest rates, which in early centuries of the republic were limited to $8^{1}/_{3}$ percent and often exceeded these legal limits, came down in the late first century B.C., at a time of peace and prosperity to 4 percent on prime credits. Thereafter as the state was weakened by political chaos and inflation they rose to over 12 percent.

The Middle Ages

After the fall of Rome and especially after the victories of the Arabs in the south and the Norsemen in the north, trade and finance in Europe all but vanished. By the eleventh century it began to revive and the revival was centered in the free cities of northern Europe and Italy that had obtained power and autonomy. They built walls. They were dominated and financed by the new merchant class of burghers.

The credit of the best merchants and free towns was generally much better than the credit of princes. Towns could pledge the wealth of their burghers in perpetuity and had to make good to preserve their sovereignty and credit. So did merchants. Princes on the other hand could not bind their subjects or pledge their successors. Their credit depended on youth, good health, and military success. Thus it was that princely loans were often made at much higher interest rates than prime commercial loans or loans to free cities. "Lend not to him that is mightier than thou."

For example the emperor Frederick II (1211–1250) usually paid 20 to 30 percent interest. Frederick the Fair of Austria (1286–1330) borrowed at 80 percent interest. In 1364 the Countess of Bar pawned her gold coronet for a loan at 50 percent. Again in 1494 Charles VIII of France paid 42, 56, and 100 percent for war loans to finance his invasion of Italy.

In contrast, commercial loans on best private credits in the fourteenth century were negotiated at 10 to 15 percent in the Netherlands and at 5 to 10 percent in Italy. At the same time the 5 percent bonds (*prestiti*, discussed later) of the republic of Venice were selling in the open market to yield from 5$\frac{1}{4}$ to 8 percent.

There were also reports of odd collateral on loans in the Middle Ages. Baldwin II, king of Jerusalem, on one occasion hypothecated his beard. Later the emperor of Constantinople borrowed in Venice on the security of the Crown of Thorns.

Commercial credit in the Middle Ages was severely hampered by the fact that all usury—any gain from lending—was usually illegal and also forbidden by the church. Merchants, fearful for their souls, gave large sums for the building of cathedrals. The prohibition, however, did not apply to the purchase and sale of incomes such as perpetual annuities; such income was not considered to be interest or usury. These perpetual annuities were the direct ancestors of our long-term bonds; the investor could not demand his principal but the borrower could redeem after a specified date. They became very popular with wealthy burghers wishing to retire and seeking safety and a fair income.

Venice

In the thirteenth century, Venice, an independent and prosperous nation-city governed by and for her seagoing merchants, financed her wars, usually with Genoa, by what we would call capital levies: assessments levied only on the wealth of the wealthy. However the taxpayer received a credit in a permanent fund that paid him 5 percent interest on face value of his tax payment until such a time as the state decided to pay him off. In the meantime, however, the taxpayer owner could sell his claim to interest at the market price. Thus were created the famous Venetian *prestiti* which were publicly traded for over 200 years and became a prime and much-sought investment. They were exempt from new assessments. All state revenues over expenses had to be applied to their redemption. Earlier loans had to be redeemed first. Considerable amounts were redeemed from time to time but new assessments usually exceeded redemptions.

In 1285 the prestiti were quoted on the rialto at a price of 75 to yield $6^5/8$ percent current income. By 1299, during a disastrous war, they declined to a price of 50 ($8^3/8$ percent). Later a sinking fund was provided. Their long record of regular payment of interest in spite of war and disaster created great confidence. In the fourteenth century the prestiti fluctuated between a high price of 102 and a low of 19 closing the century at 63. In the fifteenth century they fluctuated between 74 and 23.

The prestiti were much sought after throughout Europe. Foreign princes and capitalists bought them as a secure investment. The right to own them was a privilege that a foreigner could obtain only by act of the Council of Venice. They were widely used to endow charities and to secure dowers. They were quoted daily on the rialto and their prices accurately mirrored the fortunes of the state.

The Venetian prestiti were the first actively traded security in our history of credit. Their quotations have come down to us over a long period of centuries. They were in essence the same type of obligation as the perpetual annuities, pledging interest but not promising redemption at any date but subject to call. The Italian free cities in the Middle Ages were responsible for many such ingenious financial innovations.

The Genoese

In the sixteenth century the Genoese contributed another financial innovation. The famous Bank of St. George issued on behalf of the republic a series of perpetual securities called *luoghi*. Their income was secured by specific taxes and dividend payments varied according to the size of the tax take. A free market existed for the luoghi. They were not forced levies as were the Venetian prestiti but were popular and freely subscribed. They were in effect equity securities with highly variable dividends—stocks, not bonds, with dividends based on the state's success in collecting taxes. The luoghi were actively traded for at least a century and publicly quoted and became a favorite medium of speculation and of investment. At one time their price rose to over five times par and their current yield declined to 1.1 percent; obviously extra dividends were expected.

At this time the practice of *moltiplechi* was devised. Gifts of luoghi were made to charities and to heirs with the legatee required to hold and invest the dividends until the principal reached a specified high figure. The bank was also required to keep its reserves in luoghi.

There was a further interesting novelty: The dividends on the luoghi were declared annually but were paid one half in the fourth year after declaration and one-half in the fifth year after declaration. Thus, in the meantime the bank had the use of the earnings. Holders of those dividend claims registered them and could discount the script in the market at going rates of discount. These were pure interest rates on prime credit paper. The script was also traded actively and their rates have come down to us. They were usually low, very low for those times. Starting out in 1522 at 3 to 4 percent, these discount rates rose at times to 9 percent but were usually around 5 percent. Late in the sixteenth century they declined to 3 percent and lower, reaching a low of $1^1/8$ percent in 1619, and then they rose back to 5 percent.

Genoa prospered greatly as banker for the king of Spain. The vast hoards of Spanish gold and silver from the New World often came to Genoa and not to Spain because the king of Spain had pledged future deliveries against loans at Genoa—sometimes five years into the future. When finally the king of Spain defaulted, the Genoese bankers and investors were ruined.

Antwerp

The dynamic sixteenth century was dominated by the newly great monarchies, France and Spain, and their almost incessant wars.

These wars were financed on credit. As a consequence, a highly efficient money market developed, dominated by Italian and German bankers and centered in Antwerp, the great commercial center. There bankers performed "miracles of finance" in support of their royal patrons. They shifted vast sums from country to country as needed by the use of credit bills. The Fuggers of Augsburg obtained and controlled the mining of metals in the Tyrol in exchange for desperately needed loans. The Fugger bills at Antwerp were considered "as safe as gold." They were the bankers for Charles V.

The exchange at Antwerp dominated European transactions in bills of exchange. These were often foreign exchange bills with interest, which was illicit, sometimes concealed in the exchange rate. The exchange also dealt in other credit investments such as demand notes and loans to states and towns. At one time the exchange had 5,000 members and at times 500 ships a day would enter the port. There was, of course, an extensive trade in commodities.

The rates of interest in this international money market swung widely. Stress alternated with ease as funds were shifted via Antwerp to and from all parts of Europe. For example, short-term loans to prime governments in 1510 ranged from $7^1/2$ to 24 percent on the exchange. In 1530 the range was 12 to 24 percent for such credits. The king of France, Francis I, also borrowed heavily. He fostered a competitive money market at Lyons, dominated by Florentine bankers. He attempted to set a 15 percent legal limit on loans but at times had to pay more. Even the English Crown kept a financial agent at Antwerp, Sir Thomas Gresham, who borrowed at around 13 percent.

Finance was essential to the great wars of this century as it is today. These wars more than once came to a full stop when both sides ran out of money. The medieval financial machinery was first overstimulated by royal patronage and then destroyed by royal defaults. In 1570 the city of Antwerp, whose excellent credit had been exploited by the Spanish Crown, defaulted on its debts. In 1576 an unpaid Spanish army sacked Antwerp and ruined its commercial prosperity. At about the same time the king of France defaulted. The vast credit boom of the sixteenth century was over.

Dutch Republic

The reformation in the sixteenth century opened the way for modern credit markets by two basic changes: First, credit at interest at moderate rates was permitted. (Luther thought 5 percent was a top limit; Calvin went up to 6 percent.) Commercial credit, which had been illicit or illegal, now became open and accepted in the Protestant countries of northern Europe. Second, a high degree of local autonomy was favored by the reformers and the divine right of kings was no longer accepted. This led to governments in Protestant northern Europe that could effectively pledge the resources of their whole people free of fear of royal defaults.

These reforms first bore fruit in the new small Dutch Republic, a union of the northern provinces of the Spanish Netherlands. Her war of liberation from Spain lasted 80 years, 1568 to 1648, and ended in victory for the tiny Dutch Republic over the greatest empire in the world, backed up by all the wealth of the New World. One chief reason for the Dutch victory was no doubt her superior finance.

The Dutch burghers trusted their own government, composed as it was of Dutch burghers. Nobody trusted the king of Spain, who defaulted on his illegal loans four times in a century. The credit instruments of the Dutch provinces were meticulously serviced and could be secured only by the good name of the province. The credits of the king of Spain were secured by gold and silver from the New World on which the king sometimes borrowed five years in advance. The Dutch provinces, at the end of the seventeenth century, were paying 3 to 4 percent for long-term loans. The king of Spain at one time paid 40 percent for short-term illicit loans; it turned out that he had pledged the same property several times.

After the fall of Antwerp in 1576, the financial markets shifted to Amsterdam. The Bank of Amsterdam, founded in 1609, achieved a dominating position in the international bullion trade. Its deposits even commanded a small premium over coined money. In the seventeenth century the Dutch Republic developed a worldwide trading empire. It achieved a near monopoly of shipping and commerce. The Dutch were the carriers of the world—the middlemen, the brokers of Europe. This was made possible by the development of the new finance. Usury laws were unknown in Holland and interest rates were the lowest in Europe. A frugal, prosperous population saved regularly and invested in the securities of the Dutch provinces. They had confidence in the integrity of their leaders who could pledge the whole future surplus of all the people.

Dutch government financing was almost all at long-term annuities for one or two or three lives, or more often, perpetual annuities where the holder could never claim principal but the borrower could redeem after a certain number of years. These perpetual annuities were the direct ancestors of our long-term bonds. They were very popular. They permitted the Dutch burgher to retire from risky trade after he had "made his pile" and not only enjoy a safe income but also protect his family even to his grandsons and beyond. During the war of liberation very large sums were raised by the sale of these perpetual annuities and the money was used to hire German mercenaries to hold off the unpaid Spanish army. The Dutch themselves could handle their defense on the water and indeed their navy operated at a profit.

A remarkable series of conversions of these annuities (perpetual bonds) occurred during the seventeenth century. At the outset, sinking fund perpetual annuities were sold at $8\frac{1}{3}$ percent. This was reduced to

$7^1/7$ percent and then to $6^1/6$ percent in 1620. In the 1640s all of these annuities were called or, at the option of the holder, converted to 5 percent annuities. In 1654, all securities were converted to a rate of 4 percent. There were bondholder riots protesting the reduction of their income but the conversion was a success. Later, during the crises in the war, the prices of the 4 percent annuities declined to the point where the yield was $7^1/2$ percent but gradually recovered to par and higher. Finally at the end of the century new loans were floated at as low as 3 percent.

At the same time, the rates on short-term loans in Amsterdam came down from $6^1/6$ percent to $3^3/4$ and 3 percent. Finally at the turn of the eighteenth century the rate of interest on the Amsterdam exchange was reported as falling to 2 percent.

Great Britain: Eighteenth Century

The revolution of 1688 brought parliamentary government to Great Britain and ended the divine right of kings. The Dutch Statholder became William III of Great Britain and almost immediately Dutch finance, as the Torys contemptuously called it, was adopted and improved upon.

Up to the last decade of the seventeenth century, England had no money market, no substantial bank and no organized national debt. The Stuart kings had borrowed haphazardly from goldsmiths on short term, usually at high rates, and occasionally defaulted in the manner of medieval monarchs. Nevertheless, great wealth was accumulating and commerce was expanding. The need for reliable credit at moderate rates was pressing. Everyone in trade envied the Dutch their financial miracles and their low interest rates. The essential ingredients of Dutch finance were confidence in the ability of the government to pledge the wealth of the country as a whole behind a national debt and confidence in the integrity of the government to live up to its contracts.

In 1695 the Bank of England opened for business. It accepted deposits from the government and the public, issued bank notes payable to bearer, and honored drafts against deposits. It also discounted inland

and foreign trade bills and dealt in bullion and foreign exchange. Soon the bank helped the Treasury develop a new form of short-term obligation called *exchequer bills* with fixed interest and fixed maturity, usually a year. At the same time, the private bill market expanded rapidly under the guidance and support of the Bank of England. County banks sent the savings of agricultural communities to London to finance growing manufacturing communities. Short-term British interest rates were stabilized in the eighteenth century at around 4 to 5 percent.

More important was the development of the new funded debt, the first in English history. Early in the eighteenth century the government began selling long-term annuities in the Dutch manner—for one to three lives or for 99 years or perpetual. These were often accompanied by prizes and lotteries. The funds became very popular; wealthy British capitalists felt they were loaning money to themselves at good rates and could thus provide for retirement and perpetuate the family fortune without taking the risk of trade or the risk of poor crops. Early in the eighteenth century these perpetual annuities yielded as much as 8.7 percent but they soon came down to 6 percent, then 5 percent, then 4 percent, and by 1726 to 3 percent. Thus the Dutch experience of one century earlier was repeated.

Shortly after 1750 there was another basic innovation. Gradually almost all the outstanding annuities were called in and converted into a single issue of 3 percent consolidated annuities—the famous British consols. They are still outstanding as $2^1/2$s.

The British had made two basic improvements on Dutch finance: They created a uniform security, the consols, that therefore could be freely traded and thus became highly marketable, while each Dutch annuity was unique and not interchangeable with others; the British provided full disclosure of all details of the funded debt, including the size of the debt and tax receipts, while Dutch official financial statistics were secret.

In the eighteenth century the British 3 percent consols fluctuated widely between a high of $104^7/8$ percent [of par] and a low of $57^1/2$ percent to yield 5.22 percent. Much later, in the 1890s, they were refunded into the present $2^1/2$ percent consols which recently sold as low as 14 to yield 18 percent.

During the eighteenth and nineteenth centuries the British issued vast amounts of these perpetual bonds at various rates of interest. In effect, through the perfection of their capital market, the British borrowed and bought themselves an empire.

So successful was the system of finance initiated in seventeenth-century Holland and perfected in eighteenth-century Britain that in the nineteenth and twentieth centuries all advanced industrial nations adopted it with varying success—depending largely on the key element of confidence in government and confidence of the leading members of the financial communities in each other.

In the twentieth century this financial system was maintained with only small changes, but greatly enlarged in size. It survived the two great world wars in nations that maintained economic freedom and confidence in government. However, the recent strain of gigantic peacetime expenditures, spiraling inflation, and quantum increases in all forms of debt in many countries, notably Britain, has at times threatened the entire system and has brought back medieval interest rates.

Common Stock Commandments

CLAUDE N. ROSENBERG, JR.

Claude Rosenberg, the quintessential San Franciscan, in addition to developing Rosenberg Capital Management and RREEF, the institutional real estate firm, has served his profession in a variety of formal and informal leadership roles and is one of the industry's favorite people. Among his several books, *Stock Market Primer* has been in print the longest: over 20 years. This is Chapter 37, "Common Stock Commandments."

. . .

1. *Do not make hasty, emotional decisions about buying and selling stocks.* When you do what your emotions tell you to—on the spur of the moment—you are doing exactly what the "masses" are doing, and this is not generally profitable. It is better to wait until your emotions have returned to normal, so that you can weigh the pros and cons objectively. . . . In line with this thinking, do not be pressured to buy or sell securities by anyone. Hard-selling techniques hint there may be "stale merchandise on the shelf," and that's not what you want. If you're in doubt about buying, my advice is to *do nothing.*

2. *If you are convinced that a company has dynamic growth prospects, do not sell it just because it looks temporarily too high.* You may never be able to buy it back lower in price and you stand to miss a potential *big winner*—which is just what you should be looking for. Perhaps the gravest error I've seen made over the years is selling great companies with bright future prospects just because they temporarily looked a few points too high. . . .

3. *Do not fall in love with stocks to the point where you can no longer be objective in your appraisal of them.* Stocks are different than women. You'd be a fool to think of your wife all day the way she looks the first

Reprinted from *Stock Market Primer* (New York: Warner Books, Inc., 1981; originally published 1962), Chapter 37, pp. 320–328, by permission of the author.

thing in the morning—maybe best that you think of her as she appears all dressed up. But you do have to scrutinize stocks and think of their worst points; you have to reassess your love constantly and you have to be brutal and unemotional in your appraisal.

4.   *Do not concern yourself as much with the market in general as with the outlook for individual stocks.*   Oftentimes you will see a fine stock come down in price to an unquestionable bargain price, only to let your feeling about the general market sway you away from buying it. As they say, it is not a stock market, but instead a market for (individual) stocks. Buy a good value as it appears and do not let the general market sentiment alter your decision.

5.   *Forget about stock market "tips."*   Use your good judgment and you won't have to rely on unreliable information. I realize that this point shows no world-shattering brilliance on my part, but so often I've seen this advice ignored. I'll never forget the day I was visited by a certain client of mine at my office. He wanted a recommendation on a good stock and I suggested he buy American Photocopy Equipment, which looked very attractive to me. I related my reasoning to him about the industry, the company, etc., and I showed him all the facts and figures I had on the stock. I spent 10 or 15 minutes on the glowing outlook of this company, and then my client told me he would think about it and let me know. The next morning he called me and placed an order—for an entirely different stock, one of the "Happyjack Uranium" type. He explained he "had heard some very good things" about this stock and he wanted to own it. A year or so later his purchase was about half of his cost and he visited me again. This time he told me the "source" of his information: he had spent an hour at a very fancy cocktail lounge the evening of our original meeting and he had overheard a very confidential conversation about this stock. A fine thing, I thought (and my client agreed). Here I had spent hours researching American Photocopy and had given him the benefits of these hours— and he turned around and disregarded this in favor of a hot tip he overheard between two unknown people who had consumed an ample supply of martinis. . . .

6.   *You get what you pay for in the stock market (like everything else in life).*   Some people consider a $5.00 stock good just because it's low in

price. Nothing could be further from the truth. Most often, high-priced stocks provide far better value than low-priced stocks, in that the former generally have more earnings, dividends, etc. behind them than the low-priced issues. Likewise, high-priced stocks go into "better hands" (many are purchased by large institutional investors and others who are long-term holders), while the low-priced issues most often go into the hands of the public and speculators and gamblers, all of whom are less-informed and subject to occasional panic selling. Also remember that high-priced stocks carry one potential that cheap stocks do not—they are all potential split candidates.

7.   *Remember that stocks always look worst at the bottom of a bear market (when an air of gloom prevails) and always look best at the top of a bull market (when everybody is optimistic).*   Have strength and buy when things do look bleak and sell when they look too good to be true.

8.   *Remember, too, that you'll seldom—if ever—buy stocks right at the bottom or sell them right at the top.*   The stock market generally goes to extremes: when pessimism dominates, stocks go lower than they really should, based on their fundamentals, and when optimism runs rampant, stocks go higher than they really deserve to. Knowing this, don't expect your stocks to go up in price immediately after you buy them or to go down after you sell them, even though you are convinced that your analysis of their value is correct.

9.   *Do not buy stocks as you might store merchandise on sale.*   No doubt you've seen people scrapping and clamoring for goods on sale at stores like Macy's, Penney, etc. They fight to buy this merchandise because the goods are reduced in price and because there is limited supply of the merchandise. Too often people buy things they really don't need or really don't like and they find that they really haven't make a "good buy" at all. *But they simply couldn't resist the urge to join others in competing for something of which there was a limited supply.*

There is not a limited supply of actively traded common stocks, thus I advise you not to rush to buy as though the supply is going to dry up. If you've ever sat in a stock brokerage office and watched the "tape" (which shows the stock transactions as they take place), you'll know what I mean. A certain stock might suddenly get active and start rising in price: one minute you see it at 35, a few seconds later it's $35\frac{1}{2}$, then

36, 36^{1}/$_{4}$, 36^{1}/$_{2}$, 37. By the time it has hit 37, it is human nature to feel an almost irresistible urge to buy the stock (regardless of its fundamentals of earnings, dividends, future outlook, etc.)—to get in on the gravy train, to join the rest of the flock who are clamoring to buy the stock as though it is "sale merchandise." Resist this urge—only buy "goods" that you're sure you'll like and that meet your objectives.

10.　*There is no reason always to be in the stock market.*　After the stock market has had a long and sizable advance, it is prudent to take a few profits. Too often, after selling, the money from the sale "burns a hole in the pocket" of the investor. It's like working in a candy shop: no matter how much willpower you have, after a few weeks, the bonbons look awfully good and it's hard to resist other "bonbon" stocks. Go slowly—there are times when cash can be a valuable asset.

11.　*Seek professional advice for your investment.*　Find a broker who is honest and who you are convinced will have your best interests at heart. Make sure he knows your financial status, your objectives, and your temperament. If you don't know the right broker, consult your bank or your friends and then go in and meet the man who is recommended to you. Take the same pains to find the best broker as you would to find the best doctor for yourself. . . .

12.　*Take advantage of the research facilities your broker has to offer.*　Certainly you'll agree that *analysis is a better market tool than a pin.* The top brokerage firms spend hundreds of thousands of dollars every year to find the most attractive investments for their customers. Read the reports that are published—they will give you insight into the investment firm with whom you are dealing. Keep track of their performance over a period of years (performance over a few months may be deceiving, both because the general market may be against them and because you can't expect recommendations to bloom overnight). . . .

13.　*Remember that the public is generally wrong.*　The masses are not well informed about investments and the stock market. They have not disciplined themselves correctly to make the right choices in the right industries at the right prices. They are moved mainly by their emotions, and history has proved them to be wrong consistently. . . .

A wise investor should be wary of public overenthusiasm for anything. Don't you be "one of the herd" and be led to slaughter as have so many who have tossed sound thinking to the wind.

14. *Beware of following stock market "fads."* Along the same line of reasoning discussed in commandments 9 and 13, I want to emphasize separately this idea of following fads in the market. Remember the "sack" dresses that became the fad a decade ago? . . . Seven or eight years ago it was hula-hoops; five years ago it was trampoline centers; last year it was "Batman" and next year it will be something else. As a general rule, if you get in early in a fad you stand to make money. But if you come along after it is in full swing you are asking for trouble.

The same thing goes for the stock market. Just like sack dresses, hula-hoops, trampolines, tulip bulbs, etc., the stock market occasionally develops fads for certain industries. In almost all cases a sudden rush to buy the fad stocks pushes them to price levels that are totally unwarranted. *When you buy at the height of popularity you almost always pay prices that have little relationship to value.* . . .

15. *Do not be concerned with where a stock has already been—be instead concerned with where it is going.* Many times I've heard people say, "It must be a bargain now—it's down 20 points from its high." Where a stock *has been* is history, it's "spilt milk." Investors may have bid up ABC stock to $100 last year, but the outlook for the company may have changed entirely since then. Or it may have been emotional speculation (fad-buying) that put it up to an unreasonable price. *The important thing is what lies ahead, not what has already transpired,* and previous market prices have no bearing on the future.

16. *Take the time to supervise your stocks periodically.* Needless to say, conditions are subject to constant change. Don't shut yourself off from the outside world; take an objective look at your holdings periodically, with the thought of weeding out the "weak sisters" and adding stocks that have more potential. Your broker should be willing to make an analysis of your portfolio for you on a regular basis and I encourage you to take advantage of his service.

17. *Concentrate on quality.* While big profits are often made through buying and selling poor-quality common stocks, your success

in the stock market is far, far more ensured if you emphasize quality in your stock selections. Too many investors shy away from the top-notch companies in search of rags-to-riches performers. This, of course, is fine for a certain portion of your investment dollars, since most people can afford an *occasional* "flyer." But a person who starts out looking for flyers usually ends up, not with just one or two, but with a host of poor-quality stocks—most of which turn out unsuccessfully. These low-grade issues are certainly no foundation for a good portfolio; instead, the fine, well-managed companies should form the backbone. And don't for a minute think you can't make money without wild speculation—fabulous fortunes have been made over the years in such high-quality, *non*speculative stocks as Carnation, Coca-Cola, Procter & Gamble, and others. In other words, place your stress on the elite, not on the so-called "cats and dogs" of the marketplace. "Remember," said one wise stock market philosopher, "if you sleep with dogs, you're bound to get fleas."

Evaluation by the Rule
of Present Worth

JOHN BURR WILLIAMS

John Burr Williams is rightly credited with establishing the conceptual foundation upon which the formal discipline of investment management has been built. No mere theoretician, he was an active investor and a securities analyst. Here are the key steps in his exposition
in *The Theory of Investment Value*, published in 1938.

. . .

Let us define the investment value of a stock as the present worth of
all the dividends to be paid upon it. Likewise let us define the investment value of a bond as the present worth of its future coupons and
principal. In both cases, dividends, or coupons and principal, must be
adjusted for expected changes in the purchasing power of money. The
purchase of a stock or bond, like other transactions that give rise to the
phenomenon of interest, represents the exchange of present goods for
future goods—dividends, or coupons and principal, in this case being
the claim on future goods. To appraise the investment value, then, it
is necessary to estimate the future payments. The annuity of payments,
adjusted for changes in the value of money itself, may then be discounted
at the pure interest rate demanded by the investor.

Most people will object at once to the foregoing formula for stocks
by saying that it should use the present worth of future *earnings*, not
future *dividends*. But should not earnings and dividends both give the
same answer under the implicit assumptions of our critics? If earnings
not paid out in dividends are all successfully reinvested at compound
interest for the benefit of the stockholder, as the critics imply, then
these earnings should produce dividends later; if not, then they are

From John Burr Williams, *The Theory of Investment Value* (Cambridge, Massachusetts, 1938),
30, 542–543, by permission of the author.

money lost. Furthermore, if these reinvested earnings will produce dividends, then our formula will take account of them when it takes account of all future dividends; but if they will not, then our formula will rightly refrain from including them in any discounted annuity of benefits.

Earnings are only a means to an end, and the means should not be mistaken for the end. Therefore we must say that a stock derives its value from its dividends, not its earnings. In short, a stock is worth only *what you can get out of it.* Even so spoke the old farmer to his son:

A cow for her milk,
A hen for her eggs,
And a stock, by heck
For her dividends.

An orchard for fruit
Bees for their honey,
And stocks, besides,
For their dividends.

The old man knew where milk and honey came from, but he made no such mistake as to tell his son to buy a cow for her cud or bees for their buzz.

Long-Term Investing

JACK L. TREYNOR

Jack Treynor, as editor, made the *Financial Analysts Journal* into a
lively, challenging, and intellectually leading center of serious thought
about investing. Here, he clarifies the true role of long-term investing
and explains why even highly efficient markets are not truly efficient
in terms of profound, original insight by the investor who "buys for
keeps."

· · ·

The investor who would attempt to improve his portfolio performance
through unconventional, innovative research is currently being challenged on three fronts: (1) The efficient marketers say he will be unable to find any ideas that haven't been properly discounted by the
market. (2) Lord Keynes says that even if he finds these ideas his portfolio will be viewed as "eccentric" and "rash" by conventionally-minded
clients and professional peers. (3) The investment philistine says that
even if he stands by his ideas he won't be rewarded because actual price
movements are governed by conventional thinking, which is immune
to these ideas.

Successful response to the first challenge lies in distinguishing between two kinds of investment ideas: (a) those whose implications
are straightforward and obvious, take relatively little special expertise
to evaluate, and consequently travel quickly (e.g., "hot stocks"); and
(b) those that require reflection, judgment, special expertise, etc., for
their evaluation, and consequently travel slowly. (In practice, of course,
actual investment ideas lie along a continuous spectrum between these
two polar extremes, but we can avoid some circumlocution by focusing
on the extremes.) Pursuit of the second kind of idea—rather than the

Excerpted from the *Financial Analysts Journal* 32 (May/June 1976), pp. 56–59. Charlottesville, Virginia: Association for Investment Management and Research.

obvious, hence quickly discounted, insight relating to "long-term" economic or business developments—is, of course, the only meaningful definition for *long-term investing.*"

If the market is inefficient, it is not going to be inefficient with respect to the first kind of idea since, by definition, this kind is unlikely to be misevaluated by the great mass of investors. If investors disagree on the value of a security even when they have the same information, their differences in opinion must be due to errors in analysis of the second kind of idea. If these investors err independently, then a kind of law of averages operates on the resulting error in the market consensus. If enough independent opinions bear on the determination of the consensus price, the law of "large numbers" effect will be very powerful, and the error implicit in the consensus will be small compared to errors made on the average by the individual investors contributing to the consensus.

Under what circumstances, then, will investors' errors in appraising information available to all lead to investment opportunities for some? As the key to the averaging process underlying an accurate consensus is the assumption of independence, if all—or even a substantial fraction—of these investors make the same error, the independence assumption is violated and the consensus can diverge significantly from true value. The market then ceases to be efficient in the sense of pricing available information correctly. I see nothing in the arguments of Professor Eugene Fama or the other efficient markets advocates to suggest that large groups of investors may not make the same error in appraising the kind of abstract ideas that take special expertise to understand and evaluate, and that consequently travel relatively slowly.

According to Fama, "disagreement among investors about the implications of given information does not in itself imply market inefficiency unless there are investors who can consistently make better evaluations of available information than are implicit in market prices." Fama's statement can best be revised to read: "Disagreement among investors *due to independent errors in analysis* does not necessarily lead to market inefficiency." If the independence assumption is violated in practice, every violation represents a potential opportunity for fundamental analysis.

The assertion that the great bulk of practicing investors find long-term investing impractical was set forth almost 40 years ago by Lord Keynes:

> Most of these persons are in fact largely concerned not with most superior long term forecasts of the probable yield of an investment over its whole life, but with foreseeing changes in the *conventional basis of evaluation* a short time ahead of the general public. They are concerned not with what an investment is really worth to a man who buys it for keeps, but with what the market will evaluate it at under the influence of mass psychology three months or a year hence.

Obviously, if an investor is concerned with how the "mass psychology" appraisal of an investment will change over the next three months, he is concerned with the propagation of ideas that can be apprehended with very little analysis and that consequently travel fast.

On the other hand, the investment opportunity offered by market inefficiency is most likely to arise with investment ideas that propagate slowly, or hardly at all. Keynes went on to explain why practical investors are not interested in such ideas:

> It is the long term investor, he who most promotes the public interest, who will in practice come in for the most criticism, wherever investment funds are managed by committees or boards or banks. For it is in the essence of his behavior that he should be eccentric, unconventional and rash in the eyes of average opinion. If he is successful, that will only confirm the general belief in his rashness; and if in the short run he is unsuccessful, which is very likely, he will not receive much mercy. Worldly wisdom teaches that it is better for reputation to fail conventionally than to succeed unconventionally.

Thus Keynes not only described accurately the way most professional investors still behave; he also supplied their reasons for so behaving. He was careful never to say, however, that the long-term investor who sticks by his guns will not be rewarded.

But is the price of unconventional thinking as high as Keynes alleges? Modern portfolio theory says that an individual security can be assessed only in the context of the overall portfolio: So long as the overall portfolio has a reasonable level of market sensitivity and is reasonably well diversified, the beneficiary has nothing to fear from unconventional holdings—and still less to fear from conventional holdings bought for unconventional reasons. There is, of course, marketing advantage in holding securities enjoying wide popular esteem but, as investors as a class become more sophisticated, they are less likely to be challenged on specific holdings.

There is, finally, a school of thought that asserts that research directed toward improving our analytical tools is automatically impractical because it does not describe the behavior of a market consensus based on opinions of investors unfamiliar with these tools. This line of argument puts a premium on investment ideas that have broad appeal or are readily persuasive, while rejecting the ideas that capture abstract economic truths in terms too recondite to appeal to the mass of investors.

The investment philistine who asserts that it is impossible to benefit from superior approaches to investment analysis if the market consensus is not based on these approaches misunderstands what appraisal of a security means: An analyst's opinion of the value of a security is an estimate of the price at which, risk-adjusted, the return on the security is competitive with the returns on other securities available in the market. A superior method for identifying undervalued securities is therefore tantamount to a method of identifying securities that at their present prices offer superior long-term returns. The mere inclusion of such securities in a portfolio will guarantee a superior investment performance.

To the threefold challenge, a threefold reply is offered: (1) The efficient marketer's assertion that *no* improperly or inadequately discounted ideas exist is both unproved and unlikely. (2) Keynes' suggestion that unconventional investing is impractical is no longer valid in the age of modern portfolio theory. (3) The investment philistine who says good ideas that can't persuade the great mass of investors have no investment value is simply wrong.

The skeptical reader can ask himself the following question: If a portfolio manager . . . [is consistently right when the consensus is wrong, while] maintaining reasonable levels of market sensitivity and diversification, how long would it be before his investment record began to outweigh, in the eyes of his clients, the unconventionality of his portfolio holdings?

You Only Have to Get Rich Once

WALTER K. GUTMAN

Starting in 1949, Walter Gutman wrote one of the first and most popular Wall Street "letters." This excerpt is from his 1961 book *You Only Have to Get Rich Once*.

• • •

When computers are as familiar as cash registers, IBM will sell at a much less romantic value—you wait and see.

There is a particular moment when the value of mystery is at its greatest. When most investors are completely ignorant, they don't pay much for mystery—many of these stocks could have been bought at very reasonable prices in 1957. There is a special moment when everyone sees that something amazing is coming out of mystery and then they will pay a lot more to know more about this strange new thing. Later on, when mystery has given birth, when they know more, they will pay less. Thus most of the electronic stocks that boomed in 1959–1961 will be selling for less in 1965, and all of them, I feel sure, will be selling for less in relation to their earnings. In other words, those companies that fulfill the vision of 1959 will be much better known to investors by 1965, and their stocks will be given a rating of knowledge rather than of mystery.

For most of us, our greatest richness always has been and still remains in dreams. It may be in dreams about our future accomplishments, it may be in dreams about how wonderful it would be to meet that girl on the diving raft, it may be in dreams of our children, or dreams of the past recalled, or of revenge and future justice, or of religion and another world. We cannot hope for economic riches that are really greater than our dreams, but it is also true that economic riches can help our dreams. . . .

Because no wealth you will ever have—even if you are the richest man in the world—will equal your dreams, stocks go to particularly high levels when a lot of people think they might equal their dreams. Those stocks that are called growth stocks might better be called dream stocks. But dreams are real—we have them every day. It's a big mistake to think that dreams are unreal and what is called real life is real. If dreams were unreal, it would be possible for you to feel richer than your dreams if you were the richest man in the world. When the dream of a new industry comes true, then the dream ends and the stocks sell more conservatively, relating to what is real rather than to what was dreamed.

How Fiat Money Inflation
Came to France

====

ANDREW DICKSON WHITE

Andrew Dickson White, with the help of an endowment from Ezra Cornell, established Cornell University in 1867. In addition to being a scholar, White was a diplomat and served for six years as U.S. ambassador to Germany. This essay was originally presented to a private meeting of senators and representatives in 1876 and subsequently published in 1912. In it, White explains how in 1789, following the French Revolution, well-meaning political leaders launched their nation's economy into a disastrous inflation—for neither the first nor the last time—with all the familiar arguments, including the canard about how "this time, things are different." The more things change, . . .

· · ·

Early in the year 1789 the French nation found itself in deep financial embarrassment: there was a heavy debt and a serious deficit.

The vast reforms of that period, though a lasting blessing politically, were a temporary evil financially. There was a general want of confidence in business circles; capital had shown its proverbial timidity by retiring out of sight as far as possible; throughout the land was stagnation.

Statesmanlike measures, careful watching, and wise management would, doubtless, have ere long led to a return of confidence, a reappearance of money, and a resumption of business; but these involved patience and self-denial, and, thus far in human history, these are the rarest products of political wisdom. Few nations have ever been able to exercise these virtues; and France was not then one of these few.[1]

Excerpted from *Fiat Money Inflation in France* (Irvington-on-Hudson, New York: The Foundation for Economic Education, Inc., 1959; originally published 1912), pp. 23–36, 42–46.

There was a general search for some short road to prosperity: ere long the idea was set afloat that the great want of the country was more of the circulating medium; and this was speedily followed by calls for an issue of paper money. The Minister of Finance at this period was Necker. In financial ability he was acknowledged as among the great bankers of Europe, but his was something more than financial ability: he had a deep feeling of patriotism and a high sense of personal honor. The difficulties in his way were great, but he steadily endeavored to keep France faithful to those principles in monetary affairs that the general experience of modern times had found the only path to national safety. As difficulties arose, the National Assembly drew away from him, and soon came among the members renewed suggestions of paper money: orators in public meetings, at the clubs, and in the Assembly, proclaimed it a panacea—a way of "securing resources without paying interest." Journalists caught it up and displayed its beauties, among these men, Marat, who, in his newspaper, *The Friend of the People*, also joined the cries against Necker, picturing him—a man of sterling honesty, who gave up health and fortune for the sake of France—as a wretch seeking only to enrich himself from the public purse.

Against this tendency toward the issue of irredeemable paper Necker contended as best he might. He knew well to what it always had led, even when surrounded by the most skillful guarantees. Among those who struggled to support ideas similar to his was Bergasse, a deputy from Lyons, whose pamphlets, then and later, against such issues exerted a wider influence, perhaps, than any others. Parts of them seem fairly inspired. Anyone today reading his prophecies of the evils sure to follow such a currency would certainly ascribe to him a miraculous foresight, were it not so clear that his prophetic power was due simply to a knowledge of natural laws revealed by history.

But this current in favor of paper money became so strong that an effort was made to breast it by a compromise; and during the last months of 1789 and the first months of 1790 came discussions in the National Assembly looking to issues of notes based upon the landed property of the Church, which was to be confiscated for that purpose. But care was to be taken; the issue was to be largely in the shape of notes of 1,000, 300, and 200 livres,[2] too large to be used as ordinary currency, but of convenient size to be used in purchasing the church lands; besides this, they were to bear interest and this would tempt holders to hoard them. The Assembly thus held back from issuing smaller obligations.

Remembrances of the ruin that had come from the great issues of smaller currency at an earlier day were still vivid. Yet the pressure toward a popular currency for universal use grew stronger and stronger. The finance committee of the Assembly reported that "the people demand a new circulating medium"; that "the circulation of paper money is the best of operations"; that "it is the most free because it reposes on the will of the people"; that "it will bind the interest of the citizens to the public good."

The report appealed to the patriotism of the French people with the following exhortation: "Let us show to Europe that we understand our own resources; let us immediately take the broad road to our liberation instead of dragging ourselves along the tortuous and obscure paths of fragmentary loans." It concluded by recommending an issue of paper money carefully guarded, to the full amount of four hundred million livres, and the argument was pursued until the objection to smaller notes faded from view.

Typical in the debate on the whole subject, in its various phases, were the declarations of M. Matrineau. He was loud and long for paper money, his only fear being that the Committee had not authorized enough of it; he declared that business was stagnant, and that the sole cause was a want of more of the circulating medium; that paper money ought to be made a legal tender; and that the Assembly should rise above prejudices that the failures of John Law's paper money had caused, several decades before. Like every supporter of irredeemable paper money then or since, he seemed to think that the laws of Nature had changed since previous disastrous issues. He said: "Paper money under a despotism is dangerous; it favors corruption; but in a nation constitutionally governed, which itself takes care in the emission of its notes, which determines their number and use, that danger no longer exists." He insisted that John Law's notes at first restored prosperity, but that the wretchedness and ruin they caused resulted from their overissue, and that such an overissue is possible only under a despotism.[3]

M. de la Rochefoucauld gave his opinion that "the assignats will draw specie out of the coffers where it is now hoarded."[4]

On the other hand, Cazalès and Maury showed that the result could only be disastrous. Never, perhaps, did a political prophecy meet with more exact fulfillment in every line than the terrible picture drawn in one of Cazalès' speeches in this debate. Still the current ran stronger and stronger; Petion made a brilliant oration in favor of the report, and Necker's influence and experience were gradually worn away.

Mingled with the financial argument was a strong political plea. The National Assembly had determined to confiscate the vast real property of the French Church—the pious accumulations of 1,500 years. There were princely estates in the country, bishops' palaces, and conventual buildings in the towns; these formed between one-fourth and one-third of the entire real property of France, and amounted in value to at least two thousand million livres. By a few sweeping strokes, all this became the property of the nation. Never, apparently, did a government secure a more solid basis for a great financial future. . . .

There were two special reasons why French statesmen desired speedily to sell these lands. First, a financial reason—to obtain money to relieve the government. Second, a political reason—to get this land distributed among the thrifty middle classes, and so commit them to the Revolution and to the government that gave their title.

It was urged, then, that the issue of four hundred millions of paper, (not in the shape of interest-bearing bonds, as had at first been proposed, but in notes small as well as large), would give the treasury something to pay out immediately, and relieve the national necessities; that, having been put into circulation, this paper money would stimulate business; that it would give to all capitalists, large or small, the means for buying from the nation the ecclesiastical real estate; and that, from the proceeds of this real estate the nation would pay its debts and also obtain new funds for new necessities. Never was theory more seductive both to financiers and statesmen.

It would be a great mistake to suppose that the statesmen of France, or the French people, were ignorant of the dangers in issuing irredeemable paper money. No matter how skillfully the bright side of such a currency was exhibited, all thoughtful men in France remembered its dark side. They knew too well, from that ruinous experience, 70 years before, in John Law's time, the difficulties and dangers of a currency not well based and controlled. They had then learned how easy it is to issue it; how difficult it is to check its overissue; how seductively it leads to the absorption of the means of the workingmen and men of small fortunes; how heavily it falls on all those living on fixed incomes, salaries, or wages; how securely it creates on the ruins of the prosperity of all men of meager means a class of debauched speculators, the most injurious class that a nation can harbor—more injurious, indeed, than professional criminals whom the law recognizes and can throttle; how it stimulates overproduction at first and leaves every industry flaccid afterward; how it breaks down thrift and develops political and social immorality. All this France had been thoroughly taught by experience. Many then living had felt the result of such an experiment—the issue of paper money under John Law, a man who to this day is acknowledged one of the most ingenious financiers the world has ever known; and there were then sitting in the National Assembly of France many who owed the poverty of their families to those issues of paper. Hardly a man in the country who had not heard those who issued it cursed as the authors of the most frightful catastrophe France had then experienced. . . .

It was no mere attempt at theatrical display, but a natural impulse, which led a thoughtful statesman, during the debate, to hold up a piece of that old paper money and to declare that it was stained with the blood and tears of their fathers.

And it would also be a mistake to suppose that the National Assembly, which discussed this matter, was composed of mere wild revolutionists; no inference could be more wide of the fact. Whatever may have been the character of the men who legislated for France afterward, no thoughtful student of history can deny, despite all the arguments and sneers of reactionary statesmen and historians, that few more keen-sighted legislative bodies have ever met than this first French Constitutional Assembly. In it were such men as Sieyès, Bailly, Necker, Mirabeau, Talleyrand, Du Pont de Nemours, and a multitude of others who, in various sciences and in the political world, had already shown and were destined afterward to show themselves among the strongest and shrewdest men that Europe has yet seen.

But the current toward paper money had become irresistible. It was constantly urged, and with a great show of force, that if any nation could safely issue it, France was now that nation; that she was fully warned by her severe experience under John Law; that she was now a constitutional government, controlled by an enlightened, patriotic people—not, as in the days of the former issues of paper money, an absolute monarchy controlled by politicians and adventurers; that she was able to secure every livre of her paper money by a virtual mortgage on a landed domain vastly greater in value than the entire issue; that, with men like Bailly, Mirabeau, and Necker at her head, she could not commit the financial mistakes and crimes from which France had suffered under John Law, the Regent Duke of Orleans, and Cardinal Dubois.

Oratory prevailed over science and experience. In April 1790, came the final decree to issue four hundred millions of livres in paper money, based upon confiscated property of the Church for its security. The deliberations on this first decree and on the bill carrying it into effect were most interesting; prominent in the debate being Necker, Du Pont de Nemours, Maury, Cazalès, Petion, Bailly, and many others hardly inferior. The discussions were certainly very able; no person can read them at length in the *Moniteur*, nor even in the summaries of the parliamentary history, without feeling that various modern histories have done wretched injustice to those men who were then endeavoring to stand between France and ruin.

This sum—four hundred millions, so vast in those days—was issued in assignats, which were notes secured by a pledge of productive real estate and bearing interest to the holder at three percent. No irredeemable currency has ever claimed a more scientific and practical guarantee for its goodness and for its proper action on public finances. On the one hand, it had what the world recognized as a most practical security—a mortgage on productive real estate of vastly greater value than the issue. On the other hand, as the notes bore interest, there seemed cogent reason for their being withdrawn from circulation whenever they became redundant. . . .

As speedily as possible the notes were put into circulation. Unlike those issued in John Law's time, they were engraved in the best style of the art. To stimulate loyalty, the portrait of the king was placed in the center; to arouse public spirit, patriotic legends and emblems surrounded it; to stimulate public cupidity, the amount of interest that the note would yield each day to the holder was printed in the margin; and the whole was duly garnished with stamps and signatures to show that it was carefully registered and controlled. . . .

To crown its work the National Assembly, to explain the advantages of this new currency, issued an address to the French people. In this address it spoke of the nation as "delivered by this grand means from all uncertainty and from all ruinous results of the credit system." It foretold that this issue "would bring back into the public treasury, into commerce, and into all branches of industry strength, abundance, and prosperity."[5]

> Some of the arguments in this address are worth recalling, and, among them the following: "Paper money is without inherent value unless it represents some special property. Without representing some special property it is inadmissible in trade to compete with a metallic currency, which has a value real and independent of the public action; therefore it is that the paper money which has only the public authority as its basis has always caused ruin where it has been established; that is the reason why the bank notes of 1720, issued by John Law, after having caused terrible evils, have left only frightful memories. Therefore it is that the National Assembly has not wished to expose you to this danger, but has given this new paper money not only a value derived from the national authority but a value real and immutable, a value which permits it to sustain advantageously a competition with the precious metals themselves.[6]

But the final declaration was, perhaps, the most interesting. It was as follows: "These assignats, bearing interest as they do, will soon be considered better than the coin now hoarded, and will bring it out again into circulation." The King was also induced to issue a proclamation recommending that his people receive this new money without objection. . . .

The first result of this issue was apparently all that the most sanguine could desire: the treasury was at once greatly relieved; a portion of the public debt was paid; creditors were encouraged; credit revived; ordinary expenses were met, and, a considerable part of this paper money having thus been passed from government into the hands of the people, trade increased and all difficulties seemed to vanish. The anxieties of Necker, the prophecies of Maury and Cazalès seemed proven utterly futile. And, indeed, it is quite possible that, if the national authorities had stopped with this issue, few of the financial evils that afterwards arose would have been severely felt; the four hundred millions of paper money then issued would have simply discharged the function of a similar amount of specie. But soon there came another result: times grew less easy; by the end of September, within five months after the issue of the four hundred millions in assignats, the government had spent them and was again in distress.[7]

The old remedy immediately and naturally recurred to the minds of men. Throughout the country began a cry for another reissue of paper; thoughtful men then began to recall what their fathers had told them about the seductive path of paper-money issues in John Law's time, and to remember the prophecies that they themselves had heard in the debate on the first issue of assignats less than six months before.

At that time the opponents of paper had prophesied that, once on the downward path of inflation, the nation could not be restrained and that more issues would follow. The supporters of the first issue had asserted that this was a calumny, that *the people* were now in control, and that they could and would check these issues whenever they desired.

The condition of opinion in the Assembly was, therefore, chaotic: a few schemers and dreamers were loud and outspoken for paper money; many of the more shallow and easygoing were inclined to yield; the more thoughtful endeavored to breast the current.

Far more important than any other argument against inflation was the speech of Talleyrand. He had been among the boldest and most radical French statesmen. He it was—a former bishop—who, more than any other, had carried the extreme measure of taking into the possession of the nation the great landed estates of the Church, and he had supported the first issue of four hundred millions. But he now adopted a judicial tone—attempted to show to the Assembly the very simple truth that the effect of a second issue of assignats may be different from that of the first; that the first was evidently needed; that the second may be as injurious as the first was useful. He exhibited various weak points in the inflation fallacies and presented forcibly the trite truth that no laws and no decrees can keep large issues of irredeemable paper at par with specie.

> In his speech occur these words: "You can, indeed, arrange it so that the people shall be forced to take a thousand livres in paper for a thousand livres in specie; but you can never arrange it so that a man will be obliged to give a thousand livres in specie for a thousand livres in paper—in that fact is embedded the entire question; and on account of that fact the whole system fails."[8]

Greatest force of all, on September 27, 1790, came Mirabeau's final speech. The most sober and conservative of his modern opponents speaks of its eloquence as "prodigious." In this the great orator dwelt first on the political necessity involved, declaring that the most pressing need was to get the government lands into the hands of the people, and so to commit to the nation and against the old privileged classes the class of landholders thus created.

Through the whole course of his arguments there is one leading point enforced with all his eloquence and ingenuity—the excellence of the proposed currency, its stability, and its security. He declares that, being based on the pledge of public lands and convertible into them, the notes are better secured than if redeemable in specie; that the precious metals are only employed in the secondary arts, while the French paper money represents the first and most real of all property, the source of all production, *the land*; that while other nations have been obliged to emit paper money, none have ever been so fortunate as the French nation, for the reason that none had ever before been able to give this landed security; that whoever takes French paper money has practically a mortgage to secure it— and on landed property that can easily be sold to satisfy his claims, while other nations have been able only to give a vague claim on the entire nation. "And," he cries, "I would rather have a mortgage on a garden than on a kingdom!"

Other arguments of his are more demagogical. He declares that the only interests affected will be those of bankers and capitalists, but that manufacturers will see prosperity restored to them. Some of his arguments seem almost puerile, as when he says, "If gold has been hoarded through timidity or malignity, the issue of paper will show that gold is not necessary, and it will then come forth." But, as a whole, the speech was brilliant; it was often interrupted by applause; it settled the question. People did not stop to consider that it was the dashing speech of an orator and not the matured judgment of a financial expert; they did not see that calling Mirabeau or Talleyrand to advise upon a monetary policy, because they had shown boldness in danger and strength in conflict, was like summoning a prize fighter to mend a watch.

In vain did Maury show that, while the first issues of John Law's paper had brought prosperity, those that followed brought misery; in vain did he quote from a book published in John Law's time, showing that Law was at first considered a patriot and friend of humanity; in vain did he hold up to the Assembly one of Law's bills and appeal to their memories of the wretchedness brought upon France by them; in vain did Du Pont present a simple and really wise plan of substituting notes in the payment of the floating debt that should not form a part of the circulating medium; nothing could resist the eloquence of Mirabeau. Barnave, following, insisted that "Law's paper was based upon the phantoms of the Mississippi; ours, upon the solid basis of ecclesiastical lands" and he proved that the assignats could not depreciate further. Prudhomme's newspaper poured contempt over gold as security for the currency, extolled real estate as the only true basis, and was fervent in praise of the convertibility and self-adjusting features of the proposed scheme.

In spite of this plausibility and eloquence, a large minority stood firm to their earlier principles; but on September 29, 1790, by a vote of 508 to 423, the deed was done. . . .

Notes

1. For proof that the financial situation of France at that time was by no means hopeless, see Storch, *Economie Politique*, vol. iv., p. 159.
2. Editors' Note: The livre was the common coin of exchange in France at the beginning of the period White describes. The franc became the official monetary unit in 1795, with conversion at the rate of 81 livres to 80 francs.
3. See *Moniteur*, April 10, 1790.
4. *Ibid.*, April 15, 1790.
5. See *Addresse de l'Assemblée nationale sur les emissions d'assignats monnaies*, 5.
6. *Ibid.*, 10.
7. Von Sybel, *History of the French Revolution*, vol. i, 252; also, Levasseur, *Histoires des classes ouvrières et de l'industrie en France de 1789 à 1870*, vol. i (Paris: 1903), 137 and following.
8. See speech in *Moniteur*; also in Appendix to Thiers' *History of the French Revolution*.

U.S. Equity Returns from Colonial Times to the Present

ROGER G. IBBOTSON
GARY P. BRINSON

The power of compound interest—and of long-term investing in equities—is nowhere better demonstrated than in this delightful illustration from *Investment Markets* by Gary Brinson and Roger Ibbotson.

• • •

If George Washington had put just $1 from his first presidential salary check into U.S. equities, his heirs would have been millionaires about five times over by the mid-1980s. U.S. stocks have provided a phenomenal return to investors over the long run. Partly because of this past success, the American equity market is the largest and most closely studied market in the world. Currently, in the mid-1980s, well over 100 million shares are traded each day on the New York Stock Exchange (NYSE), with more than 100 million additional shares traded in the over-the-counter (OTC) market and on other stock exchanges. The value of outstanding equities exceeds $2 trillion.

From price appreciation alone, equities yielded a return, called a *capital appreciation return*, of 2.9 percent, compounded annually, between the 1780s and the 1980s. Without dividends reinvested, a nominal dollar invested in 1789 would have grown to almost $450 in the 1980s. . . .

Total returns, in contrast to capital appreciation returns, include dividend reinvestment as well as price appreciation. Assuming dividends were paid from the 1790s to the 1870s at the same rate as from the 1870s to the 1980s, the compound total return was 8.2 percent per

Reprinted from *Investment Markets—Gaining the Performance Advantage* (1987), Chapter 5, pp. 65, 67, by permission of McGraw-Hill Publishing Company, New York.

CONCEPTS AND MARKET HISTORY

Frequency Distribution of U.S. Equity Total Returns, 1790–1985

Summary

Positive Years: 140 or 71%
Negative Years: 56 or 29%
Standard Deviation: 19.6%

```
                              1984
                              1978
                              1970
                              1960
                              1956
                              1953  1972
                              1948  1971
                              1947  1968
                              1939  1965  1983
                              1934  1964  1982
                        1926  1929  1959  1979
                        1981  1923  1952  1976
                        1977  1916  1942  1967
                        1969  1912  1921  1963
                        1966  1911  1909  1961
                        1962  1906  1905  1955
                        1946  1902  1900  1951
                        1941  1896  1899  1950
                        1940  1895  1897  1949
                        1932  1894  1886  1944
                        1914  1892  1878  1943
                        1913  1889  1872  1938
                        1910  1888  1871  1925
                        1890  1882  1868  1924
                        1887  1881  1865  1922
                        1883  1875  1861  1919
                        1877  1874  1855  1918
                        1873  1870  1845  1901
                        1869  1867  1844  1898
                        1859  1866  1840  1891
                  1957  1853  1864  1835  1885
                  1973  1838  1851  1829  1880  1985
                  1920  1837  1849  1824  1856  1980
                  1903  1831  1848  1823  1856  1975
                  1893  1828  1847  1821  1834  1945
                  1884  1825  1846  1820  1830  1936
                  1876  1819  1833  1818  1817  1928
            1974  1858  1812  1827  1813  1809  1927
            1930  1842  1811  1826  1806  1800  1915  1958  1954
            1917  1841  1797  1822  1803  1799  1904  1935  1933
            1907  1839  1796  1816  1802  1798  1852  1908  1862
 1931 1937  1857  1836  1795  1815  1793  1794  1850  1879  1808      1843
 1807 1801  1854  1810  1792  1805  1791  1790  1832  1863  1804      1814
─────────────────────────────────────────────────────────────────────────
 -50%  -40%  -30%  -20%  -10%   0%   10%   20%   30%   40%   50%   60%   70%   80%
```

Ranges of Yearly Returns in Percent

year, resulting in a value [for that nominal dollar] of almost $5 million by year-end 1985.

Nonetheless, this spectacular return came at a substantial risk to investors. Total returns were negative in about 29 percent of the years. These returns have a standard deviation of over 19 percent, another indication of their relatively wide variability. The distribution of annual total returns since 1790 is displayed as a histogram.

Part Two

Advice, Opinions, and Commentary

No Tears for "The Market"

MIKE ROYKO

Mike Royko is a tough, straight-talking social and political observer
whose biography of Chicago's Mayor Richard Daley is a classic of its
genre. He is also an economist and a columnist for the *Chicago Tribune,* in which this hard-hitting piece on the 1980s divergence between "The Market" and reality appeared. His focus was the takeover
frenzy then impacting stock values.

* * *

I can't help it. While it might sound cruel and sadistic, when the stock
market takes one of its periodic head-first dives, I enjoy the spectacle.
Not that I really understand it. It baffles me that one day a big corporation can be worth $10 billion. But a day or two later, it is suddenly
worth only $8 billion.

It is still making the same products that are selling for the same price
in the same quantity. The same people are coming to work and getting
the same paychecks. Yet, on paper, the company is worth far less today
than it was yesterday.

But what I do understand is that when this happens on a grand scale,
to hundreds or thousands of companies, somebody is taking a financial
bath, getting clobbered, maybe even losing their shirt, trousers, underwear, driver, and limo.

I'd feel bad if I thought that little old widows in three-room flats
were being wiped out. Or if those who sweep streets, empty bedpans,
or put out fires were losing their nest eggs.

But, from what I read, that isn't the case. The average person is not
on the phone telling a broker to buy, sell, go short, go long, go medium,
stop, start, hop, skip, or whatever all that jargon is.

My guess is that if I called most of the people I know, and asked them

Reprinted from *The Chicago Tribune,* October 16, 1989, Sec. 1, Col. 1, p. 3, by permission
of Tribune Media Services.

if they just took a bath in the market, they'd say: "No, I took a shower in my washroom."

That's because most people have wised up. They'd no more get involved with that strange creature called *The Market* than they'd buy a gold watch or chain from some seedy guy standing in a doorway.

The Market. All you have to do is look at the headlines or listen to the daily broadcasts and you think you are hearing the latest medical report on someone who ought to be in therapy, on tranquilizers, or strapped down by the attendants. It sounds like a manic-depressive-psycho-head case.

"The Market up on heavy trading this morning, buoyed by reports of . . . The Market closed sharply down on light trading this evening, in the wake of reports . . . The Market reacted nervously to reports that the President found a pimple on his neck . . . The Market bounced back on reports that the President saw a dermatologist."

What kind of way to do business is that?

No, if we get another Black Monday, Gray Tuesday, or Olive-Drab Wednesday, I won't be shedding tears for those with the vanishing bottom lines. Just as I never offer sympathy for those who try to fill inside straights.

The last time The Market went from manic to depressive, we were told it was caused by computers going berserk or some such thing. If that was the reason, why didn't somebody crawl behind the computer and pull out the plug? That's what I'd do if my TV started spewing smoke.

This time we're told that the sudden drop was caused by the fear that there won't be any more greed-oozing takeovers. If that is so, it's a delight.

That means that the stock prices of companies have been going up and up and up not because anybody thinks that what they make or sell is getting better or more popular. It's because they think that a Wall Street land shark has an eye on a company and is circling. And that the land shark intends to borrow a fortune at high interest rates, break up the company, sell off chunks of it to pay off the big debt, and walk away with a fat profit. In the process, productive careers will be ruined, workers will find their lives turned upside down, companies might no longer exist, but the land sharks and those who finance them will have full bellies.

And that's why—despite the hysteria of Black Monday—the prices of stocks have been creeping upward. It's been a guessing game. Will this or that company be taken over? One little rumor, and the stock becomes manic. No, the rumor goes, now the company is no longer a tasty morsel. So the same stock sinks into a blue funk.

Now on Wall Street, LaSalle Street, and all the other places the sharks lurk, they're screaming: "Nobody is going to take over nothing anymore for ever and ever."

And suddenly those who wanted to be in on the kill are in a panic. What? No more feeding frenzies? No more ripping and shredding of slow-swimming companies? Let me out! We keep hearing that the small investor no longer is interested in the stock market. Of course he isn't. Little fish know that it isn't safe to swim with the sharks.

A Persistent Delusion

HENRY W. DUNN

Henry Dunn of Scudder, Stevens & Clark spoke out against what he called the Persistent Delusion that stock market forecasting could be done successfully, and urged his fellow investment counselors to insist on the separation of investing and stock market guessing. (Readers will also enjoy his long and graceful sentences.)

. . .

There is hardly anything more important to the future standing and usefulness of the investment counsel profession than that every reasonable effort should be made to disabuse the public mind, as far as possible, of the widespread belief or assumption, unwarranted and erroneous in fact, that competent investment management is largely a matter of anticipating stock market movements, and hence that the chief function of investment counsel is successful stock market guessing.

That statement, however, is altogether too condensed for all its implications to be immediately apparent. In attempting to deal with the situation to which I refer, it should, I believe, first of all be made clear, if means can be found to do that effectively, that investment counsel, properly so described, professes to be qualified to give advice on investment, and not on the quite different and much more adventurous activities of stock market trading—a fundamental distinction that, in my opinion, a large section of the public entirely fails to recognize or appreciate. It is necessary to go further, however, in order to give that distinction practical importance in the public mind, and to make known as widely as possible what I regard as the plain truth: that, with all the effort that has been expended on attempts to discover or devise new and better methods of forecasting or to develop greater skill in the use of the old methods, guessing the next move of the stock market, with

Reprinted with permission of Scudder, Stevens & Clark.

due reference to the two vital factors of direction and timing, still remains little more than a gamble. . . .

[M]y main thesis involves not only an assertion of the prevalence and persistence among the general public of an always wishful and more or less confident belief in the predictability by experts of coming stock market movements, but also the further assertion that this persistent belief, or mixture of hope and belief, is in fact a delusion.

To present definite records of factual research sufficient to prove beyond doubt or argument a negative proposition of that character would be an almost impossible task. Enough is certainly known of the past failures of various forecasting methods so that the burden of proof may fairly be thrown on the man who seriously claims to have perfected the necessary technique. In other words, I propose to stand on the assertion I have made, and like the political orators, challenge successful contradiction.

If, however, there should be among my hearers any who still retain a good deal of confidence in their own forecasting ability, I will add for their benefit a word of caution and warning. In a field presenting as many difficult problems as the field of investment, in which there are many uncertainties besides those of stock market guessing—and a good many rules at one time generally accepted and successfully followed have had to be later modified or abandoned to meet changes in underlying conditions none too easily or promptly recognized—there seem to me to be some lessons taught by long and responsible investment experience that, I am almost tempted to say, are effectively taught in no other way. . . .

The long-run unreliability of stock market predictions as a basis for either investment or trading policy is, I believe, one of the lessons taught by long and responsible experience, and nonetheless effectively because various systems may at times have appeared to work fairly well for periods just long enough to mislead the unwary. I am willing to rest my conclusions on this point on what I believe would be the overwhelming testimony of those whose experience has been sufficiently extended for an adequate test of ultimate results.

When to Sell—and When Not To

PHILIP A. FISHER

**Philip Fisher's *Common Stocks and Uncommon Profits* first appeared
in 1958. In it, he presented the case for growth stock investing and
explained the advantages of his "scuttlebutt" method for learning about
companies by talking to competitors, suppliers, and, particularly, former
employees. The book is full of practical Do's and Don'ts for individual
investors. In these excerpts, Fisher explains what to look for in a
prospective investment and identifies the only investment reasons ever
to sell a stock.**

. . .

There are many good reasons why an investor might decide to sell common stocks. He may want to build a new home or finance his son in
a business. Any one of a number of similar reasons can, from the standpoint of happy living, make selling common stocks sensible. This type
of selling, however, is personal rather than financial in its motive. As
such it is well beyond the scope of this book. These comments are only
designed to cover that type of selling that is motivated by a single
objective—obtaining the greatest total dollar benefit from the investment dollars available.

There are three reasons, and three reasons only, for the sale of any
common stock. The first of these reasons should be obvious to anyone.
This is when a mistake has been made in the original purchase and it
becomes increasingly clear that the factual background of the particular company is, by a significant margin, less favorable than originally
believed. The proper handling of this type of situation is largely a matter
of emotional self-control. To some degree it also depends upon the
investor's ability to be honest with himself.

From Philip A. Fisher, *Common Stocks and Uncommon Profits* (Woodside, California, 1984;
originally published 1958), 15–51, 82–91. All rights reserved by PSR Publications, 301
Henrik Road, Woodside, CA 94062. PSR Publications is a division of Fisher Investments,
Inc.

Two of the important characteristics of common stock investment are the large profits that can come with proper handling, and the high degree of skill, knowledge, and judgment required for such proper handling. Since the process of obtaining these almost fantastic profits is so complex, it is not surprising that a certain percentage of errors in purchasing are sure to occur. Fortunately the long-range profits from really good common stocks should more than balance the losses from a normal percentage of such mistakes. They should leave a tremendous margin of gain as well. This is particularly true if the mistake is recognized quickly. When this happens, losses, if any, should be far smaller than if the stock bought in error had been held for a long period of time. Even more important, the funds tied up in the undesirable situation are freed to be used for something else that, if properly selected, should produce substantial gains.

However, there is a complicating factor that makes the handling of investment mistakes more difficult. This is the ego in each of us. None of us likes to admit to himself that he has been wrong. If we have made a mistake in buying a stock but can sell the stock at a small profit, we have somehow lost any sense of having been foolish. On the other hand, if we sell at a small loss we are quite unhappy about the whole matter. This reaction, while completely natural and normal, is probably one of the most dangerous in which we can indulge ourselves in the entire investment process. More money has probably been lost by investors holding a stock they really did not want until they could "at least come out even" than from any other single reason. If to these actual losses are added the profits that might have been made through the proper reinvestment of these funds if such reinvestment had been made when the mistake was first realized, the cost of self-indulgence becomes truly tremendous.

Furthermore this dislike of taking a loss, even a small loss, is just as illogical as it is natural. If the real object of common stock investment is the making of a gain of a great many hundreds percent over a period of years, the difference between, say, a 20 percent loss or a 5 percent profit becomes a comparatively insignificant matter. What matters is not whether a loss occasionally occurs. What does matter is whether worthwhile profits so often fail to materialize that the skill of the investor or his advisor in handling investments must be questioned.

While losses should never cause strong self-disgust or emotional upset, neither should they be passed over lightly. They should always be reviewed with care so that a lesson is learned from each of them. If the particular elements which caused a misjudgment on a common stock purchase are thoroughly understood, it is unlikely that another poor purchase will be made through misjudging the same investment factors.

We come now to the second reason why sale should be made of a common stock. . . . Sales should always be made of the stock of a company that, because of changes resulting from the passage of time, no longer qualifies . . . to about the same degree it qualified at the time of purchase. This is why investors should be constantly on their guard. It explains why it is of such importance to keep at all times in close contact with the affairs of companies whose shares are held.

When companies deteriorate in this way they usually do so for one of two reasons. Either there has been a deterioration of management, or the company no longer has the prospect of increasing the markets for its product in the way it formerly did. Sometimes management deteriorates because success has affected one or more key executives. Smugness, complacency, or inertia replace the former drive and ingenuity. More often it occurs because a new set of top executives do not measure up to the standard of performance set by their predecessors. Either they no longer hold to the policies that have made the company outstandingly successful, or they do not have the ability to continue to carry out such policies. When any of these things happen the affected stock should be sold at once, regardless of how good the general market may look or how big the capital gains tax may be.

Similarly it sometimes happens that after growing spectacularly for many years, a company will reach a stage where the growth prospects of its markets are exhausted. From this time on it will only do about as well as [the] industry as a whole. It will only progress at about the same rate as the national economy does. This change may not be due to any deterioration of the management. Many managements show great skill in developing related or allied products to take advantage of growth in their immediate field. They recognize, however, that they do not have any particular advantage if they go into unrelated spheres of activity. Hence, if after years of being experts in a young and growing industry, times change and the company has pretty well exhausted the growth prospects of its market, its shares have deteriorated in an important way from the standards outlined under our frequently mentioned fifteen points. Such a stock should then be sold.

In this instance, selling might take place at a more leisurely pace than if management deterioration had set in. Possibly part of the holding might be kept until a more suitable investment could be found. However, in any event, the company should be recognized as no longer suitable for worthwhile investment. The amount of capital gains tax, no matter how large, should seldom prevent the switching of such funds into some other situation that, in the years ahead, may grow in a manner similar to the way in which this investment formerly grew.

There is a good test as to whether companies no longer adequately qualify in regard to this matter of expected further growth. This is for the investor to ask himself whether at the next peak of a business cycle, regardless of what may happen in the meantime, the comparative per-share earnings (after allowances for stock dividends and stock splits but not for new shares issued for additional capital) will probably show at least as great an increase from present levels as the present levels show from the last known peak of general business activity. If the answer is in the affirmative, the stock probably should be held. If in the negative, it should probably be sold.

For those who follow the right principles in making their original purchases, the third reason why a stock might be sold seldom arises, and should be acted upon only if an investor is very sure of his ground. It arises from the fact that opportunities for attractive investment are extremely hard to find. From a timing standpoint, they are seldom found just when investment funds happen to be available. If an investor has had funds for investment for quite a period of time and found few attractive situations into which to place these funds, he may well place some or all of them in a well-run company that he believes has definite growth prospects. However, these growth prospects may be at a slower average annual rate than may appear to be the case for some other seemingly more attractive situation that is found later. The already-owned company may in some other important aspects appear to be less attractive as well.

If the evidence is clear-cut and the investor feels quite sure of his ground, it will, even after paying capital gains taxes, probably pay him handsomely to switch into the situation with seemingly better prospects. The company that can show an average annual increase of 12 percent for a long period of years should be a source of considerable financial satisfaction to its owners. However, the difference between these results and those that could occur from a company showing a 20 percent average annual gain would be well worth the additional trouble and capital gains taxes that might be involved.

A word of caution may not be amiss, however, in regard to too readily selling a common stock in the hope of switching these funds into a still better one. There is always the risk that some major element in the picture has been misjudged. If this happens, the investment probably will not turn out nearly as well as anticipated. In contrast, an alert investor who has held a good stock for some time usually gets to know its less desirable as well as its more desirable characteristics. Therefore, before selling a rather satisfactory holding in order to get a still better one, there is need of the greatest care in trying to appraise accurately all elements of the situation.

At this point the critical reader has probably discerned a basic investment principle that by and large seems only to be understood by a small minority of successful investors. This is that once a stock has been properly selected and has borne the test of time, it is only occasionally that there is any reason for selling it at all. However, recommendations and comments continue to pour out of the financial community giving other types of reasons for selling outstanding common stocks. What about the validity of such reasons?

Most frequently given of such reasons is the conviction that a general stock market decline of some proportion is somewhere in the offing. . . . [P]ostponing an attractive purchase because of fear of what the general market might do will, over the years, proves very costly. This is because the investor is ignoring a powerful influence about which he has positive knowledge through fear of a less powerful force about which, in the present state of human knowledge, he and everyone else is largely guessing. If the argument is valid that the purchase of attractive common stocks should not be unduly influenced by fear of ordinary bear markets, the argument against selling outstanding stocks because of these fears is even more impressive. . . . Furthermore, the chance of the investor being right in making such sales is still further diminished by the factor of the capital gains tax. Because of the very large profits such outstanding stocks should be showing if they have been held for a period of years, this capital gains tax can still further accentuate the cost of making such sales.

There is another and even more costly reason why an investor should never sell out of an outstanding situation because of the possibility that an ordinary bear market may be about to occur. If the company is really a right one, the next bull market should see the stock making a new peak well above those so far attained. How is the investor to know when to buy back? Theoretically it should be after the coming decline. However, this presupposes that the investor will know when the decline will end. I have seen many investors dispose of a holding that was to show stupendous gain in the years ahead because of this fear of a coming bear market. Frequently the bear market never came and the stock went right on up. When a bear market has come, I have not seen one time in ten when the investor actually got back into the same shares before they had gone up above his selling price. Usually he either waited for them to go far lower than they actually dropped, or, when they were way down, fear of something else happening still prevented their reinstatement.

This brings us to another line of reasoning so often used to cause well-intentioned but unsophisticated investors to miss huge future profits. This is the argument that an outstanding stock has become overpriced and therefore should be sold. What is more logical than this? If a stock is overpriced, why not sell it rather than keep it?

Before reaching hasty conclusions, let us look a little bit below the surface. Just what is overpriced? What are we trying to accomplish? Any really good stock will sell and should sell at a higher ratio to current earnings than a stock with a stable rather than an expanding earning power. After all, this probability of participating in continued growth is obviously worth something. When we say that the stock is overpriced, we may mean that it is selling at an even higher ratio in relation to this expected earning power than we believe it should be. Possibly we may mean that it is selling at an even higher ratio than are other comparable stocks with similar prospects of materially increasing their future earnings.

All of this is trying to measure something with a greater degree of preciseness than is possible. The investor cannot pinpoint just how much per share a particular company will earn two years from now. He can at best judge this within such general and nonmathematical limits as "about the same," "up moderately," "up a lot," or "up tremendously." As a matter of fact, the company's top management cannot come a great deal closer than this. Either they or the investor should come pretty close in judging whether a sizable increase in average earnings is likely to occur a few years from now. But just how much increase, or the exact year in which it will occur, usually involves guessing on enough variables to make precise predictions impossible.

Under these circumstances, how can anyone say with even moderate precision just what is overpriced for an outstanding company with an unusually rapid growth rate? Suppose that instead of selling at 25 times earnings, as usually happens, the stock is now at 35 times earnings. Perhaps there are new products in the immediate future, the real economic importance of which the financial community has not yet grasped. Perhaps there are not any such products. If the growth rate is so good that in another 10 years the company might well have quadrupled, is it really of such great concern whether at the moment the stock might or might not be 35 percent overpriced? That which really matters is not to disturb a position that is going to be worth a great deal later.

Again our old friend the capital gains tax adds its bit to these conclusions. Growth stocks that are recommended for sale because they are supposedly overpriced nearly always will cost their owners a sizable capital gains tax if they are sold. Therefore, in addition to the risk of losing a permanent position in a company that over the years should continue to show unusual further gains, we also incur a sizable tax liability. Isn't it safer and cheaper simply to make up our minds that momentarily the stock may be somewhat ahead of itself? We already have a sizable profit in it. If for a while the stock loses, say, 35 percent of its current market quotation, is this really such a serious matter? Again, isn't the maintaining of our position rather than the possibility of temporarily losing a small part of our capital gain the matter that is really important?

There is still one other argument investors sometimes use to separate themselves from the profits they would otherwise make. This one is the most ridiculous of all. It is that the stock they own has had a huge advance. Therefore, just because it has gone up, it has probably used up most of its potential. Consequently they should sell it and buy something that hasn't gone up yet. Outstanding companies, the only type that I believe the investor should buy, just don't function this way. How they do function might best be understood by considering the following somewhat fanciful analogy:

Suppose it is the day you were graduated from college. If you did not go to college, consider it to be the day of your high school graduation; from the standpoint of our example it will make no difference whatsoever. Now suppose that on this day each of your male classmates had an urgent need of immediate cash. Each offered you the same deal. If you would give them a sum of money equivalent to 10 times whatever they might earn during the first 12 months after they had gone to work, that classmate would for the balance of his life turn over to you one-quarter of each year's earnings! Finally let us suppose that, while you thought this was an excellent proposition, you only had spare cash on hand sufficient to make such a deal with three of your classmates.

At this point, your reasoning would closely resemble that of the investor using sound investment principles in selecting common stocks. You would immediately start analyzing your classmates, not from the standpoint of how pleasant they might be or even how talented they might be in other ways, but solely to determine how much money they might make. If you were part of a large class, you would probably eliminate quite a number solely on the ground of not knowing them suffi-

ciently well to be able to pass worthwhile judgment on just how financially proficient they actually would get to be. Here again, the analogy
with intelligent common stock buying runs very close.

Eventually you would pick the three classmates you felt would have
the greatest future earning power. You would make your deal with them.
Ten years have passed. One of your three has done sensationally. Going
to work for a large corporation, he has won promotion after promotion.
Already insiders in the company are saying that the president has his
eye on him and that in another 10 years he will probably take the top
job. He will be in line for the large compensation, stock options, and
pension benefits that go with that job.

Under these circumstances, what would even the writers of stock
market reports who urge taking profits on superb stocks that "have gotten
ahead of the market" think of your selling out your contract with this
former classmate, just because someone has offered you 600 percent on
your original investment? You would think that anyone would need to
have his head examined if he were to advise you to sell this contract
and replace it with one with another former classmate whose annual
earnings still were about the same as when he left school 10 years before.
The argument that your successful classmate had had his advance while
the advance of your (financially) unsuccessful classmate still lay ahead
of him would probably sound rather silly. If you know your common
stocks equally well, many of the arguments commonly heard for selling
the good one sound equally silly.

You may be thinking all this sounds fine, but actually classmates are
not common stocks. To be sure, there is one major difference. That
difference increases rather than decreases the reason for never selling
the outstanding common stock just because it has had a huge rise and
may be temporarily overpriced. This difference is that the classmate is
finite, may die soon, and is sure to die eventually. There is no similar
life span for the common stock. The company behind the common
stock can have a practice of selecting management talent in depth and
training such talent in company policies, methods, and techniques in
a way that will retain and pass on the corporate vigor for generations.
Look at Du Pont in its second century of corporate existence. Look at

Dow years after the death of its brilliant founder. In this era of unlimited human wants and incredible markets, there is no limitation to corporate growth such as the life span places upon the individual.

Perhaps the thoughts behind this chapter might be put into a single sentence: If the job has been correctly done when a common stock is purchased, the time to sell it is—almost never.

Three Ways to Succeed as an Investor

CHARLES D. ELLIS

Charley Ellis has long encouraged investors to commit to determining and staying with a truly long-term investment policy. This excerpt from a 1988 address to the Empire Club in Toronto is yet another such appeal.

· · ·

There are three ways in which you might try to achieve superior results: one is physically difficult; one is intellectually difficult; and one is emotionally difficult.

Warren Buffett, John Templeton, Dean LeBaron, and Warren Goldring and a very few others have staked out the intellectually difficult way of beating the market.

Intellectually difficult investing is pursued by those who have a deep and profound understanding of the true nature of investing, see the future more clearly, and take long-term positions that turn out to be remarkably successful. We admire them, but usually only in retrospect. At the time of their doing their best work, we see them as misguided. We do not want to do what they are doing because it looks so unpromising.

Most of the crowd is deeply involved in the physically difficult way of beating the market. See if you don't recognize the physically difficult right away. They come to the office earlier; they stay later. They read a larger number of reports more rapidly. They go to more breakfast meetings and more luncheon meetings and more dinner meetings. They are on the telephone, making more calls and receiving more calls than all the rest. They carry huge briefcases home at night, determined to get ahead by reading more reports before the morrow. In every way they possibly can, they put enormous physical energy into trying to beat the

Reprinted from a 1988 speech to the Empire Club in Toronto, by permission of the author.

market by outworking the competition. What they don't seem to recognize is that so is almost everyone else.

Being incapable of doing the intellectually difficult, and reluctant about the physically difficult, I have set about the emotionally difficult approach to investing. This straightforward, untiring approach is simply to work out the long-term investment policy that's truly right for you and your particular circumstances and is realistic given the history of the capital markets, commit to it, and—here is the emotionally difficult part—hold on.

When your friends turn to you and say, "Wow! Have I got an opportunity for you! This is a great time to buy!" be absolutely uninterested. And when they turn to you and say, "Oh, Lord, this is it. It's going to be one hell of a crash. Get out now while you can!" you must simply not be interested, absolutely sound asleep. No intellectual effort; no physical effort; but for most, emotionally far too difficult. It suits me just fine. It requires no great genius and no great brawn, but it works.

The Value of Patience

JAMES H. GIPSON

Jim Gipson has developed a successful investment management firm and written a "plain-talk" book on investing, Winning the Investment Game. This excerpt, extolling the value of patience, is drawn from a chapter called "The Virtues of Investing."

. . .

Patience is a virtue with a strange distribution among investors. Young investors have all the time in the world to enjoy the long-term benefits of patient investing, but they generally are the least patient. They want instant gratification and immediate results. They want everything right now, including instant investment performance. Young investors who own stocks are likely to check their prices on a daily or hourly basis even when they are not actively buying or selling.

Old investors do not have much time left and are actuarially unlikely to enjoy the long-term results of patient investing. Their lives are entering their twilight years, yet they invest as if there will be an infinite number of tomorrows. Old investors tend to be patient investors despite the apparent lack of payoff from that patience.

For both young and old, temperament plays a larger role in their investing than most care to acknowledge. The young in a hurry in their business and social lives are likely to be in a hurry to see investment results too. The old who are patient in most other aspects of life are likely to be patient in investing too.

For the investors of any age who can rise above their own temperaments and choose rational courses of action that are most likely to enrich them, there are compelling arguments for choosing patience.

Patience is necessary simply by nature of the investing game itself.

Reprinted from *Winning the Investment Game* (1984), Chapter 10, pp. 155–157, by permission of McGraw-Hill Publishing Company, New York.

Over short periods of one to two years, luck is probably more important than skill. Stock prices have a large random element to them, analogous to Brownian motion in physics. That random motion of stock prices is a more important determinant of profits and losses than are skill and strategy in the short run. Only over periods of three to five years do the random movements of stock prices cancel each other out, leaving the net result of the investor's intelligence and diligence. . . .

Patience focuses an investor's attention on the goal of compounding money over a long period. Compounding can be magic, even when the compounding rate is modest. Investors who compound their money in real terms at 7 percent per year will double it in 10 years; in 40 years they will have 16 times their original amount. If the Indians and their descendants who sold Manhattan for $24 had been successful in compounding their money at 7 percent after taxes for the last 350 years, they would have about $30 billion today.

That $30 billion demonstrates more than the magic of compounding at even moderate rates of return. The complete absence of any pools of private capital remotely approaching $30 billion suggests that long-term compounding is an extraordinarily difficult feat. Even if one or two generations of investors are capable enough to accumulate and compound a respectable pool of assets, one of the heirs is likely to dissipate or lose it all.

The mortal enemy of compounding is the wipeout. A respectable rate of compounding for a lifetime can be lost with a single bad investment decision. The odds are that an investor will make that decision, or one of the investor's heirs will. Reducing the odds of a wipeout and raising the rate of compounding are the twin goals of this essay.

Patience has more than the long-term advantage of focusing an investor's attention on the goals of long-term compounding and avoiding a wipeout. Patience also helps control short-term brokerage costs as well. The patient investor is less likely to buy and sell often, thereby reducing the 6 percent that a real estate broker charges or the roughly 3 to 4 percent that a normal stock broker charges for a round trip to sell one stock and buy another (discount brokers charge much less, and a stockholder should use one). A toll charge of 3 to 6 percent may seem small in relation to the total amount of an investor's principal, but it is large in relation to the annual income and profit received. If, for example, an impatient stockholder makes 10 percent per year in profits and turns over his portfolio twice a year at an average cost of 3 percent per turn, then 60 percent of his annual profits go to his broker! At the end of each year investors should add up their brokerage commissions along with their net profits, and then compare the two figures to see whether it is they or their brokers who are making the most money off the investments.

Human Foibles

GEORGE ROSS GOOBEY

George Ross Goobey, a compelling presence and an engaging speaker and storyteller, has been called upon often to share with others the lessons learned as one of Britain's leading investors over the past half century. Here he counsels against being captives of our preconceptions and preferences.

. . .

There is an old and, I think, misleading adage that runs "always take a profit and you will never make a loss." As a long-term investor I have found it more profitable to run profits and cut losses. What I am really leading up to saying is that in considering whether one should sell an investment it is much better to ignore the price paid and to endeavour to judge the future of the Company on the facts of the situation in which the original cost of your own particular investment plays no part whatsoever. Unfortunately, however, human nature being what it is this cost factor seems to play the most important part and one is much more ready to sell an investment standing above the price paid for it than vice versa.

I am often asked to advise which security or securities in a portfolio should be sold when it is necessary to raise funds and it is quite apparent that the questioners' own ideas are to sell the stock or stocks which are "standing at a profit," quite regardless of the particular Company's future investment prospects. I remember saying to one such enquirer on one of these occasions when he was obviously anxious to sell his best stocks because they were standing at a profit over what he had paid for them "I think you would get a better result by using a pin to make your choice," but if he approached his problem from the right angle, namely, the "forward looking" rather than the "backward jobbing" he would find that he had decided to sell in most cases those that were

---

Reprinted from an unpublished paper, 1963, by permission of the author.

standing at a loss on what he had paid for them. Time after time when I am confronted with a portfolio of investments I find that the majority are quite sound holdings, but at the bottom of the list there are a few worthless shares. On enquiry one usually elicits the explanation that although the holder had been frequently advised that the future of these shares was in danger, he could not bring himself to sell them at a loss on what had been paid for them with the result that eventually they had become entirely worthless.

There is also a type of investor who gets even more keen to buy when the price of a share falls below the price of his original purchase— "averaging" as it is called. It is a sort of human vanity that cannot admit that the original purchase was wrong and that therefore it must be an even better investment to purchase more shares at a cheaper price.

On the Threat of Change

ARTHUR ZEIKEL

Arthur Zeikel, president of Merrill Lynch Asset Management and co-author of the leading textbook, *Investment Analysis and Portfolio Management,* is a regular and thoughtful observer of the investing scene. Here, he leads us to an answer to the question, "Why are so many of us wrong so much of the time?"

• • •

Why are so many of us wrong so much of the time? Surely, one reason is that we accommodate change poorly. More for emotional than logical reasons, we tend to base our expectations on the status quo. All too often, our expectations fail to materialize. John Maynard Keynes put it this way: "The facts of the existing situation enter, in a sense disproportionately, into the formation of our long-term expectations: our usual practice being to take the existing situation and to project it into a future modified only to the extent that we have more or less definite reasons for expecting a change."

We compound the problem by tending to become overly protective of our own judgments. Not because they are right, or even likely to be right, but because they are ours. This in turn leads to an unwillingness to accept new information for what it's worth. Frequently, it's worth a great deal, and our reluctance to consider new information with an open mind makes it harder to recognize the flaws in our old operating premise. Instead, we tend to develop a "defensive" interpretation of new developments, and this cripples our capacity for making good judgments about the future.

Investors, portfolio managers, and the like have even more than the normal problems to contend with. For one thing, they are continually forced to deal with change. Their principal task is, or should be, build-

Reprinted from *The Financial Analysts Journal,* Vol. 31, No. 6, November/December 1975, 3–7. Charlottesville, Virginia: Association for Investment Management and Research.

ing an accurate concept of the future, a task fraught with uncertainty. For another, the myriad opinions available at any time, usually from reliable sources, inevitably include embracing those ideas whose time has passed. . . .

Most of us harbor an almost natural, instinctive resistance to change. We find it much more comfortable to deal with past certainties, no matter how unpleasant, than contemplate the unknowns of the future. To this extent we try to preserve the present for as long as possible. As a result, our primary response to change is reactive, not anticipatory. Something has to happen first, before we are willing to respond. That is why, as Peter Bernstein recently noted, "Single events may prompt investors to resolve indecision and act—but the fundamental environment has to be such that people are looking for a reason to act positively." Humphrey Neill suggests that "sudden events quickly crystallize opinion."

Indecision has probably cost investors more than bad judgment. It is hard for people who reach a decision after careful analysis of their information to change their minds easily—or quickly. Thus we go, according to Claude Rosenberg, ". . . to the greatest extremes to support original judgments—even after they have been proved incorrect." Rather than keeping a free and open mind we set our opinions too firmly, thereby preventing an explanation of information contrary to our expectations.

People's responses reflect their insecurities and desires for self-protection. Fear of being wrong, for example, influences the way people react to new information. We have to learn how to be wrong more gracefully and to accept errors of judgment, particularly in forecasting, as normal—in fact, inevitable. Only then can our orientation toward that aspect of reality that is change be more adequate. Rather than practicing the "human tendency to rationalize mistakes," we will be better able to accept change for what it is: "the disparity between the course of events and our expectation or our hopes and fears." It has to be recognized, and accepted, that change is not an implicit criticism of our personal investment in the status quo, but rather an inevitable part of reality. On the other hand, it usually requires some fresh thinking and, very often, a new response.

To be sure, most of us would rather react to than initiate a new point of view. In dealing with this very problem, Thomas Kuhn accurately points out in *The Structure of Scientific Revolutions* that "the man who embraces a new paradigm at an early stage must often do so in defiance of the evidence provided by problem-solving. He must, that is, have faith that the new paradigm will succeed with the many large problems that confront it, knowing only that the older paradigm has failed with a few. A decision of that kind can only be made on faith.

Many investors get "nickeled and dimed" into penury by failing to appreciate that the first loss is not only the best, but usually the smallest. They must learn to avoid defensive rationalization of their past bad judgments. When things change, they change, and it is better to recognize it, by admitting error and shifting, than fighting reality until conventional opinion converges on the new view and sweeps the old one away. A good rule to practice is that, once a pattern of expectation is accepted and taken for granted, its reasonableness should be questioned all the more: Circumstances change faster than is commonly recognized.

Mistakes of the First 25 Years

WARREN E. BUFFETT

Warren Buffett emerges as a two-time contributor to this collection primarily because he has so much of value to say and because he says it so very well. Here, in the 1989 Annual Report, he shares the lessons he has learned during his first quarter century as Berkshire Hathaway's principal, and controlling, shareholder.

• • •

To quote Robert Benchley, "Having a dog teaches a boy fidelity, perseverance, and to turn around three times before lying down." Such are the shortcomings of experience. Nevertheless, it's a good idea to review past mistakes before committing new ones. So let's take quick look at the last 25 years.

My first mistake, of course, was in buying control of Berkshire. Though I knew its business—textile manufacturing—to be unpromising, I was enticed to buy because the price looked cheap. Stock purchases of that kind had proved reasonably rewarding in my early years, though by the time Berkshire came along in 1965 I was becoming aware that the strategy was not ideal.

If you buy a stock at a sufficiently low price, there will usually be some hiccup in the fortunes of the business that gives you a chance to unload at a decent profit, even though the long-term performance of the business may be terrible. I call this the "cigar butt" approach to investing. A cigar butt found on the street that has only one puff left in it may not offer much of a smoke, but the "bargain purchase" will make that puff all profit.

Unless you are a liquidator, that kind of approach to buying businesses is foolish. First, the original "bargain" price probably will not turn out to be such a steal after all. In a difficult business, no sooner is

---

Excerpted from the "Chairman's Letter," *Berkshire Hathaway, Inc. 1989 Annual Report*, by permission of the author.

one problem solved than another surfaces—never is there just one cockroach in the kitchen. Second, any initial advantage you secure will be quickly eroded by the low return that the business earns. For example, if you buy a business for $8 million that can be sold or liquidated for $10 million and promptly take either course, you can realize a high return. But the investment will disappoint if the business is sold for $10 million in 10 years and in the interim has annually earned and distributed only a few percent on cost. Time is the friend of the wonderful business, the enemy of the mediocre.

You might think this principle is obvious, but I had to learn it the hard way—in fact, I had to learn it several times over. Shortly after purchasing Berkshire, I acquired a Baltimore department store, Hochschild, Kohn, buying through a company called Diversified Retailing that later merged with Berkshire. I bought at a substantial discount from book value, the people were first class, and the deal included some extras—unrecorded real estate values and a significant LIFO inventory cushion. How could I miss? So-o-o—three years later I was lucky to sell the business for about what I had paid. After ending our corporate marriage to Hochschild, Kohn, I had memories like those of the husband in the country song, "My Wife Ran Away With My Best Friend and I Still Miss Him a Lot."

I could give you other personal examples of "bargain-purchase" folly, but I'm sure you get the picture: It's far better to buy a wonderful company at a fair price than a fair company at a wonderful price. . . . I was a slow learner. But now, when buying companies or common stocks, we look for first-class businesses accompanied by first-class managements.

That leads right into a related lesson: Good jockeys will do well on good horses, but not on broken-down nags. Both Berkshire's textile business and Hochschild, Kohn had able and honest people running them. The same managers employed in a business with good economic characteristics would have achieved fine records. But they were never going to make any progress while running in quicksand.

I've said many times that when a management with a reputation for brilliance tackles a business with a reputation for bad economics, it is the reputation of the business that remains intact. I just wish I hadn't been so energetic in creating examples. My behavior has matched that admitted by Mae West: "I was Snow White, but I drifted."

A further related lesson: Easy does it. After 25 years of buying and supervising a great variety of businesses, . . . I have *not* learned how to solve difficult business problems. What we have learned is to avoid them. To the extent we have been successful, it is because we concentrated on identifying one-foot hurdles that we could step over rather than because we acquired any ability to clear seven-footers.

The finding may seem unfair, but in both business and investments it is usually far more profitable to simply stick with the easy and obvious than it is to resolve the difficult. On occasion, tough problems must be tackled as was the case when we started our Sunday paper in Buffalo. In other instances, a great investment opportunity occurs when a marvelous business encounters a one-time huge, but solvable, problem as was the case many years back at both American Express and GEICO. Overall, however, we've done better by avoiding dragons than by slaying them.

My most surprising discovery: the overwhelming importance in business of an unseen force that we might call "the institutional imperative." In business school, I was given no hint of the imperative's existence and I did not intuitively understand it when I entered the business world. I thought then that decent, intelligent, and experienced managers would automatically make rational business decisions. But I learned over time that isn't so. Instead, rationality frequently wilts when the institutional imperative comes into play.

For example: (1) As if governed by Newton's First Law of Motion, an institution will resist any change in its current direction; (2) Just as work expands to fill available time, corporate projects or acquisitions will materialize to soak up available funds; (3) Any business craving of the leader, however foolish, will be quickly supported by detailed rate-of-return and strategic studies prepared by his troops; and (4) The behavior of peer companies, whether they are expanding, acquiring, setting executive compensation or whatever, will be mindlessly imitated.

Institutional dynamics, not venality or stupidity, set businesses on

these courses, which are too often misguided. After making some expensive mistakes because I ignored the power of the imperative, I have
tried to organize and manage Berkshire in ways that minimize its influence. . . .

After some other mistakes, I learned to go into business only with
people whom I like, trust, and admire. As I noted before, this policy of
itself will not ensure success: A second-class textile or department-store
company won't prosper simply because its managers are men that you
would be pleased to see your daughter marry. However, an owner—or
investor—can accomplish wonders if he manages to associate himself
with such people in businesses that possess decent economic characteristics. Conversely, we do not wish to join with managers who lack
admirable qualities, no matter how attractive the prospects of their
business. We've never succeeded in making a good deal with a bad
person.

Some of my worst mistakes were not publicly visible. These were
stock and business purchases whose virtues I understood and yet didn't
make. It's no sin to miss a great opportunity outside one's area of competence. But I have passed on a couple of really big purchases that were
served up to me on a platter and that I was fully capable of understanding. For Berkshire's shareholders, myself included, the cost of this thumb
sucking has been huge.

Our consistently conservative financial policies may appear to have
been a mistake, but in my view were not. In retrospect, it is clear that
significantly higher, though still conventional, leverage ratios at Berkshire would have produced considerably better returns on equity than
the 23.8 percent we have actually averaged. Even in 1965, perhaps we
could have judged there to be a 99 percent probability that higher
leverage would lead to nothing but good. Correspondingly, we might
have seen only a 1 percent chance that some shock factor, external or
internal, would cause a conventional debt ratio to produce a result falling
somewhere between temporary anguish and default.

We wouldn't have liked those 99:1 odds—and never will. A small
chance of distress or disgrace cannot, in our view, be offset by a large
chance of extra returns. If your actions are sensible, you are certain to

get good results; in most such cases, leverage just moves things along faster. . . . I have never been in a big hurry: We enjoy the process far more than the proceeds—though we have learned to live with those also.

We hope in another 25 years to report on the mistakes of the first 50. If we are around in 2015 to do that, you can count on this section occupying many more pages than it does here.

Mr. Market, Investment Success, and You

WARREN E. BUFFETT

Warren Buffett's affection for Ben Graham, with whom he studied and worked early in his career, is seen again in this passage from the 1987 Annual Report of Berkshire Hathaway.

• • •

Whenever Charlie [Munger] and I buy common stocks for Berkshire's insurance companies, we approach the transaction as if we were buying into a private business. We look at the economic prospects of the business, the people in charge of running it, and the price we must pay. We do not have in mind any time or price for sale. Indeed, we are willing to hold a stock indefinitely so long as we expect the business to increase in intrinsic value at a satisfactory rate. When investing, we view ourselves as business analysts—not as market analysts, not as macroeconomic analysts, and not even as security analysts.

Our approach makes an active trading market useful, since it periodically presents us with mouth-watering opportunities. But by no means is it essential: a prolonged suspension of trading in the securities we hold would not bother us any more than does the lack of daily quotations on World Book or Fechheimer. Eventually, our economic fate will be determined by the economic fate of the business we own, whether our ownership is partial or total.

Ben Graham, my friend and teacher, long ago described the mental attitude toward market fluctuations that I believe to be most conducive to investment success. He said that you should imagine market quotations as coming from a remarkably accommodating fellow named Mr. Market who is your partner in a private business. Without fail, Mr.

Excerpted from the "Chairman's Letter," *Berkshire Hathaway, Inc. 1987 Annual Report*, by permission of the author.

Market appears daily and names a price at which he will either buy your interest or sell you his.

Even though the business that the two of you own may have economic characteristics that are stable, Mr. Market's quotations will be anything but. For, sad to say, the poor fellow has incurable emotional problems. At times he feels euphoric and can see only the favorable factors affecting the business. When in the mood, he names a very high buy-sell price because he fears that you will snap up his interest and rob him of imminent gains. At other times he is depressed and can see nothing but trouble ahead for both the business and the world. On these occasions he will name a very low price, since he is terrified that you will unload your interest on him.

Mr. Market has another endearing characteristics: He doesn't mind being ignored. If his quotation is uninteresting to you today, he will be back with a new one tomorrow. Transactions are strictly at your option. Under these conditions, the more manic-depressive his behavior, the better for you.

But, like Cinderella at the ball, you must heed one warning or everything will turn into pumpkins and mice: Mr. Market is there to serve you, not to guide you. It is his pocketbook, not his wisdom, that you will find useful. If he shows up some day in a particularly foolish mood, you are free to either ignore him or to take advantage of him, but it will be disastrous if you fall under his influence. Indeed, if you aren't certain that you understand and can value your business far better than Mr. Market, you don't belong in the game. As they say in poker, "If you've been in the game 30 minutes and you don't know who the patsy is, *you're* the patsy."

Ben's Mr. Market allegory may seem out-of-date in today's investment world, in which most professionals and academicians talk of efficient markets, dynamic hedging, and betas. Their interest in such matters is understandable, since techniques shrouded in mystery clearly have value to the purveyor of investment advice. After all, what witch doctor has ever achieved fame and fortune by simply advising, "Take two aspirin"?

The value of market esoterica to the consumer of investment advice is a different story. In my opinion, investment success will not be produced by arcane formulae, computer programs, or signals flashed by the price behavior of stocks and markets. Rather an investor will succeed by coupling good business judgment with an ability to insulate his thoughts and behavior from the supercontagious emotions that swirl about the marketplace. In my own efforts to stay insulated, I have found it highly useful to keep Ben's Mr. Market concept firmly in mind.

Diversification of Investments

GERALD M. LOEB

Gerald Loeb was for many years one of Wall Street's favorite observers, and his book *The Battle for Investment Survival* an enduring favorite. Here is an excerpt—as short and direct as Loeb himself always was.

. . .

I think most accounts have entirely too much diversification of the wrong sort and not enough of the right. I can see no point at all to a distribution of so much percent in oils, so much in motors, so much in rails, etc., nor do I see the point of dividing a fund from a quality angle of so much in "governments," and so on down the list to that so-called very awful, speculative, non-dividend-paying common stock. Some geographical diversification might be justified for large funds.

This sort of thing might be necessary when capital reaches an unwieldy total, or it might be necessary where no intelligent supervision is likely. Otherwise, it is an admission of not knowing what to do and an effort to strike an average.

The intelligent and safe way to handle capital is to concentrate. If things are not clear, do nothing. When something comes up, follow it *to the limit*, subject to the method of procedure that follows. If it's not worth following to the limit, it is not worth following at all. My thought, of course, is always start with a large cash reserve; next, begin in one issue in a small way. If it does not develop, close out and get back to cash. But if it does do what is expected of it, expand your position in this one issue on a scale up. After, but not before, it has safely drawn away from your highest purchase price, then you might consider a second issue.

The greatest safety lies in putting all your eggs in one basket and

From Gerald M. Loeb, *The Battle for Investment Survival* (Burlington, Vermont, 1935–1937, 1943, 1952–1957, 1965), by permission of John Wiley & Sons.

watching the basket. You simply cannot afford to be careless or wrong. Hence, you act with much more deliberation. Of course, no thinking person will buy more of something than the market will take if he wants to sell, and here again, the practical test will force one into the listed leaders where one belongs. A smart trader isn't going to put all his capital into poor collateral, either.

In the old days when brokers' loans were at fantastic heights, the banks used to get a quick idea of the finances of the brokers by the makeup of their loans. If the collateral was all bundles of big active leaders, the bank's opinion was high. But if it was a mixture of new, untried specialties, then the expression was, "So and so is getting to the bottom of his box." Why buy securities that your broker will try to hide in the bottom of his box if his finances permit? Diversification is a balm to many who don't mind taking a chance on something a little sour in a mixed list, figuring on the better ones to pull it out and make a good average.

So buy only staples in securities; the kind that are "not included in this sale." I am thinking now of men's clothing in which all sort of fancy ties, suitings and shirtings are sold at abnormal mark-ups early in the season and for what they are really worth at the close. But certain solid-colored ties, white shirts, plain blue and grey suits, conservatively cut, are practically always excluded from the sale. Securities are not so different, and it is important to deal only in those that always, because of their nature or distribution, have a certain amount of residual interest. Be careful that in "diversifying" you are not supplying the bid for varying groups of narrow market issues that are the style for the moment because there is a special profit in trying to make them so.

Of course, we always have to remember that "one man's meat is another man's poison." The greatest safety for the capable, I might say, lies in putting all one's eggs in one basket and watching the basket. The beginner and those that simply find their investment efforts unsuccessful must resort to orthodox diversification.

I always feel that the less active a stock and the further distant the market, the more potential profit I need to see in it to make it worth buying. If one thinks he sees a potential profit of 100 percent in an active New York Stock Exchange leader, certainly one would have to expect more to go to a regional exchange or over-the-counter or to a foreign market. This is a fundamental and logical principle.

Another angle of diversification nowadays is the fear of atom bombing and what it might do to property. Investors have looked to geographical diversification because of these fears whereas in more normal times, purely profit motives made for concentration. It is purely a personal matter whether an investor feels that efforts at safety from bombing are more important than trying to get the maximum out of investing.

There is a further diversification that I've never seen mentioned and that is important to consider. This is diversification as between the position of varying companies in their business cycle or as between their shares in their market price cycle. This is a very important consideration because dividing one's funds between three or four different situations that happen all to be in the same sector of their cycle can often be discouraging or dangerous. After all, the final determinant of investment success or failure is market price. For example, industries that are in the final stages of a boom with rapidly increasing earnings, dividends, and possibly split-ups, often offer shares high in price but apparently rapidly going higher. There is a sound justification for an investor who knows what he is doing to buy into such a situation, especially for short-term gains, but it would be quite dangerous for him to put all of his funds in three or four such situations. Taken the other way, naturally we all seek deflated and cheap bargains, but very often shares like this will lie on the bottom much longer than we anticipate and if every share we own is in this same category, we may do very badly in a relatively good market.

Investment Strategy

BARTON M. BIGGS

Barton Biggs has reached that rare level of peer recognition where the first name is enough: In conversations among investment professionals in Tokyo, London, New York, and San Francisco, he is known simply as "Barton."

. . .

I believe that an investment manager is complete in terms of knowledge of his profession and the business world after 10 or 15 years of managing money. In that time he has read 100,000 or so research reports and heard at least as many "stories." He has accumulated the conventional wisdom of the market and has a working knowledge of how industries function. He has had his share of winners and bloody noses, his back is permanently twisted from whipsaws, and he has gotten whatever benefit there is to get from being run up and down the market flagpole countless times.

In other words, in that time he has acquired the seminal knowledge and experience and is a seasoned veteran of the investment business. Reading another 100,000 reports, attending another thousand analyst meetings, and collecting some bruises and a limp are merely supportive input—they keep him current but do not deepen his perception or improve his performance capability. The problem is, as that old cynic George Bernard Shaw put it, "Men are wise in proportion, not to their experience, but to their capacity for experience." . . .

We all know that within an investment organization, communication is essential, not only because the investment managers are receiving different information from diverse sources but because, as Oliver Wendell Holmes expressed it: "Many ideas grow better when

Reprinted from Morgan Stanley & Co. Letterhead, New York, January 25, 1977, with permission from Morgan Stanley & Co., Inc.

transplanted into another mind than in the one where they sprung up." . . .

An organizational problem with which the money manager has to contend is the deluge of reading material that descends on him daily. For the veteran investor who has read the 100,000 reports and knows the critical variables of the major industries, there is nothing to be derived from reading another long report about the structure of the paper industry unless it has some new insight. The problem is there is no way of finding this out except by reading, or at least scanning, the report. "Maintenance" information, in other words, what the next couple of quarters' earnings are going to be, has to be assimilated because you need to know what expectations are.

The other problem is that investment managers tend to become compulsive readers. Getting through a stack of reports and statements becomes an accomplishment in and of itself that is, of course, ridiculous. But I think we should all realize that in a job where there is no way to measure labor expended, there is a natural reaction toward any symbol of actually having accomplished something. And working through a pile of reports is accomplishing something. The trouble is that it may be of no benefit. The important thing, obviously, is to get something out of what you are reading.

A corollary of this is a bad habit I get into. I tend to set aside the reports and articles that I know I really want to read carefully, with the idea that I am going to go through all the "maintenance" stuff and the junk quickly and then focus on the heavyweight material. What happens, unfortunately, is that the maintenance material takes longer than it should, and I end up carrying around the good reports in my briefcase for a week or so because I simply haven't had the time to devote to them. In other words, I've processed the junk and haven't read the good reports.

I believe the only answer to this problem is to discipline yourself not to be compulsive; you don't have to look at every piece of research that is sent you. Discard the junk; ignore "maintenance." Instead, you are far better off to read a much smaller amount of good material with care and thoughtfulness. Devote the time that is needed to comprehend thoroughly what the analysis is saying. I think this is much harder than it sounds, but it represents the kind of discipline that has to be applied.

Contrary Opinion in Stock Market Techniques

EDWARD C. JOHNSON, II

Mr. Johnson—or, more formally, Edward C. Johnson, II—devoted his career to the Fidelity Funds, taking control in the early 1940s when assets under management were less than $5 million. Assets now exceed $300 billion. Mr. Johnson's approach to investing was informal to the point of appearing rumpled and was extraordinarily eclectic: He knew a lot about many things and was interested in all of them.

. . .

We approach the problem of investment first and foremost from a money-making point of view. We are not interested in fancy ideas and theories; we are interested in things that work. You might call us empirical pragmatists. Those are almost too heavy words for anyone to swallow, but I hope they convey a picture. Our almost religion is that we believe strongly in analysis of the present. The past is dead. We can learn from it, trying not to indulge in the "backward" successes we might have made. The future is a dream. That may be as may be. If you come to think of it, the present (I talk like a Zen Buddhist now) the present is really the only thing that anybody can actually use. So many people spend their lives thinking about the future ahead that they are hardly conscious of the present. Now there is not much you can do with the future. You can't love it, you can't taste it, you can only dream about it. This is our actual approach; we don't try to forecast. We can't buy or sell securities a month from now; we can only do it today. So what do we do today? That is enough for us to know.

The present we try to use, however, is not a static affair. It is dynamic, full of motion. It is the analysis of these dynamics and motion that is completely vital. To analyze correctly in this way the present . . . is

From a transcript of the First Annual Contrary Opinion Foliage Forum (Manchester, Vermont, 1963). Reprinted by permission of the estate of Edward C. Johnson, II.

to take advantage of the future without the desperate chances inherent in successful forecasting.

We approach the practical investing problem from two angles. First is so-called fundamental research. Let's now look at Contrary Opinion itself. I got to considering it last night. I began to wonder what made Contrary Opinion useful and what was the kind of Contrary Opinion we were interested in. For example: The sun rises tomorrow. I suppose that the general opinion is that the sun will rise tomorrow and it is obvious that here is not an opinion that we wish to be contrary to. Same way with opinions about the weather. Why? Because the opinion itself has no effect on the fact. The general opinion that the sun is going to rise, of course, has no effect on the sun rising, nor has the opinion on the state of the weather any effect on the weather. So may we not say that the test for usefulness of Contrary Opinion is the extent to which the opinion affects the fact under consideration. For example, in contrast to the sun and weather let us look at the stock market. Obviously the general opinion on whether the stock market is going up or down has a profound effect on the action of the market itself. The more unanimous the opinion, the greater the what might called inverse effect on prices will be. . . .

Next I'd like to discuss a rather subtle application of the principle of Contrary Opinion. Let us look at a certain kind of what might be called emotional involvement. Emotional involvement is a very broad thing—it comes up constantly in many forms. For example, an analyst gets emotionally involved with a company he goes to see, a psychiatrist gets emotionally involved with his patient, and the sexes get emotionally involved with each other (to put it mildly). This is something we have to allow for. When we find an analyst is getting that way—and you can tell almost by the tone of his voice and the way he looks when he talks about a company that this is happening—we cannot afford to satisfy the deep human instincts of faithfulness and trust that underlie emotional involvement. Because of the very nature of our business we have to follow the "love 'em and leave 'em" principle.

When troubles loom ahead for a company, what is one's natural instinct? You want to take off your coat and get out with management to tackle and solve the difficulties. But unfortunately that isn't our business, which is to keep investment dollars working in the most productive media. The men running the company involved of course stay with it through thick and thin, but our question always has to be whether other pastures may not be greener. We have the ability to change businesses that the ordinary man in a particular business does not. This is one of the things that makes our business so unnatural, but also, strangely, very satisfying too. So fascinating is our business that we have difficulty holding very good men because a man who can fairly consistently on balance make substantial money in securities is rare and he is coveted by the whole world. One of the things that may hold him, I think, is the fascination of the business of investing and the universality of it. The stock market represents everything that anybody has ever hoped, feared, hated, or loved. It is all of life. You leave that and you go to the XYZ Bottling Co. and the rest of your life is bottles. . . .

We are essentially men of action. Do something about it! We are also men of science—tremendous men of science. But when we turn to art we find that it is not reasoning and not scientific; it is basically a matter of individual emotion and feeling for universality, channeled into a particular mode of expression such as painting, music, or philosophy as the latter involves understanding of the human soul. It is really an instinctive sense of things that exist but are too complicated to reason out. Here Americans appear deficient, somewhat as the Romans were. Thus you take the psychiatrist today—here you have an example of the attempt to apply the scientific method to the human mind. And it just plain doesn't work, because the conscious and subconscious human mind is so vast—the stock market, by the way, is just a bunch of minds—that there is no science, no IBM machine, no anything of that sort, that can tame it. What this means to us in practical affairs is that if we are able to do the thing that Americans find very hard to do—that is, understand ourselves (and consequently others) to some degree—we have really a chance of becoming effective stock operators. That is a hard thing and a rare thing.

Now coming down from these theoretical heights, let's look at the so-called technical aspect of markets. I suppose that word is a good one. The technical side of the stock market is an attempt to understand the demand-supply situation in securities as distinct from the fundamental, which, of course, is the thing I was telling you about: going to see companies and checking industries and facts. There are a great number of "technical indicators." There is nothing secret about any of them (that are worth using). There is nothing very complicated. You can't get complicated anywhere in this business without being lost; each complication begets 10 others, and so on.

You have these various tools: We have a number of test tubes that we experiment with and look at—such as the simplest of all, moving averages of stock prices. Take for example, say, a 12-month moving average of [the] Dow Jones Industrial Average. If any one of you people wanted to close your mind to everything else—never mind about all the forecasts—just the moving average, and use a few simple techniques, that moving average would get you into all big bull markets and would keep you out of all big bear markets. It would be far from perfect, but workable. Did you ever hear of anyone who ever did this in practical operation? I never did.

For light here let's look at the ancient Greeks. The Greeks were always great favorites of mine and, as you know, they used to have many gods and goddesses; and it was a trick to know which god or goddess to back. You remember Paris had a choice to make, for he had a golden apple to be given to the fairest goddess, and here were three leading goddesses standing in front of him—to whom should he give the apple? Foolishly he gave it to Venus. If he had given it to Athene or even Hera it would have been far better for everyone, including himself, because he already had a devoted girlfriend who was far from ugly or ill favored. But he chose Venus and so destroyed his whole family and his whole city and nation because of it. You see, any choosing among gods or goddesses isn't easy. To choose one was to antagonize another. The Hebrews, on the other hand, looked to a single God, just one, and that did make life simpler at the cost of what one may learn or gain or lose through choosing for himself.

There's no one god in the investment world, so how are you going to decide which one of these indicators you are going to pick? . . . I wonder if, in the realm of art, too much thinking may not often be more responsible for trouble than too little thinking. If you will make the thinking that you do so simple as to choose some one "god" among all these technical things, then you have a chance. Remember the words: "Your God is a jealous God," and that is especially true in this kind of work. Various services put much stress on looking at many indicators and [g]oing along with a weighted majority. I submit to you that there's no mathematical way of averaging or weighing your indicators for practical stock market operation.

A violin to me is just wood and a bunch of strings. It takes an artist to play on it. These technical things are nothing but tools—nothing but the violin. They are no good without the player. Now this means that we don't want an orthodox investment approach. [A]n orthodox investment approach, handling as it does stupendous amounts of investment funds, more or less has to obtain average investment results. There isn't any other way of doing it. Unusual results in securities, as I say, have to be looked for in the basically artistic camp, which is relatively small in number as are all artistic groups.

Part Three

Visions and Amusements

How Mr. Womack Made a Killing

JOHN TRAIN

John Train's thoughtful and wise writings on investments and investment managers are both instruction and pleasure. Here is one of his many tales worth telling.

. . .

Everybody who finally learns how to make money in the stock market learns in his own way.

I like this tale of his own personal enlightenment sent in by reader Melvid Hogan, of Houston:

Right after I was discharged from the Army at the close of World War II and went into the drilling-rig building business, on the side (and at first as a hobby) I began buying and selling stocks. At the end of each year I always had a net loss. I tried every approach I would read or hear about: technical, fundamental, and combinations of all these . . . but somehow I always ended up with a loss.

It may sound impossible that even a blind man would have lost money in the rally of 1958—but *I* did. In my in-and-out trading and smart switches I lost a lot of money.

But one day in 1961 when, discouraged and frustrated, I was in the Merrill Lynch office in Houston, a senior account executive sitting at a front desk whom I knew observed the frown on my face that he had been seeing for so many years and motioned me over to his desk.

"Would you like to see a man," he asked wearily, "who has never lost money in the stock market?"

The broker looked up at me, waiting.

"Never had a loss?" I stammered.

"Never had a loss on balance," the broker drawled, "and I have handled his account for near 40 years." Then the broker gestured to a hulking man dressed in overalls who was sitting among the crowd of tape watchers.

Reprinted by permission of *Forbes* Magazine, Vol. 122, No. 7, October 2, 1978. New York: Forbes, Inc., 1978.

"If you want to meet him, you'd better hurry," the broker advised. "He only comes in here once every few years except when he's buying. He always hangs around a few minutes to gawk at the tape. He's a rice farmer and hog raiser from down at Baytown."

I worked my way through the crowd to find a seat by the stranger in overalls. I introduced myself, talked about rice farming and duck hunting for a while (I am an avid duck hunter), and gradually worked the subject around to stocks.

The stranger, to my surprise, was happy to talk about stocks. He pulled a sheet of paper from his pocket with his list of stocks scrawled in pencil on it that he had just finished selling and let me look at it.

I couldn't believe my eyes! The man had made over 50 long-term capital gain profits on the whole group. One stock in the group of 30 stocks had been shot off the board, but others had gone up to 100 percent, 200 percent, and even 500 percent.

He explained his technique, which was the ultimate in simplicity. When during a bear market he would read in the papers that the market was down to new lows and the experts were predicting that it was sure to drop another 200 points in the Dow, the farmer would look through a Standard & Poor's Stock Guide and select around 30 stocks that had fallen in price below $10—solid, profit-making, unheard-of companies (pecan growers, home furnishings, etc.)—and paid dividends. He would come to Houston and buy a $25,000 "package" of them.

And then, one, two, three, or four years later, when the stock market was bubbling and the prophets were talking about the Dow hitting 1,500, he would come to town and sell his whole package. It was as simple as that.

During the subsequent years as I cultivated Mr. Womack (and hunted ducks on his rice fields) until his death last year, I learned much of his investing philosophy.

He equated buying stocks with buying a truckload of pigs. The lower he could buy the pigs, when the pork market was depressed, the more profit he would make when the next seller's market would come along. He claimed that he would rather buy stocks under such conditions than pigs, because pigs did not pay a dividend. You must feed pigs.

He took "a farming" approach to the stock market in general. In rice farming, there is a planting season and a harvesting season; in his stock purchases and sales he strictly observed the seasons.

Mr. Womack never seemed to buy stock at its bottom or sell it at its top. He seemed happy to buy or sell in the bottom or top range of its fluctuations. He had no regard whatsoever for the cliché Never Send Good Money After Bad when he was buying. For example, when the bottom fell out of the bottom of the market of 1970, he added another $25,000 to his previous bargain price positions and made a virtual killing on the whole package.

I suppose that a modern stock market technician could have found a lot of alphas, betas, contrary opinions, and other theories in Mr. Womack's simple approach to buying and selling stocks. But none I know put the emphasis on "buy price" that he did.

I realize that many things determine if a stock is a wise buy. But I have learned that during a depressed stock market, if you can get a cost position in a stock's bottom price range it will forgive a multitude of misjudgments later.

During a market rise, you can sell too soon and make a profit, sell at the top and make a very good profit, or sell on the way down and still make a profit. So, with so many profit probabilities in your favor, the best cost price possible is worth waiting for.

Knowing this is always comforting during a depressed market, when a "chartist" looks at you with alarm after you buy on his latest "sell signal."

In sum, Mr. Womack didn't make anything complicated out of the stock market. He taught me that you can't be buying stocks every day, week, or month of the year and make a profit, any more than you could plant rice every day, week, or month and make a crop. He changed my investing lifestyle and I have made a profit ever since.

Everybody Ought to Be Rich

JOHN J. RASKOB

John J. Raskob, senior financial executive at General Motors, proposed to form Equities Security Company to enable the ordinary
workingman "the same chance that the rich banker has of profiting
by the rise in values of the common stocks of America's most successful companies." The idea, described as "the greatest vision of Wall
Street's greatest mind," would enable an investor to put up $200 in
cash, borrow $300 from a finance subsidiary, and buy $500 in stock—
repaying the loan at $25 a month. Although most commentators were
delighted, Raskob fortunately decided to wait for somewhat lower prices
before launching the venture. Here is his proposition—from an inter-
view with Samuel Crowther in the *Ladies Home Journal* dated August
1929.

. . .

Being rich is, of course, a comparative status. A man with a million
dollars used to be considered rich, but so many people have at least that
much in these days, or are earning incomes in excess of a normal return
from a million dollars, that a millionaire does not cause any comment.

Fixing a bulk line to define riches is a pointless performance. Let us
rather say that a man is rich when he has an income from invested
capital that is sufficient to support him and his family in a decent and
comfortable manner—to give as much support, let us say, as has ever
been given by his earnings. That amount of prosperity ought to be
attainable by anyone. A greater share will come to those who have
greater ability. . . .

The common stocks of this country have in the past ten years increased enormously in value because the business of the country has
increased. Ten thousand dollars invested ten years ago in the common
stock of General Motors would now be worth more than a million and

Originally published in *Ladies Home Journal* (August 1929), pp. 9, 36. New York: Meredith
Corporation.

a half dollars. And General Motors is only one of many first-class industrial corporations.

It may be said that this is a phenomenal increase and that conditions are going to be different in the next 10 years. That prophecy may be true, but it is not founded on experience. In my opinion the wealth of the country is bound to increase at a very rapid rate. The rapidity of the rate will be determined by the increase in consumption, and under wise investment plans the consumption will steadily increase.

. . . Suppose a man marries at the age of 23 and begins a regular savings of $15 a month—and almost anyone who is employed can do that if he tries. If he invests in good common stocks and allows the dividends and rights to accumulate, he will at the end of 20 years have at least $80,000 and an income from investments of around $400 a month. He will be rich. And because anyone can do that I am firm in my belief that anyone not only can be rich but ought to be rich.

The obstacles to being rich are two: The trouble of saving, and the trouble of finding a medium for investment.

If Tom is known to have $200 in the savings bank then everyone is out to get it for some absolutely necessary purpose. More than likely his wife's sister will eventually find the emergency to draw it forth. But if he does withstand all attacks, what good will the money do him? The interest he receives is so small that he has no incentive to save, and since the whole is under his own jurisdiction, he can depend only upon his own will to save. To save in any such fashion requires a stronger will than the normal.

If he thinks of investing in some stock he has nowhere to turn for advice. He is not big enough to get much attention from his banker, and he has not enough money to go to a broker—or at least he thinks that he has not.

Suppose he has $1,000; the bank can only advise him to buy a bond, for the officer will not take the risk of advising a stock and probably has not the experience anyway to give such advice. Tom can get really adequate attention only from some man who has a worthless security to sell, for then all of Tom's money will be profit. . . .

Recently I have been advocating the formation of an equity securities corporation; that is, a corporation that will invest in common stocks only under proper and careful supervision. This company will buy the common stocks of first-class industrial corporations and issue its own stock certificates against them. This stock will be offered from time to time at a price to correspond exactly with the value of the assets of the corporation and all profit will go to the stockholders. The directors will be men of outstanding character, reputation, and integrity. At regular intervals—say quarterly—the whole financial record of the corporation will be published together with all of its holdings and the cost thereof. The corporation will be owned by the public and with every transaction public. I am not at all interested in a private investment trust. The company would not be permitted to borrow money or go into any debt.

In addition to this company, there should be organized a discount company on the same lines as the finance companies of the motor concerns to be used to sell stock of the investing corporation on the installment plan. If Tom had $200, this discount company would lend him $300 and thus enable him to buy $500 of the equity securities investment company stock. . . . That would take his savings out of the free-will class and put them into the compulsory-payment class and his savings would no longer be fair game for relatives, for swindlers, or for himself. . . .

It is difficult to see why a bond or mortgage should be considered as a more conservative investment than a good stock, for the only difference in practice is that the bond can never be worth more than its face value or return more than the interest, while a stock can be worth more than was paid for it and can return a limitless profit.

One may lose on either a bond or a stock. If a company fails it will usually be reorganized and in that case the bonds will have to give way to new money and possibly they will be scaled down. The common stockholders may lose all, or again they may get another kind of stock that may or may not eventually have a value. In a failure, neither the bondholders nor the stockholders will find great cause for happiness— but there are very few failures among the larger corporations. . . .

The old view of debt was quite as illogical as the old view of investment. It was beyond the conception of anyone that debt could be constructive. Every old saw about debt—and there must be a thousand of them—is bound up with borrowing instead of earning. We now know that borrowing may be a method of earning and beneficial to everyone concerned. Suppose a man needs a certain amount of money in order to buy a set of tools or anything else that will increase his income. He can take one of two courses. He can save the money and in the course of time buy his tools, or he can, if the proper facilities are provided, borrow the money at a reasonable rate of interest, buy the tools and immediately so increase his income that he can pay off his debt and own the tools within half the time that it would have taken him to save the money and pay cash. That loan enables him at once to create more wealth than before and consequently makes him a more valuable citizen. By increasing his power to produce he also increases his power to consume and therefore he increases the power of others to produce in order to fill his new needs and naturally increases their power to consume, and so on and on. By borrowing the money instead of saving it he increases his ability to save and steps up prosperity at once. . . .

That is exactly what the automobile has done to the prosperity of the country through the plan of installment payments. The installment plan of paying for automobiles, when it was first launched, ran counter to the old notions of debt. It was opposed by bankers, who saw in it only an incentive for extravagance. It was opposed by manufacturers because they thought people would be led to buy automobiles instead of their products.

The results have been exactly opposite to the prediction. The ability to buy automobiles on credit gave an immediate step up to their purchase. Manufacturing them, servicing them, building roads for them to run on, and caring for the people who use the roads have brought into existence about $10 billion of new wealth each year. . . .

The great wealth of this country has been gained by the forces of production and consumption pushing each other for supremacy. The personal fortunes of this country have been made not by saving but by producing. . . .

The way to wealth is to get into the profit end of wealth production in this country.

If Freud Were a Portfolio Manager

BYRON R. WIEN

Byron Wien writes on investment strategy for Morgan Stanley. Previously, he spent two decades as a portfolio manager at two investment counsel firms.

• • •

A few weeks ago I was in Vienna to meet with some Austrian portfolio managers. I had a free hour before lunch and used it to go over to the stately apartment house at 19, Berggasse where Sigmund Freud lived and worked for almost half a century. A part of the great psychoanalyst's former apartment is open to the public as a kind of museum, and the original waiting room furniture and the general feel of the place are still there, but the famous couch, his writing desk, and his large, high-quality collection of antiquities are now in London where Freud moved in 1938 to escape the Nazis. The examination room and study walls have photo enlargements of the original furnishings, so one can stand there and envision what it must have been like to be in the presence of the man whose insights had such a profound effect on the way we understand ourselves as well as on the literature of much of the last century.

In the stillness of the study, I began to think about Freud's combining his speculations about human psychology with his clinical observations. He accomplished much because he successfully anticipated the next step in his developing theories, and he did that by analyzing everything that had gone before very carefully. This is the antithesis of the way portfolio managers approach their work. Although the investment business makes extensive use of computer-generated information about stocks, groups, portfolios, performance, risk, the

Reprinted from Morgan Stanley Letterhead, New York, July 7, 1986, with permission of the author and Morgan Stanley & Co., Inc.

economy, and the market, very little of that data-crunching power is directed toward the analysis of past decisions. I think most of us have developed patterns of mistake-making, that, if analyzed carefully, would lead to better performance in the future. Instead, portfolio managers tend to assume that poor decisions are random events in an ever-changing environment. They reason that, since circumstances in the future will never be the same as they were in the past, they are not likely to repeat previous mistakes. Future misjudgments, they think, will come from faulty responses to new phenomena. In an effort to encourage investment professionals to determine their error patterns, I have gathered the data and analyzed my own follies, and I have decided to let at least some of my weaknesses hang out. Perhaps this will inspire you to collect the information on your own decisions over the past several years to see if there aren't some errors that you could make less frequently in the future.

Here are some of the recurring investment mistakes. Perhaps you will hear some familiar chimes ringing.

Selling too early. All of us do this once in a while. I tend to fall into the trap in attempting to fine-tune the portfolio. Last year, I thought the drug, food, and media groups were overextended and it made sense to cut back somewhat. I had concluded that the economy was weak and therefore continued to be bullish on disinflation stocks generally, and these stable growers were the leaders of that concept. So here was a case where what I thought was profit-taking prudence was in conflict with my core investment concept. It is true that you never lose money taking a profit, but you can lose precious performance points. Make sure you're not making a change to look busy.

The turnaround with the heart of gold. For years I have been a sucker for laggard groups and stocks that have an outside chance of making it big. Many of us have a contrarian streak in us that results from the conviction that in America good things happen to the frail. When I was a child, I often dreamed of hitting home runs after being the last picked for a softball game. I was frequently the last picked but hit few homers. Why can't I remember how hard it is to turn around a major company in the competitive international business environment that exists today?

Overstaying a winner. I have had a lot of good stock ideas in my career or, more accurately, I have recognized quite a few solid opportunities when analysts have shown them to me. I have also held more than a few round-trip tickets on some very good stocks, because I have assumed that what has treated me well in the past would continue to do so in the future. More often than not, this happens because I become complacent about my knowledge of the fundamentals. Sometimes portfolio managers become so thirsty for new ideas that they don't properly maintain their knowledge of the developments taking place in the companies they have held for a long time.

Underestimating the seriousness of a problem. As Dennis Sherva has said about emerging growth stocks, "The first bad quarter is rarely the last." More often than not, it seems, the right response to a negative surprise is to sell and keep an eye on the situation from the sidelines. We can all come up with exceptions like Digital Equipment, which snapped back after the troubling September 1983 quarter, but, with smaller companies, a disappointment usually results from a set of conditions that will take time to repair and other stockholders may not have your patience. Sometimes the first day's plunge after a negative announcement is followed by a brief recovery, but if you're going to stay around for things to really improve, you'd better have plenty of other good stocks and very tolerant clients.

Freud said that "Psychoanalysis warns us to abandon the unfruitful factors of fate and has taught us regularly to discover the cause of neurosis." By studying printouts of all of your decisions over the past market cycle, I think you will uncover patterns that will enable you to improve the quality of your judgments in the future. Better yet, have one of your colleagues look over the printout and give you his analysis of your recurring transgressions. Try it. It may not help, but, as my grandmother used to say, "It couldn't hurt."

High Finance or the Point of Vanishing Interest

C. NORTHCOTE PARKINSON

Parkinson's law—that work expands to fill the time available for its completion—was also the title for a delightful book spoofing government and business. In Chapter 3 on high finance, Parkinson examines how spending decisions are made by finance committees. Some fund managers claim to have observed comparable treatment of asset allocation decisions by investment committees.

•'• •

People who understand high finance are of two kinds: those who have vast fortunes of their own and those who have nothing at all. To the actual millionaire a million dollars is something real and comprehensible. To the applied mathematician and the lecturer in economics (assuming both to be practically starving) a million dollars is at least as real as a thousand, they having never possessed either sum. But the world is full of people who fall between these two categories, knowing nothing of millions but well accustomed to think in thousands, and it is of these that finance committees are most comprised. The result is a phenomenon that has often been observed but never yet investigated. It might be termed the Law of Triviality. Briefly stated, it means that the time spent on any item of the agenda will be in inverse proportion to the sum involved.

On second thought, the statement that this law has never been investigated is not entirely accurate. Some work has actually been done in this field, but the investigators pursued a line of inquiry that led them nowhere. They assumed that the greatest significance should attach to the order in which items of the agenda are taken. They assumed, further, that most of the available time will be spent on items one to seven and that the later items will be allowed automatically to pass. The result is well known. The derision with which Dr. Guggenheim's lecture was received at the Muttworth Conference may have been thought excessive at the time, but all further discussions on this topic have tended to show that his critics were right. Years had been wasted in a research of which the basic assumptions were wrong. We realize now that position on the agenda is a minor consideration, so far, at least, as this problem is concerned. We consider also that Dr. Guggenheim was lucky to escape as he did, in his underwear. Had he dared to put his lame conclusions before the later conference in September, he would have faced something more than derision. The view would have been taken that he was deliberately wasting time.

If we are to make further progress in this investigation we must ignore all that has so far been done. We must start at the beginning and understand fully the way in which a finance committee actually works. For the sake of the general reader this can be put in dramatic form thus:

CHAIRMAN   We come now to Item Nine. Our Treasurer, Mr. McPhail, will report.

MR. MCPHAIL   The estimate for the Atomic Reactor is before you, sir, set forth in Appendix H of the subcommittee's report. You will see that the general design and layout has been approved by Professor McFission. The total cost will amount to $10,000,000. The contractors, Messrs. McNab and McHash, consider that the work should be complete by April, 1959. Mr. McFee, the consulting engineer, warns us that we should not count on completion before October, at the earliest. In this view he is supported by Dr. McHeap, the well-known geophysicist, who refers to the probable need for piling at the lower end of the site. The plan of the main building is before you—see Appendix IX—and the blueprint is laid on the table. I shall be glad to give any further information that members of this committee may require.

| CHAIRMAN | Thank you, Mr. McPhail, for your very lucid explanation of the plan as proposed. I will now invite the members present to give us their views. |

It is necessary to pause at this point and consider what views the members are likely to have. Let us suppose that they number eleven, including the Chairman but excluding the Secretary. Of these eleven members, four—including the chairman—do not know what a reactor is. Of the remainder, three do not know what it is for. Of those who know its purpose, only two have the least idea of what it should cost. One of these is Mr. Isaacson, the other is Mr. Brickworth. Either is in a position to say something. We may suppose that Mr. Isaacson is the first to speak.

MR. ISAACSON	Well, Mr. Chairman. I could wish that I felt more confidence in our contractors and consultant. Had we gone to Professor Levi in the first instance, and had the contract been given to Messrs. David and Goliath, I should have been happier about the whole scheme. Mr. Lyon-Daniels would not have wasted our time with wild guesses about the possible delay in completion, and Dr. Moses Bullrush would have told us definitely whether piling would be wanted or not.
CHAIRMAN	I am sure we all appreciate Mr. Isaacson's anxiety to complete this work in the best possible way. I feel, however, that it is rather late in the day to call in new technical advisers. I admit that the main contract has still to be signed, but we have already spent very large sums. If we reject the advice for which we have paid, we shall have to pay as much again. (Other members murmur agreement.)
MR. ISAACSON	I should like my observation to be minuted.
CHAIRMAN	Certainly. Perhaps Mr. Brickworth also has something to say on this matter?

Now Mr. Brickworth is almost the only man there who knows what he is talking about. There is a great deal he could say. He distrusts that round figure of $10,000,000. Why should it come out to exactly that? Why need they demolish the old building to make room for the new approach? Why is so large a sum set aside for "contingencies"? And who is McHeap, anyway? Is he the man who was sued last year by the Trickle and Driedup Oil Corporation? But Brickworth does not know where to begin. The other members could not read the blueprint if he referred to it. He would have to begin by explaining what a reactor is and no one there would admit that he did not already know. Better to say nothing.

MR. BRICKWORTH　I have no comment to make.

CHAIRMAN　Does any other member wish to speak? Very well. I may take it then that the plans and estimates are approved? Thank you. May I now sign the main contract on your behalf? (Murmur of agreement.) Thank you. We can now move on to Item Ten.

Allowing a few seconds for rustling papers and unrolling diagrams, the time spent on Item Nine will have been just two minutes and a half. The meeting is going well. But some members feel uneasy about Item Nine. They wonder inwardly whether they have really been pulling their weight. It is too late to query that reactor scheme, but they would like to demonstrate, before the meeting ends, that they are alive to all that is going on.

CHAIRMAN　Item Ten. Bicycle shed for the use of the clerical staff. An estimate has been received from Messrs. Bodger and Woodworm, who undertake to complete the work for the sum of $2,350. Plans and specifications are before you, gentlemen.

MR. SOFTLEIGH　Surely, Mr. Chairman, this sum is excessive. I note that the roof is to be of aluminum. Would not asbestos be cheaper?

MR. HOLDFAST　I agree with Mr. Softleigh about the cost, but the roof should, in my opinion, be of galvanized iron. I incline to think that the shed could be built for $2,000, or even less.

MR. DARING   I would go further, Mr. Chairman. I question whether this shed is really necessary. We do too much for our staff as it is. They are never satisfied, that is the trouble. They will be wanting garages next.

MR. HOLDFAST   No, I can't support Mr. Daring on this occasion. I think that the shed is needed. It is a question of material and cost. . . .

The debate is fairly launched. A sum of $2,350 is well within everybody's comprehension. Everyone can visualize a bicycle shed. Discussion goes on, therefore, for 45 minutes with the possible result of saving some $300. Members at length sit back with a feeling of achievement.

CHAIRMAN   Item Eleven. Refreshments supplied at meetings of the Joint Welfare Committee. Monthly, $4.75.

MR. SOFTLEIGH   What type of refreshment is supplied on these occasions?

CHAIRMAN   Coffee, I understand.

MR. HOLDFAST   And this means an annual charge of—let me see—$57?

CHAIRMAN   That is so.

MR. DARING   Well, really, Mr. Chairman. I question whether this is justified. How long do these meetings last?

Now begins an even more acrimonious debate. There may be members of the committee who might fail to distinguish between asbestos and galvanized iron, but every man there knows about coffee—what it is, how it should be made, where it should be bought—and whether indeed it should be bought at all. This item on the agenda will occupy the members for an hour and a quarter, and they will end by asking the Secretary to procure further information, leaving the matter to be decided at the next meeting.

It would be natural to ask at this point whether a still smaller sum—

$20, perhaps, or $10—would occupy the Finance Committee for a proportionately longer time. On this point, it must be admitted, we are still ignorant. Our tentative conclusion must be that there is a point at which the whole tendency is reversed, the committee members concluding the sum is beneath their notice. Research has still to establish the point at which this reversal occurs. The transition from the $50 debate (an hour and a quarter) to the $20 debate (two and a half minutes) is indeed an abrupt one. It would be the more interesting to establish the exact point at which it occurs. More than that, it would be of practical value. Supposing, for example, that the point of vanishing interest is represented by the sum of $35, the Treasurer with an item of $62.80 on the agenda might well decide to present it as two items, one of $30.00 and the other of $32.80, with an evident saving of time and effort.

Conclusions at this juncture can be merely tentative, but there is some reason to suppose that the point of vanishing interest represents the sum the individual committee member is willing to lose on a bet or subscribe to a charity. An inquiry on these lines conducted on racecourses and in Methodist chapels, might go far toward solving the problem. Far greater difficulty may be encountered in attempting to discover the exact point at which the sum involved becomes too large to discuss at all. One thing apparent, however, is that the time spent on $10,000,000 and on $10 may well prove to be the same. The present estimated time of two and a half minutes is by no means exact, but there is clearly a space of time—something between two and four and a half minutes—that suffices equally for the largest and the smallest sums.

Much further investigation remains to be done, but the final results, when published, cannot fail to be of absorbing interest and of immediate value to mankind.

Seven Rules for Investors

NIGEL LAWSON

Nigel Lawson wrote this tongue-in-cheek piece long before he became Britain's Chancellor of the Exchequer, but it illustrates the originality and wit that served him well in government. He now serves as vice chairman of BZW.

. . .

I am delighted that my colleague "Capitalist" is doing so well with his portfolio of shares. His careful system of selection is plainly a very sound one. But I can't help feeling that—like most accountants—he is obsessed with figures, with the purely statistical facts.

Earnings growth rates and dividend yields are all very well in their way. But the shrewd investor will want to look beyond mere figures, just as the trained psychoanalyst looks beyond the patient's words to discover truths deep in his subconscious.

Happily, I am not alone in this view. So great an authority as the well-known investment trust expert, Mr. George Touche, remarked in the midst of a learned, 25-page address on investment to the Institute of Chartered Accountants at Oxford last summer that "general impressions may be obtained from many sources, apart from the conclusions to be drawn from financial results. The cult of a chairman's personality, combined with constant repetition of his photograph, rarely inspires confidence in the management of a company."

Sole Contribution

So we have investment rule number one:

Reprinted with permission of Telegraph Group Limited, London, 1963.

Avoid companies whose chairman's photograph is published more than four times a year.

Unfortunately this was Mr. Touche's only contribution to the important science of nonstatistical investment analysis. But I strongly recommend the following as rule number two:

Avoid companies that publish their balance sheet in front of their profit and loss account in the annual report.

The Companies Act stipulates that both these be published, but it does not lay down the order in which they should appear. So companies invariably put first the document of which they are proudest (or least ashamed).

Obviously a company that is prouder of its assets than its profits is one to be avoided at all costs. This is the very hallmark of an unprogressive company earning an inadequate rate of return (if any) on its capital employed.

How many fortunes might have been saved, for example, had investors noticed that Pressed Steel publishes the parent company's balance sheet in front of the consolidated profit and loss account. You would not catch a growth stock like Elliott-Automation doing that. Again, the Lancashire Cotton Corporation, short of profits but long on assets, publishes its balance sheet first; whereas expansionist ICI . . . but I needn't elaborate. . . .

But perhaps at this stage I ought to warn investors that this particular rule, although in my experience invaluable, is not an infallible guide. Take the two cement companies, for example. Associated Portland Cement puts its profit and loss account first, Rugby Portland Cement its balance sheet. And yet it is Rugby that has by far the better growth record. The explanation of this superficially startling phenomenon brings us to rule number three:

Invest in companies whose chairman is less than 5'8" tall.

What you must look for is the Napoleon of industry—those dynamic individuals who make up for lack of physical stature by making their companies grow instead. Sir Isaac Wolfson and Mr. Charles Clore are obvious examples.

This is also the explanation of the cement conundrum. Rugby's chairman Sir Halford Reddish qualifies with flying colours under the height rule. But APC's Mr. John Reiss, although a charming gentleman and fine chairman, is over six feet tall.

The question of average height is also of material importance in determining the geographical spread of your investments. It is no accident that the small Japanese have the fastest rate of growth in the world, the medium size Europeans the next most rapid, and the tall British and Americans the slowest growth rate. . . .

Points System

It is always advisable, therefore, when considering a purchase of any share, to ask your stockbroker to let you know the precise height of the company's chairman. Buy you should also take a scientific interest in the rest of the board. Which brings us to rule number four:

Assess the board on the points system as follows—one point for every director, and an extra point for every peer, admiral, general or air marshal. More than 15 points disqualifies, or more than twenty in the case of banks and insurance companies.

Plainly no board meeting will ever reach rapid agreement if there are too many directors; equally, an excessive number of peers and military gentlemen is dangerous because such people were taught by their nannies to believe that trade is no calling for a gentleman.

The shares of Sun Alliance Insurance, for example, are lower today than they were four years ago; whereas those of Legal and General have doubled. The Sun Alliance has 33 members, including eight peers: 41 points, which means instant disqualification. Legal and General's board, however, has only 16 members, including one peer and one admiral. Eighteen points is all right for insurance.

Inner Three

Then again the Rank Organisation board runs to 18 points (which means disqualification for an industrial company) whereas the *Financial Times*, another leading group in the entertainment field, easily qualifies with nine points in spite of its three peers. But you have to be careful. The Unilever board contains 24 members, which might lead an unsuspecting investor to look elsewhere. But in fact an inner board of only three is what really counts.

This should complete your study of the company's report and accounts, except perhaps for two minor points, rules five and six:

Avoid companies who hold their annual general meetings at awkward times or in unlikely places.

Avoid companies who have just moved into a lush new head office.

The first of these is obvious. A company that announces that the annual meeting will be at 8:30 A.M. at Chipping Sodbury Town Hall is evidently not going out of its way to encourage shareholder participation.

The second derives from one of Prof. Parkinson's laws, viz that new offices are built just as the company reaches its peak, from where it can only decline.

. . . In 1961, when the Bowater Paper Corporation moved into its lavish Knightsbridge skyscraper, profits fell sharply and the company lost its growth stock rating.

But as well as the annual report, it is also well worth paying attention to the announcement of preliminary figures. Here we come to my final, and most important, rule seven:

Longer to Add

Bad figures always take longer to add up than good ones.

From this follows a simple conclusion: you should sell any share in a company whose preliminary profit figures fail to be published within five days of the date on which they were published the previous year. By following this simple rule, you will save far more money than you lose.

Shareholders in both Lombard Banking and Firth Cleveland, for example, could have sold in advance of bad news on three separate occasions, as the following table indicates:

Lombard Banking:

3/2/1960	Profits up 80 p.c.
3/9/1961	Profits down 25 p.c.
3/16/1962	Profits down 40 p.c.
3/17/1963	Profits unchanged

Firth Cleveland:

5/31/1961	Profits up by one third
6/7/1962	Profits down by one third

It will be interesting to see what 1963 brings.

Here, then, are my seven rules for investment for Easter. There are, of course, some others. But that's another story.

The Day They Red-Dogged Motorola

"ADAM SMITH"

There are two ways to understand institutional block trading. One is to actually do it at Salomon Brothers or Goldman Sachs and the other is to read this classic by Jerry Goodman writing as "Adam Smith."

. . .

When John Kenneth Galbraith sits down to write the history of the great Johnson Bear Market, as he is bound to some day, he ought to pay some attention to September 27, 1966. That is going to be one of those days like December 7, 1941, peculiar to a history, the day Wall Street stopped believing in anything, at least for this Bear Market, and you can mark it by minutes on the clock, just the way it happens in the disaster stories when the water goes gurgling into the Titanic. September 27 was the day they red-dogged Motorola.

At the moment it was happening I was having lunch at the Bankers Club with a friend of mine who runs a hot go-go fund. By this I mean an investment fund that is supposed to go up fast so that the pressure is on to pick the stock that will move. Then they compare your performance with the other "growth" funds month by month and sometimes week by week. Not recommended for widows. Orphans, maybe, young rich orphans with time to grow. It pays to have lunch with such operators on a friendly basis; sometimes you can get a bit of a ride on what they're promoting. Anyway, my friend—I'll call him Charlie—is sitting there stirring his coffee telling me the bearish news from all over, such as that one of the major New York City banks is busted except for its float, i.e. it is kiting money over the weekends and if they ever speed up the United States mail the bank is in trouble. "Kiting over the weekend" means writing checks on Friday on money

From *The Wisdom of Adam Smith*, Benjamin A. Rogge, ed. (Indianapolis, Indiana, 1976), 111–112.

that doesn't exist and rushing to cover the checks with new funds by Monday morning.

"They're out," Charlie says. "They can't go to the Fed because the Fed would slam the window on their fingers if they look at their loans, so they have been scrambling around Europe sopping up the Euro-dollars."

If you understand what Charlie said, fine, and if you don't, it doesn't have much to do with Motorola except set a nice, dark, ominous atmosphere, John Kenneth Galbraith please note. Money is tight and Wall Street doesn't like the Viet Nam war at all. Then a fellow we both know comes by and says Motorola is getting red-dogged down on the floor of the Exchange. Already there is a little crowd around the Dow Jones broad tape in the ante room, where the carpet is worn.

Meanwhile, a couple of blocks away at 15 William Street, the boys are spilling what is left of the tuna fish in order to get to the phones. All this from a speech by Mr. Robert W. Galvin from Franklin Park, Illinois. Mr. Galvin is the chairman of the board of Motorola, one of the 1966 flyers, and he is addressing the sage and august New York Society of Security Analysts. Motorola makes color TV sets, and that's growth, and semiconductors, and that's growth, and two-way radios, and that's growth. Growth, growth, growth. Six months ago all this growth is worth $234 a share. On September 27 it's worth $140. A bad gassing, but how much worse can things be? They're going to earn $8 a share. It says so in Standard & Poor's. Business, Mr. Galvin says, is so good it's bad. They have all the orders they can handle—they just have trouble producing the goods—shortages here, labor problems there. They can sell all the color TVs they can make, they just can't make them fast enough. Earnings will be up—but to $5.50, $6 on the outside. Everything else is rosy.

The sage and august analysts look at each other for a moment: $6? $6? What happened to the other $2? Then it is like the end of the White House news conference, except nobody has even said, "Thank you, Mr. President." They are all running for the phones. Except they are security analysts, not newsmen, so they use the Olympic heel-and-toe walk instead of the outright sprint. There is the question-and-answer period, but Mr. Galvin's audience has been depleted.

Back at the Bankers Club, Charlie has melted into a phone booth and is giving orders to his girl. "Sell 10,000 Motorola," he is saying; that's about a million three. I can tell the girl has the portfolio in front of her and is looking for Motorola, and I can even hear (because I am making a special attempt to do so) her saying, "But we don't *own* any Motorola." Charlie is going to short the Motorola, so he hollers a bit. He'll buy it back some other time. Right now the important thing is to sell it, whether or not you own it. This is one of the pressures of a performance fund.

We stand there watching the tape, and there goes MOT, 137, 136, oof, 134. Big blocks are appearing.

"There goes Gerry Tsai's Motorola," says some wise man behind us. That's the *in* thing to say. Gerry Tsai, who is head of the Manhattan Fund, has that $450 million sitting there bubbling away, and he does move in and out fast, but how anybody can tell it's *his* Motorola is beyond me. He might have sold it long before. It's useful, though. You can always sound wise by saying, "Gerry Tsai is buying," or "Gerry Tsai is selling." He has replaced the "They" from the old days, when "They" were about to put a stock up or down. Gerry Tsai better watch out, though, because if you're They, things have to be good. I know a chartist who says the Dow Jones is going to 380. If it does, I would go long apples because there will be plenty of demand from all the street corner salesmen, and they will be looking for a scapegoat. There will be a book sponsored by the John Birch Society called *The Protocols of the Elders of Shanghai*, in which it is proved that Gerry Tsai was really Mao Tse Tung, and there will be a public ceremony in front of the Federal Reserve Bank while Gerry Tsai is exorcised of demons by a god-fearing chaplain just before they drive the water buffalos he is tied to in opposite directions.

Now down on the Floor the pressure is on the specialist. He is standing there on the floor at Post 18, his Hippocratic Oath bidding him make an orderly market in Motorola, and suddenly there he is, like an adolescent fantasy, a quarterback in Yankee Stadium with the crowd roaring. Only it's the wrong dream. The crowd is roaring because all his receivers are covered, his defense has evaporated, and the red-dog is on: two tons of beef descending on him, tackles grunting and linebackers growling "*killll.*" Nothing to do but buckle, eat the ball, and hope you're still alive when they stop blowing the whistle. Guys are bearing down on the specialist and he can tell that if he bends over in a reflex from the first chunk of Motorola that hits him in the stomach, they will hit him over the head with the rest. That's not an orderly market. So they blow the whistle. No more trading in Motorola.

Charlie is chagrined. He needed an uptick to get off his short; they've had that rule since the Great Cash. In the good old days without that rule the bears could all get together and short the stock right down to 0 and into negative territory practically.

"Gee, and I was going to go to Europe next week," Charlie says. Now he thinks he better stick around. I ask Charlie for a prognostication. (Remember, this is September 27 and I am writing this the second week of October, so you have a two-week free ride. This is because of what they call "lead time" in this magazine, which is, I gather, that it takes the printers two weeks to put all the pages together.)

Charlie likes to sound like the Oracle of Delphi, not in print, of course, because that can catch up with you, but just to his friends.

"Everything is going to par," Charlie says. Par is 100, or it used to be and everybody still calls it that, and "everything" means the high flyers that the performance boys have to be in or they lose their union cards. Say: Motorola, Xerox, Fairchild Camera, Polaroid—just look at the list of 10 most active stocks and there they are. Well, the flyers have about 40 points to drop before they hit par and naturally Charlie doesn't mean every one, because they aren't all selling at the same price, but that's a steep drop. "After Motorola, nobody will believe anything," Charlie says. "Tomorrow, they will start saying Fairchild has terrible problems, Xerox gives you cancer, handling Polaroid film makes you sterile." So everything is going to par. At that point John Jerk and his brother will figure the way to make money is to go short.

In more polite circles, John Jerk and his brother are called "the little fellows" or "the odd-lotters"; or "the small investors." I wish I knew Mr. Jerk and his brother. They live in some place called the Hinterlands, and everything they do is wrong. They buy when the smart people sell, they sell when the smart people buy, and they panic at exactly the wrong time. There are services that make a very good living just out of charting the activity of Mr. J. and his poor brother. If I knew them I would give them room and board and consult them like they used to ask the original Jeep in the prewar Popeye comic strip, before a Jeep was a car. I would push the pheasant and champagne through the little hatch of his cell and ask Mr. J. what he was going to do that morning, and if he said, "buy," I would know to sell, and so on.

Charlie and I drifted back to his office. "It's a terrible market for everybody but me," Charlie said. "Nobody believes anything. They don't believe Johnson, they don't believe anything in Washington, they believe taxes are going to go up but not enough, they don't believe we'll ever get out of Viet Nam, and after Motorola, nobody will believe any earnings. Let Peat Marwick the CPA's certify them, they still won't believe them."

This is what the French sociologist Emile Durkheim called *anomie*. In market terms it means anxiety builds up as the market drops, and then as you get all the noise about "resistance levels" and so on and the market goes plunging through them, you get *anomie*. Like alienation, only it means "Where's the bottom? Where's the bottom? Where's the bottom?" Nobody knows where the bottom is; nobody can remember where the top was; they're all way out there in the blue, riding on anxiety and a shoeshine. The Dow Jones Average is going to 0. Only Charlie is in good shape; his fund is a hedge fund and he is short.

"At par," Charlie intones, "there will be a rally, while we chase John Jerk and his brother."

The translation of this is that Mr. J., having lost on the stocks he owned, will try to make up his losses by selling short, and then as Charlie buys, the stocks go up, giving Mr. J. a loss on the short sales. Then he panics and he has to buy all the way up with Charlie chasing him.

Times have changed since the Fifties. Way back then, an "institution" was something with a lot of money that lived in Boston or Philadelphia, and it waited until stocks got seasoned, and then it bought and tucked away the stock. They were run by guys who wore sleeve garters and said "my good man." Now you have computers that tell you exactly what each fund is worth every minute, and a bunch of swingers running them. In the old days the brokerage houses had some hot ideas, and some of their customers bought them, and then the good gray funds would pick out the right seasoned stock for the widows and orphans.

No more. Now the guys in the brokerage houses are running into the Regency Hotel where Tsai lives before they clear away the breakfast dishes in case Gerry Tsai has made some notes on the tablecloth while he was drinking his grapefruit juice.

That's a good way to lose, too, because with everything swinging so fast some of these funds buy in the morning and they feel it's sacrilegious to hold stocks overnight. Gerry Tsai is out before the tablecloth goes to laundry. It all adds up to the *anomie*.

I sat in Charlie's office while he canceled his European vacation. At 3:29 the specialist re-opened Motorola, just as the bell rang. That's like a boxer who manages to get on one knee just as the referee says 10. Motorola re-opened and closed at 119, down $19^1/4$ on the day. In the marketplace it was worth $114 million less at 3:30 P.M. than it was at 10:00 A.M., and say $684 million less than it had been a few months before. And it was the same company, more or less, and this year is better than last year and next year will be better than this year.

Now you can talk about tight money and Viet Nam and taxes all you want, but something happened on September 27. It started happening before, of course, when the banks started getting all loaned up and then all the whistles and shrieks and bells and yellow smoke signals of the indicators went off late last spring. On September 27, the bell was tolling for belief.

And what now? Well, the odd-lot figures say Mr. J. and his brother are short a lot of stock, and Charlie has the hounds ready. Our trader says the tape has to stand still for 40 days and 40 nights to prepare the way for the next bull market. Charlie is going to Europe in November. We have come to the moment in Peter Pan when the play stops and Mary Martin or whoever comes to the footlights and says, "Do you believe? Do you believe?" The only times I saw Peter Pan, everybody believed.

Some day, maybe not so far away, Charlie will be back from Europe. Mr. J. will be in the Hinterlands, pantless, and the first daisy will push through the soil and say, "I believe," and the game will be on again.

I'll tell you about that when we get to it.

There Are Only Three
Ways to Get Rich

FRED J. YOUNG

Fred Young was a key member of the Trust Department of the Harris Bank and continues to inform and entertain with talks and a book having the encouraging title, *How to Get Rich and Stay Rich*. Here are some excerpts.

. . .

There Are Only Three Ways to Get Rich

1.   Inherit it. If you can see that you are going to inherit it, then you have it made. You can skip to the part of this book about staying rich. Someone else has already made the sacrifice of spending less than they earned to create this wealth for you. You should be grateful. You didn't have anything to do about it; your ancestry is completely beyond your control. You are fortunate indeed.

2.   Marry it. This is an area in which you do have some control. This is something you can work on, but you have to get started on it before you get involved with some poor person. This can be quite a project, and I have seen both men and women work this approach to wealth quite effectively. I see nothing wrong with it. I grew up in an area and at a time when most people, boys and girls, firmly believed that the Good Lord made someone especially for them. Growing up for these young people was largely a search for their "intended." Well, if your intended, when you find him or her, happens to have a lot of money, you should graciously accept the situation. Don't fight it.

From Fred J. Young, *How to Get Rich and Stay Rich* (Hollywood, Florida, 1983), 31–32, 41, 43–44, 83, 113–114, by permission of Lifetime Books, Inc.

3.   If you are not going to inherit it, and you have already blown the chance for wealth through marriage, then you have only one chance left to get rich. You spend less than you earn and invest the difference in something that you think will increase in value and make you rich.

What should you invest in? Most rich people I know got rich from investments in one or more of the following:
a.   Real estate
b.   Own their own business
c.   Common stocks
d.   Savings accounts (thanks to the magic of compound interest rates) . . .

Any time you have a choice between good luck and good judgment, you should take good luck. Good luck, by definition, denotes success. Good judgment can still go wrong. . . .

A very important ingredient of successful stock investing is courage. The courage to buy when others are selling; the courage to buy when stocks are hitting new lows; the courage to buy when the economy looks bad; courage to buy at the bottom. If you look back over the years, you will note that the times when the gloom was the thickest invariably turned out to have been the best times to buy stocks.

But most people like to buy when everything is rosy and stocks are hitting new highs. That takes no courage. There is a great tendency to think that stocks will continue doing whatever it is they have been doing. If they have been going up, they will continue going up forever, think the masses. If they are hitting new lows, they will continue hitting new lows forever. Maybe they will continue declining a while longer after you buy them, but you are not likely to be able to know when the bottom has been reached. So your best bet is to pick a level you are willing to pay and proceed with part of your investment funds. If they go lower, you can buy more at even better prices. If they turn and go up, then you will make a profit on what you have.

The Emperor's New Clothes

HANS CHRISTIAN ANDERSEN

The wonder of market crashes is that prices get so amazingly high before they collapse. Here, we receive the wisdom of Hans Christian Andersen in a familiar story about seeing what is truly there—not just seeing what we hope to see. But, must investment professionals depend on others to identify the reality that they are paid to perceive?

. . .

Many years ago there lived an emperor, who cared so enormously for beautiful new clothes that he spent all his money upon them, that he might be very fine. He did not care about his soldiers, nor about the theatre, nor about driving in the park except to show his new clothes. He had a coat for every hour of the day; and just as they say of a king, "He is in council," one always said of him, "The emperor is in the wardrobe."

In the great city in which he lived it was always very merry; every day a number of strangers arrived there. One day two cheats came: they gave themselves out as weavers, and declared that they could weave the finest stuff any one could imagine. Not only were their colours and patterns, they said, uncommonly beautiful, but the clothes made of the stuff possessed the wonderful quality that they became invisible to any one who was unfit for the office he held, or was incorrigibly stupid.

"Those would be capital clothes!" thought the emperor. "If I wore those, I should be able to find out what men in my empire are not fit for the places they have; I could distinguish the clever from the stupid. Yes, the stuff must be woven for me directly!"

And he gave the two cheats a great deal of cash in hand, that they might begin their work at once.

Reprinted from *The Journal of Portfolio Management* 3 (Winter 1977), pp. 78–79. New York: Institutional Investor, Inc.

As for them, they put up two looms, and pretended to be working; but they had nothing at all on their looms. They at once demanded the finest silk and the costliest gold; this they put into their own pockets, and worked at the empty looms till late into the night.

"I should like to know how far they have got on with the stuff," thought the emperor. But he felt quite uncomfortable when he thought that those who were not fit for their offices could not see it. He believed, indeed, that he had nothing to fear for himself, but yet he preferred first to send some one else to see how matters stood. All the people in the whole city knew what peculiar power the stuff possessed, and all were anxious to see how bad or how stupid their neighbors were.

"I will send my honest old minister to the weavers," thought the emperor. "He can judge best how the stuff looks, for he has sense, and no one discharges his office better than he."

Now the good old minister went out into the hall where the two cheats sat working at the empty looms.

"Mercy preserve us!" thought the old minister, and he opened his eyes wide. "I cannot see anything at all!" But he did not say this.

Both the cheats begged him to be kind enough to come nearer, and asked if he did not approve of the colours and the pattern. Then they pointed to the empty loom, and the poor old minister went on opening his eyes; but he could see nothing, for there was nothing to see.

"Mercy!" thought he, "can I indeed be so stupid? I never thought that, and not a soul must know it. Am I not fit for my office?—No, it will never do for me to tell that I could not see the stuff."

"Do you say nothing to it?" said one of the weavers.

"Oh it is charming—quite enchanting!" answered the old minister, as he peered through his spectacles. "What a fine pattern, and what colours! Yes, I shall tell the emperor that I am very much pleased with it."

"Well, we are glad of that," said both the weavers; and then they named the colours, and explained the strange pattern. The old minister listened attentively, that he might be able to repeat it when he went back to the emperor. And he did so.

Now the cheats asked for more money, and more silk and gold, which they declared they wanted for weaving. They put all into their own pockets, and not a thread was put on the loom; but they continued to work at the empty frames as before.

The emperor soon sent again, dispatching another honest statesman, to see how the weaving was going on, and if the stuff would soon be ready. He fared just like the first: he looked and looked, but, as there was nothing to be seen but the empty looms, he could see nothing.

"Is not that a pretty piece of stuff?" asked the two cheats; and they displayed and explained the handsome pattern which was not there at all.

"I am not stupid!" thought the man—"it must be my good office, for which I am not fit. It is funny enough, but I must not let it be noticed." And so he praised the stuff which he did not see, and expressed his pleasure at the beautiful colours and the charming pattern. "Yes, it is enchanting," he said to the emperor.

All the people in the town were talking of the gorgeous stuff. The emperor wished to see it himself while it was still upon the loom. With a whole crowd of chosen men, among whom were also the two honest statesmen who had already been there, he went to the two cunning cheats, who were now weaving with might and main without fibre or thread.

"Is that not splendid?" said the two old statesmen, who had already been there once. "Does not your majesty remark the pattern and the colours?" And then they pointed to the empty loom, for they thought that the others could see the stuff.

"What's this?" thought the emperor. "I can see nothing at all! That is terrible. Am I stupid? Am I not fit to be emperor? That would be the most dreadful thing that could happen to me.—Oh, it is *very* pretty!" he said aloud. "It has our exalted approbation." And he nodded in a contented way, and gazed at the empty loom, for he would not say that he saw nothing. The whole suite whom he had with him looked and looked, and saw nothing, any more than the rest; but, like the emperor, they said, "That *is* pretty!" and counselled him to wear these splendid new clothes for the first time at the great procession that was presently to take place. "It is splendid, tasteful, excellent!" went from mouth to mouth. On all sides there seemed to be general rejoicing, and the emperor gave each of the cheats a cross to hang at his button-hole and the title of Imperial Court Weaver.

The whole night before the morning on which the procession was to take place the cheats were up, and had lighted more than sixteen candles. The people could see that they were hard at work, completing the emperor's new clothes. They pretended to take the stuff down from the loom; they made cuts in the air with great scissors; they sewed with needles without thread; and at last they said, "Now the clothes are ready!"

The emperor came himself with his noblest cavaliers; and the two cheats lifted up one arm as if they were holding something, and said, "See, here are the trousers! here is the coat! here is the cloak!" and so on. "It is as light as a spider's web: one would think one had nothing on; but that is just the beauty of it."

"Yes," said all the cavaliers; but they could not see anything, for nothing was there.

"Does your imperial majesty please to condescend to undress?" said the cheats; "then we will put on you the new clothes here in front of the great mirror."

The emperor took off his clothes, and the cheats pretended to put on him each of the new garments, and they took him round the waist, and seemed to fasten on something; that was the train; and the emperor turned round and round before the mirror.

"Oh, how well they look! how capitally they fit!" said all. "What a pattern! what colours! That *is* a splendid dress!"

"They are standing outside with the canopy which is to be borne above your majesty in the procession!" announced the head master of the ceremonies.

"Well, I am ready," replied the emperor. "Does it not suit me well?" And then he turned again to the mirror, for he wanted it to appear as if he contemplated his adornment with great interest.

The chamberlains, who were to carry the train, stooped down with their hands towards the floor, just as if they were picking up the mantle; then they pretended to be holding something up in the air. They did not dare to let it be noticed that they saw nothing.

So the emperor went in procession under the rich canopy, and every one in the streets said, "How incomparable are the emperor's new clothes! what a train he has to his mantle! how it fits him!" No one would let it be perceived that he could see nothing, for that would have shown that he was not fit for his office, or was very stupid. No clothes of the emperor's had ever had such a success as these.

"But he has nothing on!" a little child cried out at last.

"Just hear what that innocent says!" said the father; and one whispered to another what the child had said. "There is a little child that says he has nothing on."

"But he has nothing on!" said the whole people at length. And the emperor shivered, for it seemed to him that they were right; but he thought within himself, "I must go through with the procession." And so he carried himself still more proudly, and the chamberlains held on tighter than ever, and carried the train which did not exist at all.

Part Four

Innovative Ideas and Proven Paradigms

Proof That Properly Anticipated Prices Fluctuate Randomly

PAUL A. SAMUELSON

Long interested in—and active in—investing, Nobel laureate Paul Samuelson makes the definitive case on the randomness of stock price behavior. This excerpt states the issue and gives the conclusion, neatly deleting the actual proof and its use of equations.

· · ·

The Enigma Posed

"In competitive markets there is a buyer for every seller. If one could be sure that a price will rise, it would have already risen." Arguments like this are used to deduce that competitive prices must display price changes over time, $X_{t+1} - X_t$, that perform a random walk with no predictable bias.

Is this a correct fact about well-organized wheat or other commodity markets? About stock exchange prices for equity shares? About futures markets for wheat or other commodities, as contrasted to the movement of actual "spot prices" for the concrete commodity?

Or is it merely an interesting (refutable) hypothesis about actual markets that can somehow be put to empirical testing?

Or is it a valid deduction (like the Pythagorean Theorem applicable to Euclidean triangles) whose truth is as immutable as $2 + 2 = 4$? Does its truth follow from the very definition of "free, competitive markets"? (If so, can there fail to exist in New York and London actual stock and commodity markets with those properties; and must any failures of the "truism" that turn up be attributable to "manipulation," "thinness of markets," or other market imperfections?)

Reprinted from *Industrial Management Review* 6 (Spring 1965), pp. 41–49. Cambridge, Massachusetts: Industrial Management Review Association.

The more one thinks about the problem, the more one wonders what it is that could be established by such abstract argumentation. Is the fact that American stocks have shown an average annual rise of more than 5 percent over many decades compatible with the alleged "fair game" (or martingale property) of an unbiased random walk? Is it an exception that spot wheat prices generally rise (presumably because of storage costs) from the July harvest time to the following spring and drop during June? Is the fact that the price of next July's future shows much less strong seasonal patterns a confirmation of the alleged truism? If so, what about the alleged Keynes-Hicks-Houthakker-Cootner pattern of "normal backwardation," in which next July's wheat future could be expected to rise in price a little from July harvest to, say, the following March (as a result of need of holders of the crop to coax out, at a cost, risk-disliking speculators with whom to make short-hedging transactions); and what about the Cootner pattern in which, once wheat stocks become low in March, processors wishing to be sure of having a minimum of wheat to process, seek short-selling speculators with whom to make long-hedging transactions, even at the cost of having the July quotation dropping a little in price in months like April and May?

Consideration of such prosaic and mundane facts raises doubt that there is anything much in celestial *a priori* reasoning from the axiom that what can be perceived about the future must already be "discounted" in current price quotations. Indeed, suppose that all the participants in actual markets are necessarily boobs when it comes to foreseeing the unforeseeable future. Why should "after-the-fact" price changes show *any* systematic pattern, such as nonbias? Are the very mathematical notions of probability of any relevance to actual market quotations? If so, how could we decide that this is indeed so?

Whatever the answers to these questions, I think we can suspect that there is no *a priori* necessity for actual Board of Trade grain prices to act in accordance with specific probability models. Perhaps it is a lucky accident, a boon from Mother Nature so to speak, that so many actual price time series do behave like uncorrelated or quasi-random walks. Thus, Maurice Kendall[1] almost proves too much when he finds negligible serial correlation in spot grain prices. For reasons that I shall discuss, we would not be too surprised to find this property in futures price changes. But surely spot prices ought to vary with shifts in such supply and demand factors as weather, crop yields, and crop plantings; or population, income, and taste changes. Who says that the weather must itself display no serial correlation? A dry month does tend to be followed by a dryer-than-average month because of persistence of pressure patterns, etc. Perhaps it is true that prices depend on a summation of so many small and somewhat independent sources of variation that the result is like a random walk. But there is no necessity for this. And the fact, if it is one, is not particularly related to perfect competition or market anticipations. For consider a monopolist who sells (or buys) at fixed price. If the demand (or supply) curve he faces is the resultant of numerous independent, additive sources of variation each of which is limited or small, his resulting quality $\{q_t\}$ may well behave like the normal curve of error.

At this point, the reader may feel inclined to doubt that the arguments of my first paragraph have even a germ of interest for the economist. But I hope to show that such a rejection goes too far.

By positing a rather general stochastic model of price change, I shall deduce a fairly sweeping theorem in which next-period's price differences are shown to be uncorrelated with (if not completely independent of) previous period's price differences. This martingale property of zero expected capital gain will then be replaced by the slightly more general case of a constant mean percentage gain per unit time.

You never get something for nothing. From a nonempirical base of axioms you never get empirical results. Deductive analysis cannot determine whether the empirical properties of the stochastic model I posit come at all close to resembling the empirical determinants of today's real-world markets. That question I shall not here investigate. I shall be content if I can, for once, find definite and unambiguous content to the arguments of the opening paragraph— arguments that have long haunted economists' discussions of competitive markets.

Conclusion

. . . One should not read too much into the established theorem. It does not prove that actual competitive markets work well. It does not say that speculation is a good thing or that randomness of price changes would be a good thing. It does not prove that anyone who makes money in speculation is *ipso facto* deserving of the gain or even that he has accomplished something good for society or for anyone but himself. All or none of these may be true, but that would require a different investigation.

I have not here discussed where the basic probability distributions are supposed to come from. In whose minds are they *ex ante*? Is there any *ex post* validation of them? Are they supposed to belong to the market as a whole? And what does that mean? Are they supposed to belong to the "representative individual," and who is he? Are they some defensible or necessitous compromise of divergent expectation patterns? Do price quotations somehow produce a Pareto-optimal configuration of *ex ante* subjective probabilities? This paper has not attempted to pronounce on these interesting questions.

Note

1.   Maurice G. Kendall. "The Analysis of Economic Time-Series—Part I: Prices," *Journal of the Royal Statistical Society* 96, Part I (1953): 11–25; also in Paul H. Cootner (ed.), *The Random Character of Stock Market Prices* (Cambridge: The M.I.T. Press, 1964), 85–99.

A New Paradigm for Portfolio Risk

ROBERT H. JEFFREY

> "Risk" is not the same thing as "riskiness." And while agents (portfolio managers) can experience riskiness, or price volatility, only owners can experience true investment risk—the risk of being unable to meet cash obligations—as Tad Jeffrey explains.
>
> . . .

Thomas Kuhn, in his landmark book, *The Structure of Scientific Revolutions*, describes the fall of a so-called "rational model" as a paradigm shift. "Scientists in any field and in any time," he writes, "possess a set of shared beliefs about the world, and for that time the set constitutes the dominant paradigm. . . . Experiments are carried on strictly within the boundaries of these beliefs and small steps toward progress are made." Citing the example of the Ptolemaic view of the universe with the earth as its center, Kuhn observes, "Elaborate mathematical formulas and models were developed that would accurately predict astronomical events based on the Ptolemaic paradigm" but it was not until Copernicus and Kepler discovered "that the formulae worked *more easily* . . ." when the sun replaced the earth as the center of the universe model that a "paradigm shift" in astronomy began and laid the foundation for even greater steps toward progress.[1]

The thrust of this paper is to put forth a similar proposition. I shall assert, on a more mundane level, that our portfolio management process should also "work more easily" and *rewardingly* if a paradigm shift were to occur in the "rational model" or "shared belief" that portfolio risk is strictly a function of the volatility of portfolio returns.

The Case in Brief

This paper will suggest that the current paradigm is incomplete. More important, it is often misleading for a vast number of portfolio owners, because it fails to recognize that risk is a function of the characteristics of a portfolio's *liabilities* as well as of its assets and, in particular, of the cash-flow relationship between the two over time. Consequently, I shall offer a modification in the "rational model's" proxy for risk that, by including consideration of liabilities, which tend to be highly parochial, has the salutory effect of involving the portfolio owner more intimately in the risk determination process.

Finally, the paper will demonstrate how the acceptance of this modification in the definition of portfolio risk can naturally lead, in many cases, to the development of an asset mix policy tailored specifically to the particular, and often peculiar, needs of each portfolio owner. Such an asset mix is, after all, what "sophisticated" investors presumably seek but largely fail to achieve. The result is that most institutions have "look-alike" portfolios, even when the institutions themselves are markedly different.

Some of the ideas that I propose here have already been suggested, at least fragmentally, by others. Smidt, in discussing investment horizons and performance measurement, asks "How relevant are conventional risk/reward measures?"[2] and Trainer and colleagues state that the "holding period is the key to risk thresholds."[3] In fact, I have previously suggested that the holding periods or time horizons of a "major segment of institutional investors . . . [are] really infinity, at least as infinity is perceived by mortal beings."[4] Levy succinctly summarizes the concerns of those who are troubled by the current risk paradigm when he says that "time horizon is just as important as [return] variability in setting asset mixes" and suggests that "what is needed is an appropriate definition of risk."[5]

It is my hope that the messages of this paper may eventually reach portfolio owners, and specifically, their chief executive officers and governing boards who, in the last analysis, are solely responsible for determining the measure of risk that is appropriate to their respective situations. On a more ambitious level, I suggest that the concepts here are relevant to *all* owners of assets, not just financial assets, and to all types of portfolios, not just those of institutions.

The conclusion that the acceptance of a new risk paradigm may prove rewarding for many portfolio owners stems from a belief that the current misunderstanding of what truly constitutes risk in a given situation often leads to portfolios with less than optimal equity contents and, therefore, lower long-term returns than might otherwise be achieved.[6] Furthermore, the failure to understand explicitly how much volatility risk can actually be tolerated in a given situation all too often encourages owners to dampen volatility by attempts to "time the market," which, as I—among others—have noted elsewhere, typically leads to mediocre long-term performance results.[7]

The utility of developing a concept of risk that is more intuitively understandable to *all* portfolio situations becomes more apparent when we accept the following three premises (of which only the third may be unfamiliar):

1. To the extent that the market *is* mostly efficient, we can expect only modest improvements in portfolio returns from active asset management.
2. To the extent that well diversified portfolio returns *do* vary directly with volatility over long periods of time, returns are indeed a function of risk as risk is presently defined.
3. Prudent portfolio owners, when confronted with *uncertainties* as to what constitutes an appropriate level of risk, will usually err on the side of accepting too little volatility rather than too much.

Given the first two premises, it follows naturally that the most effective way to enhance returns is to determine the extent to which volatility does indeed affect the portfolio owner's true *risk* situation, and to select a portfolio that provides the maximum level of *tolerable* volatility and thus the highest possible return, given the attendant risk. Since uncertainties concerning appropriate levels of risk usually result in overstatements of the impact of volatility, any change in the "rational model" that reduces portfolio owners' uncertainty of what truly constitutes risk in their particular situations should have a positive effect on future returns.

The Problem with Volatility as a Proxy for Risk

The problem with equating portfolio risk solely to the volatility of portfolio returns is simply that the proposition says nothing about what is being risked as a result of the volatility. For purposes of analogy consider the most common example in our daily lives, the weather. The risk implications of weather volatility are usually minimal for the vast majority of the population, who are not farmers or sailors or outdoor sports promoters or backpackers undertaking a winter hike in the mountains. Feeling "rewarded" by not having the daily burden of carrying a raincoat, many commuters are content to bear the nominal risk of occasionally getting slightly damp on their short walk to the office. On the other hand, on a long backpack in the mountains, where one of the "rewards" is clearly carrying as little weight as possible, prudent hikers will nonetheless hedge their risk of serious discomfort or worse by toting several pounds of raingear and perhaps a tent.

Volatility per se, be it related to weather, portfolio returns, or the timing of one's morning newspaper delivery, is simply a benign statistical probability factor that tells nothing about risk until coupled with a consequence. Its measurement is useless until we describe that probability in terms of the "probability of what." If the "what" is of no concern to the given individual or group, then the probability of "what's" occurring is likewise of no concern, and vice versa, and vice all the gradations in between. As an editor of a journal reminded his clients some years ago, "The determining question in structuring a portfolio is the *consequence* of loss; this is far more important than the *chance* of loss."[8]

What then is the specific *consequence* whose probable occurrence should concern us?

Risk Is the Probability of Not Having Sufficient Cash with Which to Buy Something Important

Since an investment *portfolio* is, etymologically, a collection of noncash pieces of paper (see note for *portfolio's* literal meaning),[9] and since nearly everything we buy or every obligation we retire requires outlays of cash, the real risk in holding a portfolio is that it might not provide its owner, either during the interim or at some terminal date or both, with the cash he requires to make essential outlays, including meeting payments when due. (In the case of pension funds, such purchases include deferred payments for services previously rendered.) As Smidt aptly points out, "Investors are ultimately interested in the future stream of *consumption* they will be able to obtain from their portfolios" by converting noncash assets into cash.[10]

Nevertheless, since a portfolio's "cash convertibility" varies so directly with the volatility of its returns that the two terms are typically used interchangeably, one might argue that this emphasis on cash requirements in no way affects the usefulness of volatility as a proxy for risk. To so argue, however, overlooks the critical fact that *different portfolio owners have different needs for cash*, just as the commuter and the backpacker have different needs for protective clothing.

Ability to purchase, which varies directly with portfolio volatility, should not be confused with need to purchase. The latter . . . as Smidt suggests, is the portfolio's *raison d'être*, and is, or should be, the governing factor in determining the division of the portfolio's asset mix of holdings between those that are readily convertible into predictable amounts of cash and those that are not. By developing a risk paradigm that places the emphasis on "need to purchase" rather than "ability to purchase," each portfolio owner is encouraged to make a conscious decision as to whether or not to carry a raincoat (i.e., low volatile, "nearer to cash" assets). To carry a raincoat because others are carrying raincoats is simply being fashionable, and being fashionable in investment decisions typically leads to mediocre results, or worse.

From this, we can readily see that, strictly speaking, the widely used term "portfolio risk," standing by itself, is meaningless, because "the possibility of loss or injury," which is *Webster's* definition of risk, has no abstract significance. Like the weather, portfolios feel no pain; it is only *travelers* in the weather and *owners* of portfolios who bear whatever the attendant risk. What then is "owner's risk"?

Owner's risk is measured by the degree of "fit" that appears when a portfolio's minimum projected cash flows from income and principal conversions into cash are superimposed by time period on the owner's maximum future cash requirements for essential payments. Such a juxtapositioning provides a continuous series of pro forma cash flow statements. The periodic differences between the expected future cash conversion values of the assets, including their income flows, and the expected future cash requirements of the liabilities show up on the pro forma statements either as surpluses, connoting negative risk, or as deficits, connoting positive risk. As in all pro forma statements, however, the problem is not in the arithmetic, but rather in the accuracy of the assumptions used in projecting the cash flows.

A great deal of useful research has been done on the predictability, over varying time frames, of the cash conversion values of various arrays of portfolio assets. In this context, "predictability" can be roughly translated as "volatility" and "cash conversion value" as "total return." What is typically left undone, however, is an equally thorough analysis of the liability side of the equation, i.e., of the essentiality, timing, magnitude, and predictability of the portfolio owner's future cash requirements.

Summary: The Need for Cash Drives the Process

In the last analysis, risk is the likelihood of having insufficient cash with which to make essential payments. While the traditional proxy for risk, volatility of returns, does reflect the probable variability of the cash conversion value of a portfolio owner's assets, it says nothing about the cash requirements of his liabilities, or future obligations. Since fund assets exist solely to service these cash obligations, which vary widely from one fund to another in terms of magnitude, timing, essentiality, and predictability, portfolio owners are being seriously misled when they define risk solely in terms of the asset side of the equation.

Specifically, since both history and theory demonstrate that diversified portfolio returns historically and theoretically increase as return volatility increases, owners should be explicitly encouraged to determine *in their own particular situations* the maximum amount of return volatility that can be tolerated, given their own respective future needs for cash. While the theoreticians are presumably correct in directly relating volatility and returns, it is the owner's future *need for cash* that determines how much volatility he can tolerate and, therefore, the level of portfolio return that can theoretically be achieved.

My intention in emphasizing the *need for cash* has been purposely to shift responsibility for the risk-determination process from the asset manager to the portfolio owner. As one author reminds us, "Spending decisions (and thus future needs for cash) are the one input to the portfolio management equation that is totally controllable by the owner."[11] Furthermore, the cumulative effect of the owner's prior spending decisions on future needs for cash can, in most cases, best be fathomed and thus planned for, conceivably modified, and ensured against, within the owner's own shop and not by an outside agent.

Finally, by letting the need for cash drive the portfolio management process, the owner can make future spending decisions more wisely. Over time, he can develop and sustain an understandable and defendable asset mix policy that will provide him with an optimum portfolio return given his particular cash requirement situation. In one sentence, the traditional, narrow definition of portfolio risk based solely on volatility encourages owners to apply a universal risk measurement standard, for which they themselves accept little personal responsibility, to what is essentially a highly parochial problem.

Notes

1. T. Kuhn, *The Structure of Scientific Revolutions* (Chicago: University of Chicago Press, 1970), as quoted in T. J. Peters and R. H. Waterman, Jr., *In Search of Excellence* (New York: Harper and Row, 1982), 42.

2. S. Smidt, "Investment Horizons and Performance Measurement," *The Journal of Portfolio Management* (Winter 1978): 18.
3. F.H. Trainer, Jr., J.B. Yawitz, and W.J. Marshall, "Holding Period Is the Key to Risk Thresholds," *The Journal of Portfolio Management* (Winter 1979): 48.
4. R.H. Jeffrey, "Internal Portfolio Growth: The Better Measure," *The Journal of Portfolio Management* (Summer 1977): 10.
5. R.A. Levy, "Stocks, Bonds, Bills, and Inflation over 52 Years," *The Journal of Portfolio Management* (Summer 1978): 18.
6. While presumably unnecessary for readers, we note here (using Ibbotson and Sinquefield data through 1981) that the annualized total return of the S&P 500 from 1926 to 1983 was 9.6 percent vs. 3.2 percent for 90-day Treasury bills.
7. R.H. Jeffrey, "The Folly of Market Timing," *Harvard Business Review* (July–August 1984).
8. P. L. Bernstein, "Management of Individual Portfolios," in S. Levine, ed., *The Financial Analyst's Handbook* (Homewood, IL: Dow Jones-Irwin, Inc., 1975), 1373–1388.
9. *Portfolio* derives from the Latin words *portare*, to carry, and *foglio*, leaf or sheet. Since the Romans had a perfectly good word for cash, *moneta*, which they could have used for "cashbox," we can thus infer that *foglio* refers to noncash forms of paper. Etymologically then, a "portfolio," or even a so-called "investment portfolio," is not and should not be confused with cash, a distinction that most investors fail to make in the "mark-to-market" world in which we live.
10. Smidt, op. cit., p. 21.
11. J.P. Williamson and H.A.D. Sanger, "Educational Endowment Funds," in *Investment Manager's Handbook* (Homewood, IL: Dow Jones-Irwin, Inc., 1980), 839. The actual quotation is, "The spending rate is totally controllable."

How True Are the Tried Principles?

PETER L. BERNSTEIN

President of the company that bears his name and a respected researcher and commentator on economic and investment matters, Peter L. Bernstein is the editor who developed *The Journal of Portfolio Management* into a splendid forum for the exchange of ideas and experience between professional investors and academicians. Here (with apologies for deletion of much documentary data) is one of his typically original, sometimes startling, and always lucid propositions: that bonds should trade places with cash as the "residual stepchild" of asset allocation to reduce portfolio risk and improve returns.

• • •

Why is it that the conventional allocation of portfolio assets is between stocks and bonds? Why is cash the portfolio's stepchild, held in lesser amounts and used only as a buying reserve for the two long-term assets? Is there a case for making cash a primary asset in its own right? If so, is it possible that bonds or equities might then become the residual stepchild?

The answers to these questions lead to an unconventional conclusion. Bonds have no legitimate place in a portfolio except under two special and specified conditions. First, unusual short-run opportunities in the bond market do present themselves and should not be ignored. Second, bonds may best serve the unique requirements of some portfolios, especially those with high current expenditures relative to the size of their principal.

As a general statement, however, portfolios that hold only stocks and cash can provide higher long-run expected returns, with no increase in risk, as compared with the conventional portfolio that con-

Reprinted from *Investment Management Review* 3 (March/April 1989), pp. 17–24. New York: DMA Communications, Inc.

centrates its assets in stocks and bonds. This means that bonds rather than cash should be the residual stepchild of long-run portfolio asset allocation, except where unique portfolio requirements prevail.

I emphasize that this analysis focuses on what most people today refer to as *strategic* rather than tactical asset allocation. In other words, I consider the range of choice for a portfolio in equilibrium, in its long-run stance, when no unusual opportunities are available in any single sector of the capital markets. This contrasts with tactical asset allocation, which makes temporary shifts away from the strategic allocation in order to take advantage of market disequilibrium.

Diversification and Asset Choices

The overwhelming majority of investors will want to make equities the asset of choice in determining their appropriate strategic asset mix, simply because equities promise the highest rate of return over the long run.

At the same time, most investors find equities too risky to occupy 100 percent of the portfolio. That is why people diversify; they try to avoid having all their eggs in one equity basket. The essential issue that we confront here is how effectively investors can combine equities with bonds and with cash as diversifying agents.

Let us consider for a moment how diversification really works. Although diversification helps us avoid the chance that all our assets will go down together, it also means that we will avoid the chance that all assets will go up together. Seen from this standpoint, diversification is a mixed blessing.

In order to keep the mixture of the blessings of diversification as favorable as possible, effective diversification has two necessary conditions:

1. The covariance in returns among the assets must be negative; if it is positive, we will still run the risk that all assets will go down together.

2. The expected returns in all the assets should be high; no one wants to hold assets with significant probabilities of loss.

How well do bonds and cash meet these conditions?

Consider covariance first. We know that the correlation between bond and stock returns is variable, but we also know that it is positive most of the time. . . . Stock returns correlate even more weakly with cash; but, such as it is, the correlation between stocks and cash is negative. Bonds and cash also correlate weakly, but the correlation here tends to be positive.

If the correlation between bond and stock returns is positive, but stocks have higher expected returns, why does anybody bother to own bonds at all? There are two reasons. First, the long-run expected return on bonds is higher than the expected return on cash. Second, bond returns are usually less volatile than equity returns while providing a higher component of current income.

Nevertheless, bonds have three distinct disadvantages. First, bonds have lower expected returns than stocks most of the time—and this shortfall increases as we lengthen the investment horizon or holding period. Second, bond returns move in the same direction as stock returns too frequently to make bonds a perfect diversifying agent. Finally, bonds are vulnerable to negative returns (prices can fall by more than coupon income); cash suffers from no such vulnerability, in a nominal sense at least. . . .

Monthly and quarterly bond and stock returns are simultaneously positive over 70 percent of the time. This ratio increases as we lengthen the holding period, as all assets have a higher probability of positive results over the long run.

The meaning is clear: most of the time that bonds are going up, the stock market is going up. Unless bonds tend to provide higher returns on those occasions, they will be making a reliable contribution to the overall performance of the portfolio only during the relatively infrequent time periods when the bond market is going up and the stock market is going down.

How Can Cash Help?

Although cash tends to have a lower expected return than bonds, we have seen that cash can hold its own against bonds 30 percent of the time or more when bond returns are positive. Cash will always win out over bonds when bond returns are negative.

The logical step, therefore, is to try a portfolio mix that offsets the lower expected return on cash by increasing the share devoted to equities. As cash has no negative returns, the volatility might not be any higher than it would be in a portfolio that includes bonds.

. . . The results of a portfolio consisting of 60 percent stocks, 40 percent bonds, and no cash [are compared] with a portfolio consisting of 75 percent stocks, no bonds, and 25 percent cash.

The results are clearly in favor of the bond-free portfolio, which provides higher returns with almost identical levels of risk. The bond-free portfolio outperforms the cash-free portfolio in 88 out of the 138 quarters, or 64 percent of the time.

Why Bonds at All?

. . . Momentary disequilibrium in the capital markets does provide tactical opportunities for owning bonds. In addition, some portfolios, and especially those whose spending requirements are high relative to capital values, may find that prudence requires investing in the high current income that bonds provide. In addition, active bond management, which involves varying the duration and convexity of fixed-income portfolios, may also have a higher reward/risk profile than a straight cash investment.

None of these considerations dilutes the primary conclusion that long-term bonds are an unsatisfactory asset, with expected returns below stocks and with risk-reducing features below cash. The investor who includes bonds in a portfolio should therefore have clear and positive reasons for doing so; bonds have no place in the portfolio by default.

A New Theory of Risk Measurement

DANIEL BERNOULLI

Daniel Bernoulli (1700–1782) was a member of a Swiss family of distinguished mathematicians and a professor at the University of Basel. He won the prize of the French Academy no fewer than 10 times. His concept of utility, which forms the basis for all theories of portfolio management, is described in this excerpt from the paper he gave at the Imperial Academy of Sciences in Petersburg in 1738.

. . .

§1. Ever since mathematicians first began to study the measurement of risk there has been general agreement on the following proposition: *Expected values are computed by multiplying each possible gain by the number of ways in which it can occur, and then dividing the sum of these products by the total number of possible cases where, in this theory, the consideration of cases that are all of the same probability is insisted upon.* If this rule be accepted, what remains to be done within the framework of this theory amounts to the enumeration of all alternatives, their breakdown into equi-probable cases, and finally, their insertion into corresponding classifications.

§2. Proper examination of the numerous demonstrations of this proposition that have come forth indicates that they all rest upon one hypothesis: *Since there is no reason to assume that of two persons encountering identical risks,*[1] *either should expect to have his desires more closely fulfilled, the risks anticipated by each must be deemed equal in value.* No characteristic of the persons themselves ought to be taken into consideration; only those matters should be weighed carefully that pertain to the terms of the risk. The relevant finding might then be made by the highest judges established by public authority. But really there is here

---

Reprinted from *Econometrica* 22 (January 1954; originally published 1738, Petersburg), pp. 23–26. Evanston, IL: The Econometric Society.

no need for judgment but of deliberation, i.e., rules would be set up whereby anyone could estimate his prospects from any risky undertaking in light of one's specific financial circumstances.

§3. To make this clear it is perhaps advisable to consider the following example: Somehow a very poor fellow obtains a lottery ticket that will yield with equal probability either nothing or 20,000 ducats. Will this man evaluate his chance of winning at 10,000 ducats? Would he not be ill-advised to sell this lottery ticket for 9,000 ducats? To me it seems that the answer is in the negative. On the other hand I am inclined to believe that a rich man would be ill-advised to refuse to buy the lottery ticket for 9,000 ducats. If I am not wrong then it seems clear that all men cannot use the same rule to evaluate the gamble. The rule established in §1 must, therefore, be discarded. But anyone who considers the problem with perspicacity and interest will ascertain that the concept of *value* that we have used in this rule may be defined in a way that renders the entire procedure universally acceptable without reservation. To do this the determination of the *value* of an item must not be based on its *price*, but rather on the *utility* it yields. The price of the item is dependent only on the thing itself and is equal for everyone; the utility, however, is dependent on the particular circumstances of the person making the estimate. Thus there is no doubt that a gain of 1,000 ducats is more significant to a pauper than to a rich man though both gain the same amount.

§4. The discussion has now been developed to a point where anyone may proceed with the investigation by the mere paraphrasing of one and the same principle. However, since the hypothesis is entirely new, it may nevertheless require some elucidation. I have, therefore, decided to explain by example what I have explored. Meanwhile, let us use this as a fundamental rule: *If the utility of each possible profit expectation is multiplied by the number of ways in which it can occur, and we then divide the sum of these products by the total number of possible cases, a mean utility[2] [moral expectation] will be obtained, and the profit that corresponds to this utility will equal the value of the risk in question.*

§5. Thus it becomes evident that no valid measurement of the value of a risk can be obtained without consideration being given to its *utility*, that is to say, the utility of whatever gain accrues to the individual, or, conversely, how much profit is required to yield a given utility.

Notes

1. In other words, risky propositions (gambles). [Translator]
2. Free translation of Bernoulli's "emolumentum medium." Literally, "mean utility."

Timing Considerations
in Investment Policy

BENJAMIN GRAHAM
DAVID L. DODD

Ben Graham and Dave Dodd, in this 40-year-old passage from the
third edition of their *Security Analysis*, explain why they are skeptics
on "timing." "The major consideration," they say, is not when an
investor buys or sells, "but at what prices."

. . .

Timing Considerations in Investment Policy

The old rule for the ordinary investor was that he should buy sound
securities when he had funds available. If he waited for lower prices he
would be losing interest on his money; he might "miss his market,"
even if prices declined; in any case, he was turning himself into a stock
trader or speculator. Much of this view retains its validity. However,
the time when the investor should clearly *not* buy common stocks is
during the upper ranges of a bull market. For most issues this is tantamount to saying that he should not buy them at prices higher than can
be justified by conservative analysis—which is something of a truism.
But, this warning applies also to the purchase of apparent "bargain issues"
when the general price level seems dangerously high.

There remain two other major questions of investment timing. The
first is whether the investor should try to *anticipate* the movements of
the market—endeavoring to buy just before an advance begins or in its
early stages, and to sell at corresponding times prior to a decline. We
state dogmatically at this point that it is impossible for *all* investors to

Excerpted from *Security Analysis: Principles and Techniques*, 3rd edition (1951; originally
published 1934), Chapter 5, pp. 47–59, by permission of McGraw-Hill Publishing Company, New York.

follow timing of this sort, and that there is no reason for any typical investor to believe that he can get more dependable guidance here than the countless *speculators* who are chasing the same will-o'-the-wisp. Furthermore, the major consideration for the investor is not *when* he buys or sells, but at what prices.

This is an aspect of the "timing" philosophy that has been almost completely overlooked. The speculator will always be concerned about timing because he wants to make his profit in a hurry. But waiting for a profit is no drawback to an investor, as compared with having his money uninvested until a propitious buying "signal" is given, unless he thereby succeeds in buying at a sufficiently *lower price* to offset his loss of dividends. This means that *timing*, as such, does not benefit the investor unless it coincides with *pricing*. Specifically, if his aim is to buy and sell repeatedly, then his timing policy must enable him to repurchase his shares at substantially under his previous selling price. We do not believe that the popular approaches to stock-market timing—the famous Dow theory—will accomplish this for the investor. . . .

A more serious question of timing policy, in our opinion, is presented by the well-defined cyclical movements of the stock market. Should the investor endeavor to confine his buying to the lower reaches of the recurrent bear markets, and correspondingly plan to sell out in the upper ranges of the recurrent bull markets? In such a policy, timing and pricing would clearly coincide—he would be buying at the right time because he would be buying at the right price, and vice versa.

No one can tell in advance how such an investment philosophy will work out in the years to come. Presumably its theoretical justification must be sought in the market's past history. If this is studied with some care, the indications it yields will not be found too encouraging.

. . . For the first half of the past 50-year period [1900–1950] both the amplitude of the price swings and their duration were regular enough to support the idea that the investor could buy his stocks at well-defined cheap levels and sell them out at well-defined dear levels, about once every five years. But since 1925 the market swings have been much less homogeneous in their successive forms, and the time interval between one low (or high) point and the next seems to have widened considerably. In fact since the bull-market peak of 1919 there have been only three subsequent peaks in 30 years—in 1929, 1937, and 1946. Since the bear-market low in 1921 there have been only two well-defined lows—in 1932 and 1942—plus a noncharacteristic market cycle between 1938 and 1942.

The Central Value of the Dow Jones Industrial Average

We have made some hindsight calculations of results from the use of a "central-value method" of purchasing and selling, as a group, the stocks in the Dow Jones Industrial Average. This method involves an actual appraisal of the Dow Jones Unit, together with the decision to buy at a fixed discount below and to sell at a fixed premium above such value. In effect, however, it is not far different from a simple effort to wait for historically indicated low levels to buy and high levels to sell. On paper the results are rather attractive. But we do not believe that they can be projected into the future with any degree of confidence, or that they promise a sufficiently large gain to justify the risks they involve of "missing the market" and of losing investment income for a long period of time. These risks might make the enterprise an essentially speculative one, and apart from the mathematical probabilities of gain or loss, it would not be well suited to the psychology of the typical investor.

Inflation and Pensions

WILLIAM C. GREENOUGH

William Greenough provided intellectual leadership in the area of retirement income for college and university educators when he prepared the analysis, excerpted here, that led to the establishment of the
College Retirement Equities Fund (CREF)—an equity-linked com-
panion to the annuities set up under the Teachers Insurance and
Annuity Association (TIAA). Prior to the period of the publication
of this analysis, educational pension investments were almost entirely
confined to bonds.

• • •

The rapid and far-reaching economic changes during recent decades
have served to emphasize the difficulties of making adequate income
provision for old age. Prior to this century very little had been done
about retirement plans; the problem was scarcely recognized in an
expanding but still predominantly rural economy.

When Andrew Carnegie gave $10 million in 1905 to establish free
pensions for college professors, he provided a strong impetus to retirement planning not only for teachers but for other groups as well. In
1918 the Carnegie Foundation for the Advancement of Teaching and
the Carnegie Corporation of New York established a broader and more
enduring concept of contributory annuity benefits for educators through
the establishment of Teachers Insurance and Annuity Association of
America (TIAA). At that time the United States was just emerging
from the first World War. No one then foresaw the violent economic
fluctuations that were to follow, including those caused by the deepest
depression in history, a second World War, and a long period of heavy
expenditures for defense.

From William C. Greenough, A New Approach to Retirement Income (New York, New York,
1951), 7–15 by permission of the Teachers Insurance and Annuity Association of America.

When planning for old-age income the educator, or for that matter anyone, must seek a method that has the best hope of affording him real security when he can no longer rely on his own efforts to provide a livable income. Security in retirement poses a difficult problem when it means providing not only a sufficient annuity income in dollars but also a reasonable income in current purchasing power. Traditional methods of saving for retirement have been effective in providing the dollar income; they have fallen short of the goal of providing a suitable purchasing power income. During the low prices prevailing in the 1930s, annuitants and others living on fixed incomes were receiving a larger "real" or purchasing power income than they might have expected; in 1950 their real income was seriously reduced. There is little in the present situation to assure us that the purchasing power of the dollar in the year 1960, 1970, or 2000 will be the same as it is today. This suggests that an effort be made to provide more dollars as retirement income when prices are high even though that may mean reducing the number of dollars when prices are low.

Eminent authorities believe that our economic system is now "replete with built-in inflationary bias," especially in periods of war or international tension accompanied by heavy expenditures for defense. They point to the tax structure, escalator wage clauses, parity prices, budget deficits, government borrowing from commercial banks, low rates of interest, cost-plus contracts, subsidies, and the like. Some point to Keynesian economics, emphasis on full employment, the public welfare state, [and the] disinclination to return to the gold standard.

The "new era" philosophy has been with us on previous occasions, sometimes strongest just before a major turn. There is abundant evidence that the law of supply and demand has not been repealed. There are strains and stresses in the economy that could lead to a major depression sometime in the future. Although the hope of world peace looks visionary, it is by no means inconceivable that a long period of world peace could occur. It could be accompanied in America by constantly increasing productivity, higher standards of living, and declining prices.

At any one time the forces of inflation or the forces of deflation seem to be stronger. But planning for retirement income is a very long-range process. Transitory shifts in the economy are relatively unimportant; the objective must be to provide reasonable security for the retired person regardless of the direction in which the American economy moves.

The difficulty is that there seems to be no perfect protection against inflation. However, there is good reason to believe that retirement security can be substantially enhanced by broadening the scope and diversification of the investment of funds saved during working years. . . .

Contrast with Usual Investment Methods

Frequently the individual investor in common stocks purchases a single block of stock on a particular day, holds it until a later date and then sells it. He thereby does not obtain adequate diversification either among issues or over time. Most studies of common stock performance take a given list of stocks at one point in time and follow the experience through to another point. When this method of purchasing and selling stocks is used, the starting and ending dates are all-important.

The advent of the investment companies, especially the open-end mutual funds, offered the individual a chance to choose a fund that provided adequate diversification *among issues*. The individual can in some funds invest small sums periodically, thereby gaining diversification over *time* as well as among issues, unless he fails to stay with his long-range program. However, if the individual cashes out of his entire fund at one point, the market prices of common stocks at that point assume great importance.

The method of investing planned for the College Retirement Equities Fund combines a number of well-known principles into a broad new pattern. The principle of *diversification among issues* of equity investments would be obtained through pooling a portion of the annuity savings of many employers and individuals into a substantial fund invested in a great many companies in a number of industries. The principle of *diversification over time* would be obtained by accepting small payments, month by month and year by year, over a major portion of each participant's working lifetime. These payments would be directly related to salary and therefore would continue at all levels of common stock prices. Effective use would be made of the principle of *dollar cost averaging*, whereby more shares of stock are purchased by a given premium at low prices than at high. Even though salaries were reduced in many instances in the early 1930s, annuity premium income on existing policies proved more stable than payments into other investment media.

Perhaps the most interesting innovation is the *unit annuity*. Few individuals can expect to accumulate enough by retirement time to live entirely on the earnings from investments. Under ordinary conditions the retired individual dares not dip too deeply into principal because he has no way of knowing how long he and his wife will live. Some people die soon after retirement; others live 30 years or longer. Through a life annuity an individual can, with safety, use up capital as well as interest earnings and thereby obtain a substantially higher income throughout the remainder of his life.

The unit, or variable, annuity directly applies the annuity principle to a new area of investment, common stocks, allowing the individual the assurance again that he can use up both capital and dividend payments without danger of outliving his income.

General Conclusions from the Data

This economic study is, of course, based on historical data. There are cogent reasons why equities may not do as well in the future as they have in the past; there are reasons why they may do better. Not all of the inflationary forces previously mentioned would be reflected in increasing common stock prices and dividends; some are adverse to common stocks. Likewise, not all the influences toward a stable or declining price level would mean reduced performance of common stocks.

The conclusions to be drawn from the historical data will be stated with full realization that they are not necessarily a preview of the future. However, periods of inflation and deflation are included, as are periods of good and poor common stock performance, so that an indication may be gained of possible experience under varying economic conditions.

The comparisons in the study are drawn from general averages of all life insurance companies, where possible, and the large majority of common stocks. Therefore the study and the data behind it, while directly related to retirement plans in the field of higher education, of course have broader applicability for long-range investment programs and the channeling of retirement savings into productive enterprise.

The general conclusions are given at this point for the convenience of the reader and so that he may test them against the data as he proceeds. The conclusions of course were reached after studying a much larger volume of data than deemed practical to include in this report.

1.   It is unwise to commit *all* of one's retirement savings to dollar obligations, since decreases in the purchasing power of the dollar can seriously reduce the value of a fixed income annuity. Increases in the purchasing power of the dollar, on the other hand, improve the status of the owner of a fixed income annuity.

2.   It is equally unwise to commit *all* of one's retirement savings to equity investments, since variations in prices of common stocks are much too pronounced to permit full reliance on them for the stable income needed during retirement. Changes in the value of common stocks and other equities are by no means perfectly correlated with cost of living changes, but they have provided a considerably better protection against inflation than have debt obligations.

3.   Contributions to a retirement plan that are invested partly in debt obligations and partly in common stocks through an Equities Fund providing lifetime unit annuities offer promise of supplying retirement income that is at once reasonably free from violent fluctuations in amount and from serious depreciation through price level changes.

4.   The Equities Fund should make no dollar guarantees. Its liabilities should always be valued directly in terms of its assets. This is a cardinal point of the suggested arrangement for two principal reasons:

a.   It ensures that the Equities Fund is "failure proof" in the technical sense and cannot be forced into liquidation of its assets at a low point in the market. Whether the market be high or low, the Equities Fund obligations are automatically limited to the then market value of its assets. Typical pension plans whose liabilities are expressed in dollar guarantees and whose assets are partially in fluctuating securities, such as common stocks, are vulnerable in this connection.

b.   It ensures the individual participant his full pro rata share in any rise in the net asset value of the Equities Fund. Under typical pension plans invested partially in common stocks, the employer gives a fixed dollar pension assurance to his employees. Any appreciation in common stock values is normally used to reduce the employer's cost or to create reserves, whereas it is needed in a period of rising prices as an increased benefit for the employees. Through a common stock fund free from the confinements of dollar promises, a participant can have a wider opportunity to share in the development of the American economy with part of his savings. Obviously, this opportunity to share in rises must be accompanied by a willingness to share in falls of the net asset values.

5.   Common stock investments obtained through purchases month by month, at low prices as well as high, would have provided a very effective method of investing a portion of retirement funds. Most of the difficulties in individual investing in equities arise from lack of diversification both *among shares* and *over time*. So long as the period of regular payments into a fund invested in common stocks was reasonably long, so long as each person owned a portion of a large well-diversified fund and so long as there were no substantial shifts either into or out of equities at a particular moment, the experience was normally considerably better than that of a fund invested wholly or principally in debt obligations.

The Loser's Game

CHARLES D. ELLIS

"Gifted, determined, ambitious professionals have come into invest-ment management in such large numbers during the past 30 years that it may no longer be feasible for any of them to profit from the errors of all the others sufficiently often and by sufficient magnitude to beat the market averages." Thus did Charles Ellis set the stage for this classic 1975 exploration of why it is so hard to win the market game.

. . .

Disagreeable data are streaming out of the computers of Becker Secu-rities and Merrill Lynch and all the other performance measurement firms. Over and over and over again, these facts and figures inform us that investment managers are failing to perform. Not only are the nation's leading portfolio managers failing to produce positive absolute rates of return (after all, it's been a long, long bear market) but they are also failing to produce positive *relative* rates of return. Contrary to their oft articulated goal of outperforming the market averages, investment managers are not beating the market: The market is beating them.

Faced with information that contradicts what they believe, human beings tend to respond in one of two ways. Some will assimilate the information, changing it—as oysters cover an obnoxious grain of silica with nacre—so they can ignore the new knowledge and hold on to their former beliefs; and others will accept the validity of the new information. Instead of changing the meaning of the new data to fit their old concept of reality, they adjust their perception of reality to accommodate the information and then they put it to use.

Psychologists advise us that the more important the old concept of reality is to a person—the more important it is to his sense of self-

Reprinted from *The Financial Analysts Journal*, Vol. 31, No. 4, July/August 1975, 19–26. New York: Financial Analyst's Federation.

esteem and sense of inner worth—the more tenaciously he will hold on to the old concept and the more insistently he will assimilate, ignore or reject new evidence that conflicts with his old and familiar concept of the world. This behavior is particularly common among very bright people because they can so easily develop and articulate self-persuasive logic to justify the conclusions they want to keep.

For example, most institutional investment managers continue to believe, or at least say they believe, that they can and soon will again "outperform the market." They won't and they can't. And the purpose of this article is to explain why not.

My experience with very bright and articulate investment managers is that their skills at analysis and logical extrapolation are very good, often superb, but that their brilliance in extending logical extrapolation draws their own attention far away from the sometimes erroneous basic assumptions upon which their schemes are based. Major errors in reasoning and exposition are rarely found in the logical development of this analysis, but instead lie within the premise itself. This is what worried Martin Luther. It's what *The Best and the Brightest* is all about. It's what lifted LTV above $100; why the Emperor went for days without clothes; and why comedians and science fiction writers are so careful first to establish the "premise" and then quickly divert attention from it so they can elaborate the persuasive details of developing "logic."

The investment management business (it should be a profession but it is not) is built upon a simple and basic belief: Professional money managers can beat the market. That premise appears to be false.

If the premise that it is feasible to outperform the market were accepted, deciding how to go about achieving success would be a matter of straightforward logic. First, the market can be represented by an index, such as the S&P 500. Since this is a passive and public listing, the successful manager need only rearrange his bets differently from those of the S&P "shill." He can be an activist in either stock selection or market timing, or both. Since the manager will want his "bets" to be right most of the time, he will assemble a group of bright, well educated, highly motivated, hard working young people, and their collective purpose will be to beat the market by "betting against the house" with a "good batting average."

The belief that active managers can beat the market is based on two assumptions: (1) liquidity offered in the stock market is an advantage, and (2) institutional investing is a Winner's Game.

The unhappy thesis of this article can be briefly stated: Owing to important changes in the past 10 years, these basic assumptions are no longer true. On the contrary, market liquidity is a *liability* rather than an *asset*, and institutional investors will, over the long term, *under*perform the market because money management has become a Loser's Game.

Before demonstrating with mathematical evidence why money management has become a Loser's Game, we should close off the one path of escape for those who will try to assimilate the facts. They may argue that this analysis is unfair because so much of the data on performance comes from bear market experience, giving an adverse bias to an evaluation of the long-term capabilities of managers who have portfolio betas above 1.0. "Of course," they will concede with dripping innuendo, "these interesting analyses may have less to say about dynamic fund managers operating in a decent market." Perhaps, but can they present us with evidence to support their hopes? Can they shoulder the burden of proof? After many hours of discussion with protesting money managers all over America and in Canada and Europe, I have heard no new evidence or persuasive appeal from the hard judgment that follows the evidence presented below. In brief, the "problem" is not a cyclical aberration; it is a long-term secular trend.

Unfortunately, the relative performance of institutionally managed portfolios appears to be getting worse. Measuring returns from trough to trough in the market, the institutionally managed funds in the Becker sample are falling farther and farther behind the market as represented by the S&P 500 Average. It appears that the *costs* of active management are going up and that the *rewards* from active management are going down.

The basic characteristics of the environment within which institutional investors must operate have changed greatly in the past decade. The most significant change is that institutional investors have become, and will continue to be, the dominant feature of their own environment.

For the ten years ending December 31, 1974, the funds in the Becker Securities sample had a median rate of return of 0.0 percent. The S&P total rate of return over the same period was 1.2 percent per annum. (Within the Becker sample, the high fund's annual rate of return was 4.5 percent, the first quartile fund's return was 1.1 percent, the median 0.0 percent, the third quartile—1.1 percent; and the low fund's annual rate of return—5.6 percent.)

	S&P 500 Average	Becker Median	Institutional Shortfall
Last Three Market Cycles (9/30/62 to 12/31/74)	5.3%	4.1%	(0.8%)
Last Two Market Cycles (12/31/66 to 12/31/74)	2.1%	0.4%	(1.7%)
Last Single Market Cycle (9/30/70 to 12/31/74)	2.2%	(0.3%)	(2.5%)

Data: Becker Securities 1974 Institutional Funds Evaluation Service.

This change has impacted greatly upon all the major features of the investment field. In particular, institutional dominance has converted market liquidity from a source of *profits* to a source of *costs*, and this is the main reason behind the transformation of money management from a Winner's Game to a Loser's Game.

Before analyzing what happened to convert institutional investing from a Winner's Game to a Loser's Game, we should explore the profound difference between these two kinds of "games." In making the conceptual distinction, I will use the writings of an eminent scientist, a distinguished historian, and a renowned educator. They are, respectively, Dr. Simon Ramo of TRW; naval historian, Admiral Samuel Elliot Morrison; and professional golf instructor, Tommy Armour.

Simon Ramo identified the crucial difference between a Winner's Game and a Loser's Game in his excellent book on playing strategy, *Extraordinary Tennis for the Ordinary Tennis Player*. Over a period of many years, he observed that tennis was not *one* game but *two*. One game of tennis is played by professionals and a very few gifted amateurs; the other is played by all the rest of us.

Although players in both games use the same equipment, dress, rules, and scoring, and conform to the same etiquette and customs, the basic natures of their two games are almost entirely different. After extensive scientific and statistical analysis, Dr. Ramo summed it up this way: Professionals *win* points, amateurs *lose* points. Professional tennis players stroke the ball with strong, well aimed shots, through long and often exciting rallies, until one player is able to drive the ball just beyond the reach of his opponent. Errors are seldom made by these splendid players.

Expert tennis is what I call a Winner's Game because the ultimate outcome is determined by the actions of the *winner*. Victory is due to *winning more points than the opponent wins*—not, as we shall see in a moment, simply to getting a higher score than the opponent, but getting that higher score by *winning* points.

Amateur tennis, Ramo found, is almost entirely different. Brilliant shots, long and exciting rallies, and seemingly miraculous recoveries are few and far between. On the other hand, the ball is fairly often hit into the net or out of bounds, and double faults at service are not uncommon. The amateur duffer seldom *beats* his opponent, but he beats himself all the time. The victor in this game of tennis gets a higher score than the opponent, but he gets that higher score *because his opponent is losing even more points.*

As a scientist and statistician, Dr. Ramo gathered data to test his hypothesis. And he did it in a very clever way. Instead of keeping conventional game scores—"Love," "Fifteen All," "Thirty-Fifteen," etc.—Ramo simply counted points *won* versus points *lost*. And here is what he found. In expert tennis, about 80 percent of the points are won; in amateur tennis, about 80 percent of the points are *lost*. In other words, professional tennis is a Winner's Game—the final outcome is determined by the activities of the winner—and amateur tennis is a Loser's Game—the final outcome is determined by the activities of the *loser*. The two games are, in their fundamental characteristic, not at all the same. They are opposites.

From this discovery of the two kinds of tennis, Dr. Ramo builds a complete strategy by which ordinary tennis players can win games, sets, and matches again and again by following the simple stratagem of losing less, and letting the opponent defeat himself.

Dr. Ramo explains that if you choose to win at tennis—as opposed to having a good time—the strategy for winning is to avoid mistakes. The way to avoid mistakes is to be conservative and keep the ball in play, letting the other fellow have plenty of room in which to blunder his way to defeat, because he, being an amateur (and probably not having read Ramo's book) will play a losing game and not know it.

He will make errors. He will make too many errors. Once in a while he may hit a serve you cannot possibly handle, but much more frequently he will double fault. Occasionally, he may volley balls past you at the net, but more often than not they will sail far out of bounds. He will slam balls into the net from the front court and from the back court. His game will be a routine catalogue of gaffes, goofs, and grief.

He will try to beat you by winning, but he is not good enough to overcome the many inherent adversities of the game itself. The situation does not allow him to win with an activist strategy and he will instead lose. His efforts to win more points will, unfortunately for him, only increase his error rate. As Ramo instructs us in his book, the strategy for winning in a loser's game is to lose less. Avoid trying too hard. By keeping the ball in play, give the opponent as many opportunities as possible to make mistakes and blunder his way to defeat. In brief, by losing less become the victor.

In his thoughtful treatise on military science, *Strategy and Compromise*, Admiral Morrison makes the following point: "In warfare, mistakes are inevitable. Military decisions are based on estimates of the enemy's strengths and intentions that are usually faulty, and on intelligence that is never complete and often misleading." (This sounds a great deal like the investment business.) "Other things being equal," concludes Morrison, "the side that makes the fewest strategic errors wins the war."

War, as we all know, is the ultimate Loser's Game. As General Patton said, "Let the other poor dumb bastard lose his life for his country." Golf is another Loser's Game. Tommy Armour, in his great book *How to Play Your Best Golf All the Time*, says: "The way to win is by making fewer bad shots."

Gambling in a casino where the house takes at least 20 percent of every pot is obviously a Loser's Game. Stud poker is a Loser's Game but

Night Baseball with deuces, treys, and one-eyed Jacks "wild" is a Winner's Game.

Campaigning for elected office is a Loser's Game. The electorate seldom votes *for* one of the candidates but rather *against* the other candidate. Professional politicians advise their candidates: "Help the voters find a way to vote *against* the other guy, and you'll get elected."

Recent studies of professional football have found that the most effective defensive platoon members play an open, ad hoc, enterprising, risk-taking style—the proper strategy for a Winner's Game—while the best offensive players play a careful, "by the book" style that concentrates on avoiding errors and eliminating uncertainty, which is the requisite game plan for a Loser's Game. "Keep it simple," said Vincent Lombardi.

There are many other Loser's Games. Some, like institutional investing, used to be Winner's Games in the past, but have changed with the passage of time into *Loser's Games*. For example, 50 years ago, only very brave, very athletic, very strong willed young people with good eyesight had the nerve to try flying an airplane. In those glorious days, flying was a Winner's Game. But times have changed and so has flying. If you got into a 747 today, and the pilot came aboard wearing a 50-mission hat with a long, white silk scarf around his neck, you'd get off. Those people do not belong in airplanes any longer because flying an airplane today is a Loser's Game. Today, there's only one way to fly an airplane. It's simple: Don't make any mistakes.

Prize fighting starts out as a Winner's Game and becomes a Loser's Game as the fight progresses. In the first three or four rounds, a really strong puncher tries for a knockout. Thereafter, prize fighting is a gruelling contest of endurance to see who can survive the most punishment, while the other fellow gets so worn out that he literally drops to defeat.

Expert card players know that after several rounds of play, games like Gin Rummy go through a "phase change" after which discards no longer improve the relative position of the discarding player. During this latter phase, discards tend to add more strength to the opponent's hand than they remove weakness from the hand of the discarder. This changes long hands of Gin Rummy into a Loser's Game, and the correct strategy in this latter phase of the game is to evaluate discards not in terms of how much good they will do for your hand to get rid of them, but rather how much good they may do for your opponent.

Many other examples could be given, but these will suffice to make the distinction between Winner's Games and Loser's Games, to explain why the requisite player strategy is very different for the two kinds of games, and to show that the fundamental nature of a game can change and that Winner's Games can and sometimes do become Loser's Games. And that's what has happened to the Money Game. . . .

The trouble with Winner's Games is that they tend to self-destruct because they attract too much attention and too many players—all of whom want to win. (That's why gold rushes finish ugly.) But in the short run, the rushing in of more and more players seeking to win expands the apparent reward. And that's what happened in Wall Street during the 1960's. Riding the tide of a bull market, institutional investors obtained such splendid rates of return in equities that more and more money was turned over to them—particularly in mutual funds and pension funds—which fueled the continuation of their own bull market. Institutional investing was a Winner's Game and the winners knew that by playing it faster, they would increase the rate of winnings. But in the process, a basic change occurred in the investment environment; the market came to be dominated by the institutions.

In just ten years, the market activities of the investing institutions have gone from only 30 percent of total public transactions to a whopping 70 percent. And that has made all the difference. No longer are the "New Breed on Wall Street" in the minority; they are now the majority. The professional money manager isn't competing any longer with amateurs who are out of touch with the market; now he competes with other experts.

It's an impressive group of competitors. There are 150 major institutional investors and another 600 small and medium sized institutions operating in the market all day, every day, in the most intensely competitive way. And in the past decade, these institutions have become more active, have developed larger in-house research staffs, and have tapped into the central source of market information and fundamental research provided by institutional brokers. Ten years ago, many institutions were still far out of the mainstream of intensive management; today, such an institution, if any exists, would be a rare collector's item.

Competitively active institutional investing has resulted in sharply higher portfolio turnover. The typical equity portfolio turnover has gone from 10 to 30 percent. As we've already seen, this acceleration in portfolio activity plus the growth in institutional assets and the shift of pension funds toward equities have increased the proportion of market transactions of institutions from 30 to 70 percent which has, in turn, produced the basic "phase change" that has transformed portfolio activity from a source of incremental profits to a major cost, and that transformation has switched institutional investing from a Winner's Game to a Loser's Game. . . .

In plain language, the manager who intends to deliver *net* returns 20 percent better than the market must earn a gross return before fees and transactions costs (liquidity tolls) that is more than 40 percent better than the market. If this sounds absurd, [one can] show that the active manager must beat the market *gross* by 22 percent just to come out even with the market *net*.

In other words, for the institutional investor to perform as well as, *but no better than*, the S&P 500, he must be sufficiently astute and skillful to "outdo" the market by 22 percent. But how can institutional investors hope to outperform the market by such a magnitude when, in effect, they *are* the market today? Which managers are so well staffed and organized in their operations, or so prescient in their investment policies that they can honestly expect to beat the other professionals by so much on a sustained basis?

The disagreeable numbers from the performance measurement firms say there are *no* managers whose past performance promises that they will outperform the market in the future. Looking backward, the evidence is deeply disturbing: 85 percent of professionally managed funds underperformed the S&P 500 during the past 10 years. And the median fund's rate of return was only 5.4 percent—about 10 percent *below* the S&P 500.

Most money managers have been losing the Money Game. And they know it, even if they cannot admit it publicly. Expectations and promises have come down substantially since the mid-1960's. Almost nobody still talks in terms of beating the market by 20 percent compounded annually. And nobody listens to those who do.

In times like these, the burden of proof is on the person who says, "I am a winner. I can win the Money Game." Because only a sucker backs a "winner" in the Loser's Game, we have a right to expect him to explain exactly what he is going to do and why it is going to work so very well. This is not very often done in the investment management business.

Does the evidence necessarily lead to an entirely passive or index portfolio? No, it doesn't necessarily lead in that direction. Not quite. But the "null" hypothesis is hard to beat in a situation like this. At the risk of over-simplifying, the null hypothesis says there is nothing there if you cannot find statistically significant evidence of its presence. This would suggest to investment managers, "Don't do anything because when you try to do something, it is on average a mistake." And if you can't beat the market, you certainly should consider joining it. An index fund is one way. The data from the performance measurement firms show that an index fund would have outperformed most money managers.

For those who are determined to try to win the Loser's Game, however, there are a few specific things they might consider.

First, be sure you are playing your own game. Know your policies very well and play according to them all the time. Admiral Morrison, citing the *Concise Oxford Dictionary*, says: "Impose upon the enemy the time and place and conditions for fighting preferred by oneself." Simon Ramo suggests: "Give the other fellow as many opportunities as possible to make mistakes, and he will do so."

Second, keep it simple. Tommy Armour, talking about golf, says: "Play the shot you've got the greatest chance of playing well." Ramo says: "Every game boils down to doing the things you do best, and doing them over and over again." Armour again: "Simplicity, concentration, and economy of time and effort have been the distinguishing features of the great players' methods, while others lost their way to glory by wandering in a maze of details." Mies Van der Rohe, the architect, suggest, "Less is more." Why not bring turnover down as a deliberate, conscientious practice? Make fewer and perhaps better investment decisions. Simplify the professional investment management problem. Try to do a few things unusually well.

Third, concentrate on your defenses. Almost all of the information in the investment management business is oriented toward purchase decisions. The competition in making purchase decisions is too good. It's too hard to outperform the other fellow in buying. Concentrate on selling instead. In a Winner's Game, 90 percent of all research effort should be spent on making purchase decisions; in a Loser's Game, most researchers should spend most of their time making sell decisions. Almost all of the really big trouble that you're going to experience in the next year is in your portfolio right now; if you could reduce some of those really big problems, you might come out the winner in the Loser's Game.

Fourth, don't take it personally. Most of the people in the investment business are "winners" who have won all their lives by being bright, articulate, disciplined, and willing to work hard. They are so accustomed to succeeding by trying harder and are so used to believing that failure to succeed is the failure's own fault that they may take it personally when they see that the average professionally managed fund cannot keep pace with the market any more than John Henry could beat the steam drill.

There is a class of diseases that are called "iatrogenic" meaning they are doctor-caused. The Chinese finger cage and the modern straightjacket most tightly grip the person who struggles to break free. Ironically, the reason institutional investing has become the Loser's Game is that in the complex problem each manager is trying to solve, his efforts to find a solution—and the efforts of his many urgent competitors—have become the dominant variables. And their efforts to beat the market are no longer the most important part of the solution; they are the most important part of the problem.

Part Five

Speculation, Crashes, and Financial Turmoil

The Big Bull Market and the Crash

FREDERICK LEWIS ALLEN

Frederick Lewis Allen achieved great success in his popular accounts
of many of the key events that marked the 1920s and the 1930s. Here
he recalls the chaotic days that preceded and followed Black Tuesday—October 29, 1929.

. . .

The Crash

Early in September the stock market broke. It quickly recovered, however; indeed, on September 19th the averages as compiled by the *New
York Times* reached an even higher level than that of September 3rd.
Once more it slipped, farther and faster, until by October 4th the prices
of a good many stocks had coasted to what seemed first-class bargain
levels. Steel, for example, after having touched 261³/4 a few weeks earlier,
had dropped as low as 204; American Can, at the closing on October
4th, was nearly 20 points below its high for the year; General Electric
was over 50 points below its high; Radio had gone down from 114³/4
to 82¹/2.

A bad break, to be sure, but there had been other bad breaks, and
the speculators who escaped unscathed proceeded to take advantage of
the lesson they had learned in June and December of 1928 and March
and May of 1929; when there was a break it was a good time to buy.
In the face of all this tremendous liquidation, brokers' loans as compiled by the Federal Reserve Bank of New York mounted to a new
high record on October 2nd, reaching $6,804,000,000—a sure sign
that margin buyers were not deserting the market but coming into it

Reprinted from *Only Yesterday* (1931), Chapters 12 and 13, 290–336, by permission of
HarperCollins Publishers, New York. © 1931 by Frederick Lewis Allen, © 1957 by Harper
& Brothers.

in numbers at least undiminished. . . . And sure enough, prices once more began to climb.

Something was wrong, however. The decline began once more. . . . But there was little real alarm until the week of October 21st. The consensus of opinion, in the meantime, was merely that the equinoctial storm of September had not quite blown over. The market was readjusting itself into a "more secure technical position."

The expected recovery in the stock market did not come. It seemed to be beginning on Tuesday, October 22nd, but the gains made during the day were largely lost during the last hour. And on Wednesday, the 23rd, there was a perfect Niagara of liquidation. . . . The next day was Thursday, October 24th.

On that momentous day stocks opened moderately steady in price, but in enormous volume. Kennecott appeared on the tape in a block of 20,000 shares, General Motors in another of the same amount. Almost at once the ticker tape began to lag behind the trading floor. The pressure of selling orders was disconcertingly heavy. Prices were going down. . . . Presently they were going down with some rapidity. . . . Before the first hour of trading was over, it was already apparent that they were going down with an altogether unprecedented and amazing violence. In brokers' offices all over the country, tape-watchers looked at one another in astonishment and perplexity. Where on earth was this torrent of selling orders coming from?

The exact answer to this question will probably never be known. But it seems probable that the principal cause of the break in prices during that first hour on October 24th was not fear. Nor was it short selling. It was forced selling. It was the dumping on the market of hundreds of thousands of shares of stock held in the name of miserable traders whose margins were exhausted or about to be exhausted. The gigantic edifice of prices was honeycombed with speculative credit and was now breaking under its own weight. . . . There seemed to be no support whatever. Down, down, down. The roar of voices that rose from the floor of the Exchange had become a roar of panic.

. . . In the space of two short hours, dozens of stocks lost ground that had required many months of the bull market to gain. . . .

A few minutes after noon, some of the more alert members of a crowd that had collected on the street outside the Stock Exchange, expecting they knew not what, recognized Charles E. Mitchell, erstwhile defender of the bull market, slipping quietly into the offices of J. P. Morgan & Company on the opposite corner. It was scarcely more than nine years since the House of Morgan had been pitted with the shrapnel-fire of the Wall Street explosion; now its occupants faced a different sort of calamity equally near at hand.

Mr. Mitchell was followed shortly by Albert H. Wiggin, head of the Chase National Bank; William Potter, head of the Guaranty Trust Company; and Seward Prosser, head of the Bankers Trust Company. They had come to confer with Thomas W. Lamont of the Morgan firm. In the space of five minutes these five men, with George F. Baker, Jr., of the First National Bank, agreed in behalf of their respective institutions to put up 40 million apiece to shore up the stock market. The object of the $240 million pool thus formed, as explained subsequently by Mr. Lamont, was not to hold prices at any given level, but simply to make such purchases as were necessary to keep trading on an orderly basis. Their first action, they decided, would be to try to steady the prices of the leading securities that served as bellwethers for the list as a whole. It was a dangerous plan, for with hysteria spreading there was no telling what sort of debacle might be impending. But this was no time for any action but the boldest. . . .

As the news that the bankers were meeting circulated on the floor of the Exchange, prices began to steady. Soon a brisk rally set in. Steel jumped back to the level at which it had opened that morning. But the bankers had more to offer the dying bull market than a Morgan partner's best bedside manner.

At about half-past one o'clock Richard Whitney, vice president of the Exchange, who usually acted as floor broker for the Morgan interests, went into the "Steel crowd" and put in a bid of 205—the price of the last previous sale—for 10,000 shares of Steel. He bought only 200 shares and left the remainder of the order with the specialists. Mr. Whitney then went to various other points on the floor, and offered the price of the last previous sale for 10,000 shares of each of 15 or 20 other stocks, reporting what was sold to him at that price and leaving the remainder of the order with the specialist. In short, within a space of a few minutes Mr. Whitney offered to purchase something in the neighborhood of $20 or $30 million worth of stock. Purchases of this magnitude are not undertaken by Tom, Dick, and Harry; it was clear that Mr. Whitney represented the bankers' pool.

The desperate remedy worked. The semblance of confidence returned. Prices held steady for a while; and though many of them slid off once more in the final hour, the net results for the day might well have been worse. Steel actually closed two points higher than on Wednesday, and the net losses of most of the other leading securities amounted to less than 10 points apiece for the whole day's trading.

All the same, it had been a frightful day. At seven o'clock that night the tickers in a thousand brokers' offices were still chattering; not 'til after 7:08 did they finally record the last sale made on the floor at three o'clock. The volume of trading had set a new record—12,894,650 shares. ("The time may come when we shall see a five-million-share day," the wise men of the Street had been saying 20 months before!) Incredible rumors had spread wildly during the early afternoon—that eleven speculators had committed suicide, that the Buffalo and Chicago exchanges had been closed, that troops were guarding the New York Stock Exchange against an angry mob. The country had known the bitter taste of panic. And although the bankers' pool had prevented for the moment an utter collapse, there was no gainsaying the fact that the economic structure had cracked wide open.

Things looked somewhat better on Friday and Saturday. Trading was still on an enormous scale, but prices for the most part held. At the very moment when the bankers' pool was cautiously disposing of as much as possible of the stock that it had accumulated on Thursday and was thus preparing for future emergencies, traders who had sold out higher up were coming back into the market again with new purchases, in the hope that the bottom had been reached. But toward the close of Saturday's session prices began to slip again. And on Monday the rout was under way once more. . . .

The big gong had hardly sounded in the great hall of the Exchange at ten o'clock Tuesday morning before the storm broke in full force. Huge blocks of stock were thrown upon the market for what they would bring. Five thousand shares, 10,000 shares appeared at a time on the laboring ticker at fearful recessions in price. Not only were innumerable small traders being sold out, but big ones too, protagonists of the new economic era who a few weeks before had counted themselves millionaires. Again and again the specialist in a stock would find himself surrounded by brokers fighting to sell—and nobody at all even thinking of buying. To give one single example: during the bull market the common stock of the White Sewing Machine Company had gone as high as 48; on Monday, October 28th, it had closed at $11\frac{1}{8}$. On that black Tuesday, somebody—a clever messenger boy for the Exchange, it was rumored—had the bright idea of putting in an order to buy at 1— and in the temporarily complete absence of other bids he actually got his stock for a dollar a share! The scene on the floor was chaotic. Despite the jamming of the communication system, orders to buy and sell— mostly to sell—came in faster than human beings could possibly handle them; it was on that day that an exhausted broker, at the close of the session, found a large waste-basket that he had stuffed with orders to be executed and had carefully set aside for safe-keeping—and then had completely forgotten. Within half an hour of the opening the volume of trading passed three million shares, by twelve o'clock it had passed eight million, by half-past one it had passed 12 million, and when the closing gong brought the day's madness to an end the gigantic record of 16,410,030 shares had been set. Toward the close there was a rally, but by that time the average prices of 50 leading stocks, as compiled by the *New York Times*, had fallen nearly forty points. Meanwhile there was a near-panic in other markets—the foreign stock exchanges, the lesser American exchanges, the grain market. . . .

The next day—Wednesday, October 30th—the outlook suddenly had providentially brightened. The directors of the Steel Corporation had declared an extra dividend; the directors of the American Can Company had not only declared an extra dividend, but had raised the regular dividend. There was another flood of reassuring statements— though by this time a cheerful statement from a financier fell upon somewhat skeptical ears. Julius Klein, Mr. Hoover's Assistant Secretary of Commerce, composed a rhapsody on continued prosperity. John J. Raskob declared that stocks were at bargain prices and that he and his friends were buying. John D. Rockefeller poured Standard Oil upon the waters: "Believing that fundamental conditions of the country are sound and that there is nothing in the business situation to warrant the destruction of values that has taken place on the exchanges during the past week, my son and I have for some days been purchasing sound common stocks." Better still, prices rose—steadily and buoyantly. Now at least the time had come when the strain on the Exchange could be relieved without causing undue alarm. At 1:40 o'clock Vice-President Whitney announced from the rostrum that the Exchange would not open until noon the following day and would remain closed all day Friday and Saturday—and to his immense relief the announcement was greeted, not with renewed panic, but with a cheer.

Throughout Thursday's short session the recovery continued. Prices gyrated wildly—for who could arrive at a reasonable idea of what a given stock was worth, now that all settled standards of value had been upset?—but the worst of the storm seemed to have blown over. The financial community breathed more easily; now they could have a chance to set their houses in order.

The Tulipmania

CHARLES MACKAY

Tulipmania is but one of two *dozen* extraordinary popular delusions
recounted in Charles Mackay's 700-page book from 1841. The tales
of John Law, the Crusades, and the South Sea Bubble are equally
instructive.

. . .

Quis furor, ô cives!—*Lucan.*

The tulip—so named, it is said, from a Turkish word, signifying a tur-
ban—was introduced into western Europe about the middle of the
sixteenth century. Conrad Gesner, who claims the merit of having
brought it into repute—little dreaming of the commotion it was shortly
afterward to make in the world—says that he first saw it in the year
1559, in a garden at Augsburg belonging to the learned Counsellor
Herwart, a man very famous in his day for his collection of rare exotics.
The bulbs were sent to this gentleman by a friend at Constantinople,
where the flower had long been a favorite. In the course of 10 or 11
years after this period, tulips were much sought after by the wealthy,
especially in Holland and Germany. Rich people at Amsterdam sent
for the bulbs direct to Constantinople, and paid the most extravagant
prices for them. The first roots planted in England were brought from
Vienna in 1600. Until the year 1634 the tulip annually increased in
reputation, until it was deemed a proof of bad taste in any man of fortune
to be without a collection of them. Many learned men, including
Pompeius de Angelis, and the celebrated Lipsius of Leyden, the author
of the treatise "De Constantia," were passionately fond of tulips. The
rage for possessing them soon caught the middle classes of society, and
merchants and shopkeepers, even of moderate means, began to vie with

Reprinted from *Extraordinary Popular Delusions and the Madness of Crowds* (New York:
Harmony Books, 1980; originally published in 1841), 89–97.

each other in the rarity of these flowers and the preposterous prices they paid for them. A trader at Harlaem was known to pay one-half his fortune for a single root, not with the design of selling it again at a profit, but to keep in his own conservatory for the admiration of his acquaintance.

One would suppose that there must have been some great virtue in this flower to have made it so valuable in the eyes of so prudent a people as the Dutch; but it has neither the beauty nor the perfume of the rose— hardly the beauty of the "sweet, sweet-pea;" neither is it as enduring as either. Cowley, it is true, is loud in its praise. He says—

> The tulip next appeared, all over gay,
> But wanton, full of pride, and full of play;
> The world can't show a dye but here has place;
> Nay, by new mixtures, she can change her face;
> Purple and gold are both beneath her care,
> The richest needlework she loves to wear;
> Her only study is to please the eye,
> And to outshine the rest in finery.

Many persons grow insensibly attached to that which gives them a great deal of trouble, as a mother often loves her sick and ever-ailing child better than her more healthy offspring. Upon the same principle we must account for the unmerited encomia lavished upon these frag- ile blossoms. In 1634, the rage among the Dutch to possess them was so great that the ordinary industry of the country was neglected, and the population, even to its lowest dregs, embarked in the tulip trade. As the mania increased, prices augmented, until, in the year 1635, many persons were known to invest a fortune of 100,00 florins in the pur- chase of 40 roots. It then became necessary to sell them by their weight in *perits*, a small weight less than a grain. A tulip of the species called *Admiral Liefken*, weighing 400 *perits*, was worth 4,400 florins; an *Admi- ral Van der Eyck*, weighing 446 *perits*, was worth 1,260 florins; a *Childer* of 106 *perits* was worth 1,615 florins; a *Viceroy* of 400 *perits*, 3,000 flor- ins; and, most precious of all, a *Semper Augustus*, weighing 200 *perits*, was thought to be very cheap at 5,500 florins. The latter was much sought after, and even an inferior bulb might command a price of 2,000 florins. It is related that, at one time, early in 1636, there were only two roots of this description to be had in all Holland, and those not of the best. One was in the possession of a dealer in Amsterdam, and the other in Harlaem. So anxious were the speculators to obtain them, that one person offered the fee-simple of 12 acres of building-ground for the Harlaem tulip. That of Amsterdam was bought for 4,600 florins, a new carriage, two grey horses, and a complete set of harness. Munting, an industrious author of that day, who wrote a folio volume of 1,000 pages upon the tulipmania, has preserved the following list of the various articles, and their value, that were delivered for one single root of the rare species called the *Viceroy*:

	Florins
Two lasts of wheat	448
Four lasts of rye	558
Four fat oxen	480
Eight fat swine	240
Twelve fat sheep	120
Two hogsheads of wine	70
Four tuns of beer	32
Two tuns of butter	192
One thousand lbs. of cheese	120
A complete bed	100
A suit of clothes	80
A silver drinking-cup	60
	2500

People who had been absent from Holland, and whose chance it was to return when this folly was at its maximum, were sometimes led into awkward dilemmas by their ignorance. There is an amusing instance of the kind related in Blainville's *Travels*. A wealthy merchant, who prided himself not a little in his rare tulips, received upon one occasion a very valuable consignment of merchandise from the Levant. Intelligence of its arrival was brought him by a sailor, who presented himself for that purpose at the counting-house, among bales of goods of every description. The merchant, to reward him for his news, munificently made him a present of a fine red herring for his breakfast. The sailor had, it appears, a great partiality for onions, and seeing a bulb very like an onion lying upon the counter of this liberal trader, and thinking it, no doubt, very much out of its place among silks and velvets, he slily seized an opportunity and slipped it into his pocket, as a relish for his herring. He got clear off with his prize, and proceeded to the quay to eat his breakfast. Hardly was his back turned when the merchant missed his valuable *Semper Augustus*, worth 3,000 florins, or about 280£ sterling. The whole establishment was instantly in an uproar; search was everywhere made for the precious root, but it was not to be found. Great was the merchant's distress of mind. The search was renewed, but again without success. At last some one thought of the sailor.

The unhappy merchant sprang into the street at the bare suggestion. His alarmed household followed him. The sailor, simple soul! had not thought of concealment. He was found quietly sitting on a coil of ropes, masticating the last morsel of his "*onion*." Little did he dream that he had been eating a breakfast whose cost might have regaled a whole ship's crew for a twelvemonth; or, as the plundered merchant himself expressed it, "might have sumptuously feasted the Prince of Orange and the whole court of the Stadtholder." Anthony caused pearls to be dissolved in wine to drink the health of Cleopatra; Sir Richard Whittington was as foolishly magnificent in an entertainment to King Henry V.; and Sir Thomas Gresham drank a diamond dissolved in wine to the health of Queen Elizabeth, when she opened the Royal Exchange; but the breakfast of this roguish Dutchman was as splendid as either. He had an advantage, too, over his wasteful predecessors: *their* gems did not improve the taste or the wholesomeness of *their* wine, while *his* tulip was quite delicious with his red herring. The most unfortunate part of the business for him was, that he remained in prison for some months on a charge of felony preferred against him by the merchant. . . .

The demand for tulips of a rare species increased so much in the year 1636, that regular marts for their sale were established on the Stock Exchange of Amsterdam, in Rotterdam, Harlaem, Leyden,

Alkmar, Hoorn, and other towns. Symptoms of gambling now became, for the first time, apparent. The stock-jobbers, ever on the alert for a new speculation, dealt largely in tulips, making use of all the means they so well knew how to employ to cause fluctuations in prices. At first, as in all these gambling mania, confidence was at its height, and every body gained. The tulip-jobbers speculated in the rise and fall of the tulip stocks, and made large profits by buying when prices fell, and selling out when they rose. Many individuals grew suddenly rich. A golden bait hung temptingly out before the people, and one after the other, they rushed to the tulip-marts, like flies around a honey-pot. Every one imagined that the passion for tulips would last forever, and that the wealthy from every part of the world would send to Holland, and pay whatever prices were asked for them. The riches of Europe would be concentrated on the shores of the Zuyder Zee, and poverty banished from the favoured clime of Holland. Nobles, citizens, farmers, mechanics, seamen, footmen, maid-servants, even chimney-sweeps and old clotheswomen, dabbled in tulips. People of all grades converted their property into cash, and invested it in flowers. . . .

At last, however, the more prudent began to see that this folly could not last for ever. Rich people no longer bought the flowers to keep them in their gardens, but to sell them again at one cent percent profit. It was seen that somebody must lose fearfully in the end. As this conviction spread, prices fell, and never rose again. Confidence was destroyed, and a universal panic seized upon the dealers. A had agreed to purchase ten *Semper Augustines* from B, at 4,000 florins each, at six weeks after the signing contract. B was ready with the flowers at the appointed time; but the price had fallen to 300 or 400 florins, and A refused either to pay the difference or receive the tulips. Defaulters were announced day after day in all the towns in Holland. Hundreds who, a few months previously, had begun to doubt that there was such a thing as poverty in the land suddenly found themselves the possessors of a few bulbs, that nobody would buy, even though they offered them at one quarter of the sums they had paid for them. The cry of distress resounded everywhere, and each man accused his neighbor. The few who had contrived to enrich themselves hid their wealth from the knowledge of their fellow-citizens, and invested it in the English or other funds. Many who, for a brief season, had emerged from the humbler walks of life, were cast back into their original obscurity. Substantial merchants were reduced almost to beggary, and many a representative of a noble line saw the fortunes of his house ruined beyond redemption.

Second Thoughts about the Tulipmania

PETER M. GARBER

Peter Garber, professor of economics at Brown University, here provides us in excerpted form with an analysis of the Tulipmania affair that yields strikingly nonstandard conclusions. Perhaps, after all, only the uninformed, late, and greedy entrants to the race got bagged—and, perhaps, they deserved it. Readers are encouraged to read Garber's entire article, which examines the famous Mississippi and South Sea episodes as well as John Law's financing methods. The whole provides trenchant perspectives on "bubbles" and on the workings of the British Parliament and the French Court in the early 1700s.

. . .

The jargon of economics and finance contains numerous colorful expressions to denote a market-determined asset price at odds with any reasonable economic explanation. Such words as "tulip mania," "bubble," "chain letter," "Ponzi scheme," "panic," "crash," and "financial crisis" immediately evoke images of frenzied and probably irrational speculative activity. Many of these terms have emerged from specific speculative episodes that have been sufficiently frequent and important that they underpin a strong current belief among economists that key capital markets sometimes generate irrational and inefficient pricing and allocational outcomes.

Before economists relegate a speculative event to the inexplicable or bubble category, however, we must exhaust all reasonable economic explanations. While such explanations are often not easily generated due to the inherent complexity of economic phenomena, the business of economists is to find clever fundamental market explanations for

Excerpted from *The Journal of Economic Perspectives* 4 (Spring 1990), pp. 35–54. Nashville, Tennessee: American Economic Association.

events; and our methodology should always require that we search intensively for market fundamental explanations before clutching the "bubble" last resort.

Thus, among the "reasonable" or "market fundamental" explanations, I would include the perception of an increased probability of large returns. The perception might be triggered by genuine economic good news, by a convincing new economic theory about payoffs or by a fraud launched by insiders acting strategically to trick investors. It might also be triggered by uninformed market participants correctly inferring changes in the distribution of dividends by observing price movements generated by the trading of informed insiders. While some of these perceptions might in the end prove erroneous, movements in asset prices based on them are fundamental and not bubble movements.

I am in these pages to propose a market fundamental explanation for the . . . Dutch tulipmania (1634-37). . . . This [being treated in the modern literature as an outburst of irrationality] may be attributable to the influence of Mackay's (1852) graphic descriptions . . . from our current perspective, though, such "irrational" speculation probably looked a lot like a normal day in a pit of the Board of Trade. . . .

Mackay (1852) passed on to economists the standard description of the tulipmania as a speculative bubble.[1] In this description, the Netherlands became a center of cultivation and development of new tulip varieties after the tulip's entry into Europe from Turkey in the mid-1500s. Professional growers and wealthy flower fanciers created a market for rare varieties in which bulbs sold at high prices. For example, a Semper Augustus bulb sold for 2,000 guilders in 1625, an amount of gold worth about $16,000 at $400 per ounce. Common bulb varieties, on the other hand, received very low prices.

By 1636, the rapid price rises attracted speculators, and prices of many varieties surged upward from November 1636 through January 1637. In February 1637, prices suddenly collapsed, and bulbs could not be sold at 10 percent of their peak values. By 1739, the prices of all the most prized bulbs of the mania had fallen to no more than 0.1 guilder. This was $^1/_{200}$ of 1 percent of Semper Augustus's peak price. The story concludes by asserting that the collapse led to economic distress in the Netherlands for years afterwards.

The standard version of the tulipmania neglects discussion about what the market fundamental price of bulbs should have been. Mackay did not report transaction prices for the rare bulbs immediately after the collapse. Instead, he recorded tulip bulb prices from 60 to 200 years after the collapse, interpreting these much lower prices as ones justified by market fundamentals. Yet the dynamics of bulb prices during the tulip episode were typical of any market for rare bulbs, even those existing today. The tulip market involved only bulbs affected by a mosaic virus that had the effect of creating beautiful, feathered patterns in the flowers. Only diseased bulbs were valued by traders and collectors, because a particular pattern could not be reproduced through seed propagation. Only through budding of the mother bulb would a pattern breed true.

A standard pricing pattern arises for new varieties of flowers, even in modern markets. When a particularly prized variety is developed, its original bulb sells for a high price. As the bulbs accumulate, the variety's price falls rapidly; after less than 30 years, bulbs sell at their reproduction cost. This pattern raises two questions. First, why did the price of bulbs increase rapidly? Second, did prices decline faster than should have been expected?

The price increases prior to February 1637 occurred as the status of a variety became clear; and as its renown increased, so would its price. After all, most new varieties were not considered particularly beautiful. This would explain the steady increase in the price of Semper Augustus.

Table 1   Guilder Prices of Tulip Bulbs, 1707, 1722, 1739

Bulb	1707	1722	1739
1. Premier Noble	409	—	1.0
2. Aigle Noir	110	0.75	0.3
3. Roi de Fleurs	251	10.9	0.1
4. Diamant	71	2.5	2.0

Source: Garber (1989).

Table 2   Post-Collapse Bulb Prices in Guilders

Bulb	Feb. 5, 1637	1642 or 1643
1. English Admiral (bulb)	700	210
2. Admirael van Eyck (bulb)	1345	220
3. General Rotgans	805	138

Source: Garber (1989).

Similarly, a shift in fashion toward the appreciation of tulips in general over a shorter period would generate rising prices for all the rare bulbs.

To form an expectation about a typical rate of price decline of tulip bulbs, I collected data on 18th century bulb price patterns for various highly valued tulip bulbs. The level of 18th century prices was much lower than during the mania. By 1707, an enormous variety of tulip bulbs had been developed; and the tulip itself had been replaced as the most fashionable flower by the hyacinth. Nonetheless, as Table 1 shows, bulb prices still were falling sharply. The average annual rate of depreciation for these bulbs was 28.5 percent before bulb prices reached floor values.

Table 2 reports prices of those bulbs for which I have been able to gather price data for years immediately after the mania. February 5, 1637 was the day on which peak prices were attained. For these bulbs from February 1637 to 1642, the average annual rate of price depreciation was 32 percent, not greatly different from the 18th century depreciation rate. If the more rapid annual rate of decline for the tulipmania bulbs was attributed entirely to the crash, and not to factors which materialized in the succeeding five years, the crash can have accounted for no more than a 16 percent price decline: large, but hardly the stuff that legends are made of.

Strangely enough, if one is to speak of tulipmania, it would be more accurate to speak of the rapid price rise and collapse in common bulbs in the last week of January and first week of February 1637. Common bulbs became objects of speculation among the lower classes in a futures market which emerged in November 1636. These markets were located in local taverns, and each sale was associated with a payment of "wine money." In January 1637, prices for some common bulb varieties increased by as much as 25 times. For example, the peak price for a bulb called Switser of .17 guilders/aas was attained on February 5, the apparent peak of the market (1 aas = $^1/_{20}$ gram). Data from notarized contracts on February 6 and 9 indicate a sudden decline to .11 guilders/aas. This represents a substantial decline from prices in the first five days of February, but it still exceeds the price of .035 guilders/aas attained on January 23. Price increases through mid-January, while rapid, were not as great as in the final two weeks of the speculation; and there is no evidence that they were out of line. Since serious traders ignored this market and participants in this market had almost no wealth, it can have been little more than a mid-winter diversion among tavern regulars mimicking more serious traders.

Finally, there is no evidence of serious economic distress arising from the tulipmania. All histories of the period treat it as a golden age in Dutch development.

Note

1. Mackay plagiarized his description from Beckmann (1846). Beckmann refers to a long sequence of research about the episode, but all sources are ultimately based on a set of three anonymously written pamphlets in dialogue form published in 1637. These pamphlets were among dozens written just after the collapse by anti-speculative partisans launched by the economic oligarchy which wished to assure that speculative capital was channeled through markets which it controlled.

Too Many Freds

DAVID L. BABSON

This dialogue took place in early 1971, as practitioners did some soul-searching about their 1970 investment actions and results, results that shook their own—as well as their clients'—faith in the profession. David Babson, outraged by the events that preceded the debacle, spoke directly and bluntly to the professional money managers assembled for the conference in a talk still referred to as "Too Many Freds."

. . .

David Babson's Presentation

Asking the performance investors of the late 1960s what went wrong is like someone, in 1720, asking John Law what went wrong with the Mississippi Bubble.

Or in 1635 asking Mynheer Vanderveer what went wrong with the Dutch Tulip Craze.

Nevertheless, this panel interests me because if we can identify what really did go wrong it may help to avoid a future speculative frenzy.

And if we are serious about getting to the bottom of what went wrong then we ought to say what really did go wrong.

So let me list a dozen things that people in our field did to set the stage for the greatest bloodbath in 40 years.

First, there was the conglomerate movement and all its fancy rhetoric about synergism and leverage. Its abuses were to the late 1960s what the public utility holding companies were to the late 1920s.

Second, too many accountants played footsie with stock-promoting managements by certifying earnings that weren't earnings at all.

Third, the "modern" corporate treasurers who looked upon their

From the Fourth Annual Investor's Conference, March 18, 1971. Reprinted by permission of Institutional Investor, Inc.

company pension funds as new-found "profit centers" and pressured their investment advisors into speculating with them.

Fourth, the investment advisors who massacred clients' portfolios because they were trying to make good on the over-promises that they had made to attract the business in the first place.

Fifth, the new breed of portfolio managers who churned their customers' holdings on the specious theory that high "turnover" was a new "secret" leading to outstanding investment performance.

Sixth, the new issue underwriters who brought out the greatest collection of low-grade junky offerings in history—some of which were created solely for the purpose of generating something to sell.

Seventh, the elements of the financial press who promoted into new investment geniuses a group of neophytes who didn't even have the first requisite for managing other people's money, namely, a sense of responsibility.

Eighth, the security salesman who peddled the items with the best "stories," or the biggest markups even though such issues were totally unsuited to their customers' needs.

Ninth, the sanctimonious partners of major investment houses who wrung their hands over all these shameful happenings while they deployed an army of untrained salesmen to forage among a group of even less informed investors.

Tenth, the mutual fund managers who tried to become millionaires overnight by using every gimmick imaginable to manufacture their own paper performance.

Eleventh, the portfolio managers who collected bonanza "incentive" fees—the "heads I win, tails you lose" kind—which made them fortunes in the bull market but turned the portfolios they managed into disasters in the bear market.

Twelfth, the security analysts who forgot about their professional ethics to become "story peddlers" and who let their institutions get taken in by a whole parade of confidence men.

These are some of the things that "went wrong." But for those who stuck to their guns, who tried to follow a progressive but realistic approach, who didn't prostitute their professional responsibilities, who didn't get seduced by conflicts of interest, who didn't get suckered into glib "concepts," nothing much really did go wrong.

At our firm we've never laid claim to being geniuses but our mutual fund, for example, is well above its peak of three years ago when I was here discussing "What's wrong with performance investing?"

So what did we learn from this list of horrors? Over the years most of the country has considered New England folks to be shrewd investment managers—and you know up our way the greatest compliment we can pay a man is not to say "He's really smart," rather it's to say "He's got a lot of common sense."

I think this sums up "what went wrong." As in earlier periods of delusion most investors tried so hard to be "smart" that they lost the "common sense" that pays off in the long run.

Thank you.

Question and Answer Session

MR. GOODMAN: David, we were talking about decline here, in the market, managed by professionals. Do you think the decline was due to the professionals? It's an institutionally dominated market?

MR. BABSON: Of course, it was due to the professionals. [1967–1968] was the first wild market, 1967–1968, when the big institutions and the people that ought to know how to manage investments got sucked into speculation. The 1969–1970 bear market was due to the professionals—nobody else.

MR. GOODMAN: What do you think we can do about this?

MR. BABSON: Well, I think a lot of the professionals ought to get out of the business, personally.

I think that anybody who went to bed with a quarter million shares of Four Seasons Nursing Homes—

MR. GOODMAN: Do you have anybody in mind?

MR. BABSON: Things like Parvin Dohrmann, and Performance Systems. I have a list here.

MR. GOODMAN: I'm not sure what the pain threshold of the audience is.

MR. BABSON: I've got a group here of about 30 companies that were—

MR. GOODMAN: Don't read them off.

MR. BABSON: No.

     —that were favorites among the professional money managers a couple of years ago. They were down 90 percent last July, and they are still down 83 percent, and it's obvious that. . .

MR. GOODMAN: Upside down, those charts would look very good.

MR. BABSON: I don't think that it was a doctor out in Pocatello, Idaho, who was all loaded up with Performance Systems or Lums or Susquehanna or Unexcelled. I think the fellows who were loaded up with them were probably located in offices not far from here.

MR. GOODMAN: I don't know anybody who has an office close to here.

     We heard a lot of talk yesterday about self-regulation and Senator Muskie seemed to indicate that the country at large was unhappy with the investment business, and if you think a lot of people should leave the investment business, I wonder how we are going to pick which people and how do we enforce this so that the country at large won't rise in its wrath and do more harmful things to the investment business than it is doing to itself.

     Does anybody want to comment?

MR. BABSON: Well, if these smart investment managers, money managers, have got clients that are as smart as they are, the clients ought to determine whether they will stay in the business or not, I should think.

MR. GOODMAN: That's a great belief in the free market. You could have said that about the clients going in, too. Then you think the people who were burned in investing in mutual funds would simply disappear or never come back again or fund another mutual fund, or what?

MR. BABSON: I think an awful lot of people will avoid the stock market for a long time to come as a result of what has happened.

There was a survey in *The Wall Street Journal* a couple of weeks ago that showed a high percentage of people will never buy stocks again. And judging from what is going on in the business today, an awful lot of accounts are trying to find new managers.

MR. GOODMAN: Isn't there just one mistake of yours that you could point to?

MR. BABSON: I could find a couple if I dug hard, but not a serious one. Our problem was not 1970, or 1969; it was 1968. Our problem in 1968 was why weren't we doing what David Meid was able to do or—

MR. GOODMAN: There was a moment of silence there.

MR. BABSON: —or the Freds—Fred Alger, Fred Carr, Fred Mates.

MR. GOODMAN: I never thought of the group that way.

MR. BABSON: They made our problems in 1968. In 1970, we didn't have any at all.

Catastrophe

JOHN BROOKS

John Brooks has written with wit and understanding of both the highs
and lows of Wall Street and investing. Here, in a chapter from *Once
in Golconda* (aptly subtitled "A True Drama of Wall Street 1920–
1938"), he tells of the disgrace of Richard Whitney. Once an Establishment power and the floor broker for J. P. Morgan & Company, Mr.
Whitney's financial troubles drove him to a criminal misappropriation
of the Gratuity (retirement) Fund of the New York Stock Exchange—
and disaster.

• • •

George Whitney devoted Thanksgiving Day to trying to salvage his
brother's shattered affairs, and perhaps, too, his shattered opinion of his
brother's character. That morning, at his insistence, Richard Whitney
came to his house and laid before him a hastily assembled set of figures
purporting to show the condition of Richard Whitney & Company as
of that moment. The figures, which Richard Whitney would later admit
were false, showed the firm to be in the black to the extent of about
$1 million. The elder brother, however did not question the *bona fides*
of the accounting—only Dick's high valuation of the enormous amount
of Distilled Liquors stock that by this time had come to constitute most
of the assets of Whitney & Company. After marking the stock down
to a more realistic valuation, George Whitney concluded that the firm
was still in the black by perhaps half a million—provided the stock
could somehow be sold. He also concluded that the Distilled Liquors
debacle demonstrated that Dick's business judgment had gone to pieces,
and that the best course now would be for Dick to get out of the brokerage business as quickly as possible, before other debacles ensued.
Someone ought to be found who would want to take over a firm with

Reprinted from *Once in Golconda: A True Drama of Wall Street 1920–1938* (New York,
Evanston, and London: Harper & Row, 1969), Chapter 11, pp. 249–269, by permission of
Harold Ober Associates, Inc. © 1969 by John Brooks.

such a fine reputation extending over two decades—some wealthy man, say, might want to put his son into it. Shocking as the notion of giving up his very foothold in the world he had lately ruled must have been to Richard Whitney, he responded like a younger brother whose elder brother had just saved him from a desperate jam by lending him a million dollars; he agreed.

The next step was taken even without waiting for the holiday to be over. George Whitney telephoned his brother's old friend Harry Simmons and asked him to come over and join the brothers that afternoon. Simmons, taken aback, pleaded that he was committed to church and then a family dinner. Nevertheless, late that afternoon he came to George Whitney's house to confer with the two brothers, the elder of whom outlined the situation and explained the plan. Nobody quite came out and said so, but it was clear enough why Simmons had been so hurriedly and urgently invited, if not summoned. Obviously the thought was that *he* might be the man to take over Richard Whitney & Company. Simmons was not having any of that. Without even looking at Richard Whitney's sheet of figures, he volunteered the information that he knew nothing about bonds—ostensibly the principal business of Whitney & Company—and therefore wasn't in the market.

A mood of disappointment settled over the conference. The conversation trailed off in discussion of various possible methods of disposing of the business; it was agreed among the three, for one thing, that a sale of the firm would be preferable to outright liquidation because of the value of its celebrated name. It was agreed that in the days following, Richard Whitney would devote himself energetically to the related matters of finding a buyer for his firm and finding a way—*some way*—of converting all that Distilled Liquors stock, delicately referred to by the conferees as the "slow assets," into cash.

No one at any time mentioned the incident of the Gratuity Fund.

The day after Thanksgiving, George Whitney mentioned to his partner [Thomas] Lamont that he had decided Dick was no longer "capable of handling a business properly and adequately," and that accordingly he was "going to get him to wind up his business." "Well," Lamont replied, with Morgan understatement, "I should think that was a good thing." That same weekend, both George Whitney and Lamont left New York for their long-planned vacations in the South. As for Simmons—who, it will be remembered, had no firm evidence that Whitney had embezzled from the Gratuity Fund, and who, indeed, stated later that at this time he had not the faintest doubts as to Richard Whitney's integrity—he had several meetings with Whitney during December at the Stock Exchange Luncheon Club, in the course of which he inquired how the plans for liquidation were coming along. Slowly, Whitney replied, mentioning one group or another that he thought might be interested in taking over the Distilled Liquors account or even the whole firm. In fact, the plans were not proceeding at all; nobody wanted the stock or the firm, and Whitney was continuing his frantic efforts to support the market price of Distilled Liquors and for this purpose of course, to borrow more money. Just before Christmas [Paul] Adler let him have another $100,000 which this time was repaid on the button a week later; but the harder-boiled Abraham, asked for the same sum, this time came through with only $15,000—almost an insult, but Whitney nevertheless took it. On January 3, 1938, Whitney had to report to George, back from the South, that his liquidation negotiations had "fallen through."

Meanwhile Richard Whitney's career as the White Knight was in its appropriately quixotic last phase. Privately defeated and dishonored, he played to the hilt the last act of his public role as man of iron principle. [Charles] Gay had decided by Thanksgiving Day that there was nothing for the Stock Exchange to do but give in gracefully to Douglas and the SEC, and reform itself from top to bottom. The alternative, he understood clearly now, was just what Douglas had warned of—a "takeover" by Washington. Early in December, with the reluctant approval of the Stock Exchange governors, Gay put together a new group, composed partly of outsiders to the Stock Exchange and headed by Carle C. Conway, chairman of the board of Continental Can, and notably including the New Dealer A. A. Berle, Jr., to make recommendations as to reorganization of the Stock Exchange. Here was an all-but-formal concession of defeat; everyone understood that the Conway committee would recommend reorganization of the Exchange along the lines proposed by the SEC, and presumed that the Exchange would have to accept the recommendation. Whitney's Law Committee stubbornly objected to both the existence of the Conway committee and its generally liberal makeup, but in vain. Majority sentiment in the Exchange leadership, while probably still privately on Whitney's side, had opted for expediency; Whitney almost alone continued to stand on principle. By the first of January the Conway committee was writing its report; on the twenty-seventh, when the report was published, it was found to recommend everything—the paid president, the technical staff, the non-member governors, the provisions for increased influence of liberals within the Exchange—that Douglas had wanted in the first place. Gay instantly endorsed the report in full, and Douglas warmly commended it. To emphasize the new mood of peace and harmony between Wall Street and Washington, the newest appointee to a seat on the SEC was Morgan-worshipping North Carolinian John Wesley Hanes, who, interestingly enough, thereby became the first deep-dyed Wall Streeter since Joe Kennedy to join the New Deal in any top-level domestic capacity.

The long war was all but over at last; a stage had been reached when hostages were being exchanged. But Whitney was not done standing on principle. On January 31 the Governing Committee met to consider the Conway report. Overwhelming sentiment was for immediate and unconditional acceptance. Only Whitney and his cohorts, their ranks thinned to a pathetic few, held out, insisting that the report be accepted only in a general way, leaving leeway for rearguard struggles on each individual provision, along the lines of the famous fight against the Securities Exchange Act. So great was Whitney's eloquence that for a moment it appeared he might still win the day. But Gay, stepping down from the presidential rostrum into the well of the governors' chamber to emphasize the gravity of what he had to say, replied with an impassioned exhortation that the Exchange at last stop maneuvering and temporizing and accept the inevitable with good grace.

Acceptance was unanimous—but for a single vote. It was, as a matter of fact, to be Whitney's last vote as a Stock Exchange governor.

During January George Whitney applied himself one last time to his brother's affairs, this time taking over the thankless task of personally

trying to manage a liquidation of Richard Whitney & Company. Had
he succeeded, he would later have been in trouble himself, since the
firm, as his brother had not told him, was insolvent. But he did not
succeed. His chief thought now was that the rescuer might be his own
firm—that Morgan's itself "might conceivably in some way" arrange to
take over the Distilled Liquors stock as collateral for a new loan giving
Whitney & Company the cash that would make it more appetizing to
a prospective buyer. If the matter were viewed as strictly a business
proposition, one formidable obstacle to this course of action was that
Whitney & Company still owed Morgan's all but $26,000 of the half-
million dollars Whitney had borrowed back in the dark ages of 1931.
Nevertheless George Whitney doggedly, and maybe by this time a little
sheepishly, asked Francis Bartow, the Morgan partner most versed in
common stocks, to look over the Whitney Distilled Liquors portfolio
with a view to seeing whether it might somehow meet his firm's standards for collateral on a new loan.

Bartow had his troubles. Digging into the affairs of Distilled Liquors,
he found that the company's assets consisted mainly of about 550,000
gallons of Jersey Lightning ("brandy," Bartow called it elegantly) and
one million gallons of cider. As he recounted later, he asked himself,
"How can any man living determine that such a volume of liquor can
be sold within six months or within a year?" Perhaps some man living
could have determined it, but Bartow could not, and neither could the
two of his other partners whom he consulted. Thus the matter of the
new loan remained in abeyance, and the crisis of Whitney & Company
dragged on.

But meanwhile something else had happened. Rumors of financial
stringency at Whitney & Company had at last reached the place where
they could do the most harm—the Stock Exchange—and set in motion an inexorable chain of events. Simmons, right after Thanksgiving,
had tortured himself with the notion that it was his duty to repeat the
tale of Whitney's slowness in producing the Gratuity Fund assets to the
Stock Exchange's Business Conduct Committee, its disciplinary body.
On reflection, though, he had decided that since Whitney had come
across with the assets and everything was now square, there was no call
for such talebearing on his part. And now there re-enters our story a

character who has been missing from it for a long time: Sell 'em Ben Smith, the bullnecked, bellowing speculator and pool operator and the public villain in the bear market of 1930 and 1931. In mid-December President Gay invited Smith, now a solid, respected member of the Exchange community, to lunch privately in his office. During the lunch Gay asked Smith what he thought could be done to create better public feeling toward the Stock Exchange.

The two men later differed on precisely how Smith had replied. Smith said, "I told him I didn't think he would ever be able to do it as long as he had the Old Guard in there. . . . I cited Mr. Whitney, and I told him that the quicker he got rid of him the better off the Exchange would be; that I felt that he was in a large measure responsible for the discredit in which the Exchange stood today. He wanted to know what I had against him, and I . . . said that he was broke and owed money all over the Street and I didn't think it was befitting for him to be one of the leading governors of the Exchange." Gay later corroborated all of this except that he vehemently denied that Smith had said that Whitney was "broke." He further commented that Smith's attitude toward Whitney, as expressed by his manner during the lunch, had been antagonistic, bitter, and angry.

Perhaps so; the self-made Irishman and the haughty Brahmin were set against each other by almost every *casus belli* that the harsh little society of Wall Street and the harsh big society of the United States could offer them. What had come between them since 1931 and 1932, when Whitney's fervent defense of short selling in Washington had been, after all—in general if not in particular—a defense of Smith? We do not know; but it is easy enough to imagine some offhand slight by the Brahmin or some tactless crudity by the Irishman, at one time or another, on the Exchange floor or somewhere else in the little world they both inhabited. At all events, because of Smith's evident hostility toward Whitney, Gay discounted much of what he had heard. In the month following the lunch he made no effort to inquire into the financial affairs of Whitney & Company. But he was, inevitably, put on the alert for such news when it came.

By the kind of irony that life contrives with ease where art wouldn't dare, the rumor that did start action was a wholly false one. One day in mid-January, John B. Shetlar, Stock Exchange specialist in the stock of Greyhound Corporation, noticed what he called "distress selling" in Greyhound. "It came in five-hundred-share lots," Shetlar would recall later, "but was continuous"; moreover, the lots, coming from many different brokers, "were thrown in for sale at the market regardless of price." Somehow or other—without evidence, but relying on the sixth sense about market operations without which no floor specialist could survive—Shetlar came to the conclusion that the distress selling originated with Richard Whitney & Company (in spite of the blind provided by the multiplicity of brokers) and was the tip-off that that firm was in dire trouble. As a matter of fact, later investigation showed that during mid-January not a single share of Greyhound was offered for sale by Whitney & Company on behalf of either itself or its customers.

If he knew that a member firm was in bad trouble, it was Shetlar's clear-cut duty as a member to notify the authorities. Conscientiously acting on his hunch, he went to Duke Wellington, in his capacities as an Exchange governor and close friend of Whitney. He told Wellington of the distress selling and of his belief as to its source, whereupon Wellington nodded and replied, "I'll take care of the matter." Wellington immediately went to the proper Exchange authority—Howland S. Davis, chairman of the Business Conduct Committee—and passed along what he had heard, pleading with Davis that, in any action that Davis might see fit to take, Wellington's name as the informant be kept out in consideration of his personal relations with Whitney. Davis agreed to that. And then a strange thing happened. Wellington had scarcely moved from the spot on the Exchange floor where he had the conversation with Davis when he was given a message that Whitney wanted to see him. Upon his meeting Whitney, the latter asked for a loan of $25,000, unsecured. Wellington, remembering the years he had waited to get back his original loan, had already turned down one request by his old friend for $100,000, the previous November. Now, with Shetlar's report to add to what he knew already, he had no doubt what he had to say. His answer was no.

The chairman of the Committee on Business Conduct went into action. Howland Davis was by background and inheritance a potential

Old Guardsman; son of an old-school gentleman broker, he had grown up in a house in Murray Hill across Madison Avenue from J. P. Morgan's and had gone to the Morgan daughters' coming-out parties; as a broker himself, he was often thought to be a "Morgan man" because he had social relations with several of the Morgan partners, but in fact his firm was never a house pet of No. 23 in a business way. Davis had met both George and Dick Whitney in their boyhood and his, and had taken an instant dislike to them—as he put it years later, he found the two boys "perfect snobs" and "pains in the neck." Still, long after that, when Davis had become a Stock Exchange governor and had thus found himself often in Dick Whitney's company, he had modified his opinion as to that brother, and even become cautiously fond of him, though never close. As to Wall Street politics, for all his connections Davis had never been an Old Guardsman, but neither was he a reformer; as an independent he had remained aloof in the 1935 Stock Exchange fight. Now, when he heard Shetlar's report via Wellington, he saw his duty. One of the reforms that the Stock Exchange had lately adopted under SEC pressure was to institute the practice of sending questionnaires about current financial condition at intervals to all member firms. As it happened, the first of the forms under the new procedure were to be mailed out in just a few days, on January 20; in the normal course, Whitney & Company was not scheduled to receive its first form until mid-May, for reply by the end of May. But Davis now directed that Whitney & Company be advanced to the top of the list, and be sent its questionnaire immediately, for reply by February 15. That, he felt, would straighten out the situation; moreover, since the firms themselves in most cases did not know the Exchange's schedule for mailing out the forms, there would be nothing particular in the early arrival of his questionnaire to arouse Whitney's suspicion that *he* was under suspicion.

Thus a false scent had set the dogs on the true trail. Whitney got his questionnaire. On February 15, the due date for its return, he requested a week's extension, which was granted. He filed his return on February 21; a quick check of it was made by the comptroller of the Exchange that same evening. Whitney's return, although necessarily far more detailed than his Thanksgiving Day accounting for his brother, nevertheless similarly contained omissions that had the force of falsifications; even so, the comptroller's preliminary analysis indicated that the firm's capital position fell far short of the requirements of the Business Conduct Committee. So the next step, routine in such cases, was taken: on February 23 a staff accountant of the Exchange was sent to the Whitney offices at 15 Broad Street to make an audit of the books.

Again, the books themselves were falsified—but insufficiently. Realizing this, Whitney on February 24 called on Davis at his apartment uptown to plead for time. He knew, he said, that his capital fell short of requirements, that his assets were injudiciously concentrated in certain specific securities, and so on. But, he explained, he was actively negotiating for a loan of about $700,000 that would enable him to correct all deficiencies; he very much disliked the prospect of having an even partially unfavorable report on his reputable firm go into the Exchange records; and in view of all this, might not the accountant now in his offices be withdrawn, to return in a few weeks when everything would be to rights?

The reply of the man who had once thought Whitney a pain in the neck, and had later grown fond of him, was that it seemed to him advisable that the accountant be permitted to continue his work in the normal way.

By February 28—five days after he had begun his digging in Whitney's office books—the Exchange accountant had extensive but not conclusive evidence of misappropriation of customers' securities. On March 1, Davis told Gay of the findings so far. The following evening, at the Metropolitan Club, Gay, Davis, Simmons, and the Stock Exchange lawyers met with Whitney's personal lawyer, L. Randolph Mason, to hash the whole thing over. Delicately, they warned Mason that there appeared to be serious doubt as to whether his client's books truly reflected his financial situation. They would be in touch. The day after that—Thursday—Whitney made a second unsuccessful attempt to influence Davis to call off his dogs. On Friday the dogs found the corpse. The Exchange comptroller reported to his superiors that he had now established positive proof that Richard Whitney was an embezzler and that his firm was insolvent.

On Saturday morning, March 5, the comptroller confronted Whitney

in person with the evidence he had uncovered. Whitney, as the comptroller put it later, gave a "tacit admission" that he had misused customers' securities. This was a feint; Whitney had not given up yet.
That afternoon he spent two hours in Gay's office playing his last card.
Readily admitting misconduct, he asked for special consideration—
specifically, that the Exchange quietly allow him to sell his member-
ship, then drop charges against him. On what grounds? Gay wanted to
know—and then Whitney made his play. "After all, I'm Richard
Whitney," he said. "I mean the Stock Exchange to millions of people."
Therefore what affected him affected the Stock Exchange—and Wall
Street. His exposure as a bankrupt was now inevitable, but his exposure
as an embezzler—it would make a mockery of the trust on which all
stock trading is based; it would be a triumph for the reformulate forces
in Washington; it would be a bonanza beyond the wildest dreams of the
SEC. . . .

This was a telling point, and Whitney emphasized it; in the course
of the two-hour session he brought the same argument up over and
over again. "I wouldn't say that Mr. Whitney was pleading," Gay
recounted later. "He assumed more of a reasoning attitude, as if he
were discussing somebody else than himself." Indeed he was: the
White Knight was discussing a thief. It is possible to imagine that Charley
Gay was sorely tempted. He had the deep conservatism of the self-
made—had grown up admiring the Wall Street Old Guardsmen with
their easy languorous charm, and had spent his life working like a peon
to try to become one of them; now he was surely no more anxious than
Whitney himself that Whitney should bring the Old Guard and its era
crashing down with him. If Whitney were allowed to resign quietly
with the announcement that he was going to retire from the bond
business and take up some other line of work, there was at least a good
chance that nothing would ever come to light about his defalcations
and that, after a brief flurry of scandal, the whole thing would blow
over and things would be back where they had been before. If, on the
other hand . . .

But Gay was also a passionately honest and conscientious man. His
horrified conscience triumphed over his desire to preserve the world he
had accepted and admired so long. Adamantly, over and over again, he

told Whitney that the drawing up of charges and specifications against him would proceed, and that they, along with the evidence, would be presented to the Business Conduct Committee on Monday morning as planned.

Through the two months preceding that Saturday afternoon, Whitney, fighting for his life and perhaps his way of life, had indulged in one last binge of cash-raising efforts, the details of which add some bizarre footnotes to his story and indeed to the history of borrowing. Turndowns on loan requests were getting to be commonplace now, and he was learning to accept them without batting an eye. "How about George?" people would ask him, bluntly, when he came to them for money. "My brother is out of town, and if he were here I wouldn't be coming to you," he would reply loftily. "Well, I am very sorry . . ." he would hear again and again, and would simply turn his heel and leave. In January the long-suffering, long-awestruck Paul Adler turned him down; unable to face the idol he saw toppling before him, Adler scrawled on a piece of Stock Exchange notepaper: "Dick, I am sorry, but we have decided that we are not willing to make any loans to anyone at this time, and I deeply regret to say so. Sincerely, Paul." In mid-February he walked up to John H. McMannus, a floor specialist far outside his normal social orbit, and asked for $100,000. McMannus, after a stunned pause, offered to make the loan provided Whitney's note be endorsed by George. Whitney offered instead his wife's endorsement—"She's worth half a million dollars," he confided without shame. McMannus said he never accepted a woman's endorsement on a note. Whitney nodded. "Don't say anything about this," he remarked casually as he turned away. McMannus said later that the episode had been one of the most surprising events of his business life: "I thought he was the essence of everything fine in the world. I was so shocked I couldn't think clearly." If he had thought clearly, McMannus realized only afterward, he would have known that he didn't have the $100,000 to loan anyway.

Late in February Whitney asked Sidney Weinberg, by this time a partner at Goldman, Sachs and well on his way to becoming the "Mr. Wall Street" of the early postwar years, for $50,000. The only trouble, or one trouble, was that Whitney seems to have thought the gentleman's name was Weinstein.

But simultaneous, and more astonishing, were several spectacular successes. In mid-February Whitney asked Alexander B. Gale, an Exchange member, for the usual amount—$100,000. Gale said he could lend only $75,000, and immediately sent along a check for that amount. Whitney, however, brazenly sent back his note for $100,000. Thus made to feel like a piker, Gale sent along the additional $25,000 to round out the note. At about the same time Whitney approached one Walter T. Rosen for the usual amount—as usual, without offering collateral. Rosen handed over the money along with a charming and flattering little speech: "I have always been much impressed by the attitude of the elder Mr. Morgan, who held the view that the personal integrity of the borrower was of far greater value than his collateral." "Mr. Morgan was entirely right," the Morgan broker graciously allowed as he took the check.

Whitney's two last borrowings were memorable for their own reasons. On March 1, four days before his Saturday showdown with Gay, he approached two partners of Brown Brothers, Harriman & Company, Knight Woolley and W. Averell Harriman—the latter not yet launched on his diplomatic career—for the usual amount. Unlike the elder Mr. Morgan, although members of an equally distinguished and aristocratic firm, Woolley and Harriman wanted collateral. Whitney promised to have the collateral delivered within a few days, and got his loan on the spot; somehow the collateral never arrived. That same day Whitney borrowed $25,000 from an old and none-too-hale friend of his, a man who has spanned our turbulent story—Colonel John W. Prentiss, the tactful mediator in the 1920 dispute between Allan Ryan and the Stock Exchange. Eighteen days later, Colonel Prentiss, unrepaid, would be dead.

And late in January Whitney had made one last, grand embezzlement—his grandest. On the twenty-sixth, without explanation, he ordered the cashier of his firm, Robert J. Rosenthal, to turn over to him a batch of securities belonging to various customers of the firm, among them the estate of his father-in-law, and having a value of about $800,000. Two days later he took these securities to the Public National Bank and, representing them as his own, pledged them as collateral for a loan of no less than $280,000.

Let us sum up in broad strokes, for the astonishing record, Whitney's true financial condition as of the first week of March, 1938. Over the preceding four months he had negotiated, all told, 111 loans aggregating $27,361,500; of this, more than $25 million had been in more or less soundly secured borrowings from commercial banks, constantly turned over as he made new loans to repay those that came due. Apart from this, he owed, entirely unsecured, $2,897,000 to George Whitney, $474,000 to J. P. Morgan & Company, and about an even million dollars to others. He owed borrowed stocks worth about $390,000. Quite apart, then, from the sums he "owed" to the customers from whom he had embezzled, he had managed to accumulate on the strength of nothing, or almost nothing, more than his character and good name net borrowings well in excess of $5 million.

In those last days he was walking up to men he didn't know on the Exchange floor and asking them in tones casual to the point of indifference to lend him his standard sum—$100,000. He also did one thing suggesting that madness or something like it was overtaking him at last. On Tuesday of the frantic week that ended with his Saturday-afternoon confrontation, he went to Ben Smith. He made no lame effort to ingratiate himself. Rather, he announced brusquely that he "wanted to get this over quickly"—as if, say, his mission were to administer a justified rebuke to an inferior. Then he said that he wanted to borrow $250,000 "on my face." Smith's reply was, in the circumstances, not startling, and can scarcely be described as ruder than the occasion called for. "I remarked he was putting a pretty high value on his face," Smith recounted later. "So he told me that was his story and his back was to the wall and he had to have $250,000. I told him he had a lot of nerve to ask me for $250,000 when he didn't even bid me the time of day. I told him I frankly didn't like him—that I wouldn't loan him a dime." Whitney nodded; that was that.

Of course. But why had he done it? What had he expected from Ben Smith but a harsh rebuff? Was this the ritual of capitulation, the beaten wolf intentionally baring his neck to the teeth of his conqueror? It could not have been; as we know, on that Tuesday Whitney was by no means ready to capitulate. The remaining assumption must be that he was as insensitive in the matter of slights received as he had so long been in that of slights delivered; that he regarded this upstart so little as to be immune to his bad opinion, and had made the approach simply because it could cost him nothing; that, as Smith said, he had a lot of nerve, a rather awesome lot, and the nerve at least had not failed.

Francis Bartow, J. P. Morgan's "Stock Exchange man," was the firm's responsible partner in the absence of Lamont, who had followed his trip South with one abroad, and George Whitney, who early in 1938 had returned to the South to resume a long convalescence from his 1937 illness. Let Bartow tell, with a fine dramatic flair, what happened Saturday night after Whitney's last-ditch attempt to persuade Gay to drop charges:

"On the afternoon of March 5, I was playing bridge with some friends at the Links Club in New York and I was called to the telephone by Richard Whitney. He said he wanted to see me as soon as possible. I explained where I was and inquired where he was and he said at his office. I suggested that he stop by and see me where I was. He said he would.

"Some time later he appeared and we sat down together to talk. As we did so, he drew from his pocket a large folded piece of paper which he proceeded to open. He said, 'I am in a jam.' I said, 'Wait a minute, is your idea in talking to me now to borrow money?' He said, 'Yes.' 'Well,' I said, 'in all frankness I will not agree to that.' I think in my mind at the moment I was a little impatient with him because I assumed he must have known that I had talked with Randolph Mason about his affairs and the promised audit report and other information had not been given to me. He said, 'Well, on Monday at ten-thirty my affairs are coming up for examination before the Business Conduct Committee.' I said, 'Now, wait a minute, stop right there. I am not the proper person for you to talk to. My advice is that you go and get Randolph Mason and tell him.'

"He folded his papers up and left me. I resumed my game with friends. I think as he left me I said to him, 'I expect to be here some time longer, if you should want me.'

"Quite a considerable time later, word was brought to me that Richard Whitney would like to speak with me in the floor below. As soon as I was free I went there. He and Randolph Mason were together. He said, 'Frank, we have been talking this over and I want to know if you have any suggestions to offer.'

"I said, 'I have already told you that I have no suggestions to offer.'

" 'Well,' he said, 'when my affairs come up for review before the Business Conduct Committee on Monday, it is conceivable some embarrassing questions will arise.'

"I said, 'What do you mean, embarrassing?'

" 'Well,' he said, 'for example, the New York Yacht Club have securities with me and I have taken those securities and I have pledged them in loans.'

"I said, 'How much does the New York Yacht Club owe you?'

"He said, 'They don't owe me anything.'

"I said, 'Do you mean that you have taken a client's securities and pledged them in loans and taken the proceeds of that and placed it in your business when they did not owe you anything?'

"He said, 'Yes, I do.'

"I said, 'That is serious.'

"He said, 'It is criminal.'

"I asked, 'Are there any other cases where this had occurred?'

"He said, 'Yes, two; the Sheldon estate of which I am an executor, and Mrs. Baird.'

"I said, 'Dick, now this is such an entirely different nature than the matter that you originally discussed with me that I will not discuss it with you any further. And I want now to go to the telephone and call my counsel.' "

Does it seem rather odd that a man, on hearing a friend and business associate confess that he has been engaged in criminal activities, should react simply by saying that he is going to call his lawyer? It does, but it should not; remember that, in a time when Wall Street was still very much on the public griddle, Whitney was the most publicized man in Wall Street and Morgan's the most publicized firm, and that private knowledge of a crime on the part of a Morgan partner raised the possibility of the Morgan firm's being considered an accessory. Bartow called the Morgan lawyer—no lesser lawyer than the former Presidential candidate John W. Davis—and made an appointment to see him that evening at his home at Glen Cove, Long Island. Then he went back to Whitney and Mason. The three of them had a hasty supper together at the Links, and just before or during the meal Whitney said to Bartow, "I would like to explain this to you. I have a loan of $280,000 at the Public National Bank. In that loan are all of the securities taken improperly from the accounts in my office—the Yacht Club, Sheldon, and Baird. If I could borrow $280,000 and pay that loan off, it would enable me to restore all of those improperly used securities and when I went before the Business Conduct Committee on Monday morning I could state truthfully that there were no irregularities in my office."

Bartow gave no immediate answer. A prudent man, he was going to wait for advice of counsel. Immediately after dinner he and Mason left Whitney at the Links and took the hour's drive to Glen Cove to see John W. Davis. Davis, after hearing the story, replied without hesitation that no one could or should do anything to help Whitney now— "Anyone who did would run the risk of taking actions that would be misconstrued," as Davis put it euphemistically.

"All right, Mr. Davis," said Bartow. "I accept your advice and counsel on that. I am glad I came to you." One other question: would it be proper to call Gay, and ask him for a one-day or perhaps even two-day delay in the meeting of the Business Conduct Committee that would consider the Whitney case?

Davis gave it as his opinion that there was no reason not to do that.

So back to New York hurried Bartow and Mason, this time for a midnight meeting, arranged on the spur of the moment, with Gay at the Metropolitan Club. They found Gay there with a Stock Exchange lawyer, who, on hearing Bartow's request, replied most emphatically that under no circumstances would there be a single minute's delay in the scheduled Monday-morning meeting. That seemed to be that. Bartow and Mason went back to the Links, where they gave a glum Dick Whitney their grim news.

On Sunday there was more frantic scrambling. Bartow takes up the story again:

"Quite early, I called my partner, Mr. Anderson, and at the same time called my partner, Charles Dickey, in his home in Philadelphia, and in a general way told them of the events of the day before and asked if they would meet me at my house in New York at two-

thirty that afternoon, and they agreed. I then called my senior partner, Mr. J. P. Morgan, at his house at Glen Cove, and made an appointment with him for twelve o'clock. I then called Mr. Randolph
Mason and told him of a meeting that was to be that afternoon at
my house and asked if he would come. I also asked—if it were possible,
I would like to have Mr. Rodewald there, as I wished to learn from
him firsthand how long, in his opinion, it would take to make
an audit.

"Mr. Mason said he would come and, if possible, arrange for Mr.
Rodewald to be there, too.

"I then motored to Glen Cove. I went to Mr. Morgan's house where
I told him of the events of the night before, and my advice from John
W. Davis, and the conclusions that Mr. Davis had reached. Mr. Morgan
was naturally shocked beyond measure and gave it as his judgment,
which was mine, that there was no course for us to follow except to
abide by the advice that we had received from counsel."

(But in view of what he already knew, can J. P. Morgan have really
been all that shocked? Or did the old gentleman put on a show for the
benefit of the junior partner?)

"I then left and returned to my house in town. Sunday afternoon Mr.
Anderson and Mr. Dickey arrived and we sat down and I told them
what I had learned in as great detail as I recalled. I then telephoned Mr.
Sunderland, who is Mr. John W. Davis' partner, and asked him if he
would come to my house. He did. About that time Mr. Mason arrived.
Some while after that Mr. Rodewald arrived. I asked Mr. Rodewald
how long, in his judgment, he thought it would take for high-class accountants to make a proper audit. He was vague and to me disappointing because he gave the impression it would take a great deal longer
than I presumed it would take. . . .

"When Mr. Sunderland arrived, I told him what I had done, and
what I planned. I asked him if he thought it was a proper and right
thing for me to do and he said, 'Under no circumstances can you or
anyone else from J. P. Morgan & Company go into the office of Richard
Whitney & Company to find out anything.'

"I then told Mr. Rodewald that the reason for his being called was
over with, and we did not need him any more and I presumed he was

busy, and he left to go about his business. A little later . . . one by one I expressed my regret at calling [Anderson, Dickey, and Mason] from their homes in the country, and they went back to where they had come from, I presume. . . .

"Late in the afternoon I determined that the time had come when I must call my partner, George Whitney, on the telephone and advise him of everything that I knew. Accordingly I put in a call to get him on the telephone in Florida, which I did. As guardedly as I could, yet as fully as I could, I told him of my knowledge. . . .

"Mr. Whitney said, 'My God!' "

"My God" indeed: there was apparently little else George Whitney could say, and nothing more he could do.

So on Monday the wheels of Stock Exchange justice turned. That morning, right on schedule, the Business Conduct Committee met, heard the evidence, and voted unanimously to present forthwith the charges against Whitney and the two of his partners who held Exchange memberships, Edwin D. Morgan, Jr. and Henry D. Mygatt, to the Governing Committee for action. Early in the afternoon the Governing Committee considered the charges and voted unanimously that they be served on the three member partners, that the accused be notified that they would have the customary 10 days to prepare their answers, and that a hearing on the charges be held at the end of the 10-day period, on March 17. The charges were served on Whitney, Morgan, and Mygatt the same day. That evening, by telephone, Gay notified the SEC in Washington of the affair.

Meanwhile, no public announcement had yet been made and there had rather astonishingly been no leaks to the press; and Whitney's remaining allies, most of them now thinking chiefly of the public disaster for Wall Street that his exposure would be, were continuing with sinking hearts their furious efforts to find some way out. Early Monday morning George Whitney called Bartow back from Florida. He was very much disturbed about not being in New York, he said; shouldn't he come at once? Bartow urged him not to, reminding him that he was still not entirely recovered from his illness, and pointing out that there was nothing he could do anyway. Later that morning, grasping at straws, Bartow—after again getting clearance from John W. Davis—called on

Roland Redmond, the Stock Exchange lawyer who was perhaps Whitney's closest friend. "Is there anything that anybody can humanly do in this thing that you know of?" Bartow asked. Redmond replied, "Absolutely not. I don't know of a solitary thing." Poor Redmond was obviously in distress; to him, as Exchange lawyer, fell the duty of drawing up the charges against his friend—a duty he had performed at his office the previous afternoon, with tears actually streaming down his face.

"We parted," Bartow recounted later. "In the afternoon of that day, Randolph Mason called me on the phone and said that he would like to see me that evening. He would probably be late, and would I wait at my house until he came, and I said I would. And that evening he did come, and I am not quite clear now why he came, because there did not seem to me any purpose in it, because the only thing he told me now was that he had been engaged all afternoon and evening on papers dealing with the proposed bankruptcy proceedings of Richard Whitney & Company the next day—and after a very brief talk he left." But in retrospect it is clear enough why Mason came to Bartow's house—he wanted to have a wake.

John Wesley Hanes, with mixed emotions, became the SEC's liaison man in the Whitney case. Chairman Douglas on Monday night, right after hearing the news from Gay, picked Hanes for the assignment on the spot and called him shortly before midnight, asking him to take it on.

Hanes took the night train to New York, sleeping little and brooding much en route. "My first and principal concern was the extent of public participation in this failure," he said later. "We were unable to find out the extent of the public interest [in Washington]. I came to New York to find out if I could get any more facts than we had in Washington." Some insisted later that he had had another major concern. Far from lusting for the Morgan broker's scalp, Hanes was indubitably as worried as his idolized friends, the men at No. 23 themselves, for the good name of Wall Street at large and J. P. Morgan & Company in particular, and there was talk in Wall Street early that morning—circulated, it is true, by the die-hard remnants of the Whitney Old Guard—that Hanes was coming to New York with the specific mission of recommending on behalf of the SEC that public announcement of the disaster be postponed while efforts were made to negotiate some kind of accommodation. Whatever his intentions may have been—and he later denied that they were these—Hanes found, on his arrival in Wall Street at nine forty-five, only 15 minutes before Stock Exchange opening time, that events were wholly beyond reversal. The place, he found, was seething with rumors about Whitney that were, if possible, even worse than the facts; from the point of view of Wall Street's public image, no announcement would be the worst possible course. Hanes accordingly recommended to the Stock Exchange authorities that they go ahead with the announcement as planned. In any case, by that time it was already inexorably in the works. Some three-quarters of an hour earlier, at nine o'clock sharp, the Business Conduct Committee had convened with Howland Davis presiding; on the carpet before it were Mason as Whitney's representative and two of Whitney's partners. Davis had opened the meeting by saying, "Gentlemen, I think the thing the committee is most interested in is whether between now and ten o'clock we have to do something with regard to the plans of Richard Whitney & Company to do business today."

Mason had said, "We don't know all the figures. . . . I am obliged to say . . . that the firm is insolvent."

The chairman then asked Kingsley Rodewald, Whitney's partner—a bewildered man who, like all Whitney's partners, had for years been kept entirely in the dark as to Whitney's defalcations and even as to the desperate financial plight of the firm—whether he had anything to say. Rodewald replied that he had not.

"Can your firm meet its obligations?" the chairman had inquired.

"No, sir," Rodewald had replied.

So the failure was formalized, ipse dixit; now the Exchange under its own rules had no choice. At ten-five, just after the start of the day's trading, Gay mounted the rostrum overlooking the floor; the secretary rang the gong that suspends trading; the hum on the floor faded into dead silence; and Gay read an announcement of the suspension of Whitney & Company for insolvency. Immediately thereafter the Exchange released a statement that did not fail to make clear that wrongdoing was involved in the holocaust:

In the course of an examination of the affairs of Richard Whitney & Company, the Committee on Business Conduct discovered on March 1, 1938, evidence of conduct apparently contrary to just and equitable principles of trade, and on Monday, March 7, 1938, at 1:30 P.M. presented to a special meeting of the Governing Committee charges and specifications. Hearing on the charges was set for March 17, 1938. This morning the firm of Richard Whitney & Company advised the Exchange that it was unable to meet its obligations and its suspension for insolvency was announced from the rostrum of the Exchange shortly after 10:00 A.M.

With the fall of its champion, the fall of the Old Guard was accomplished.

Of the Private Cheats Used to Deceive One Another

DANIEL DEFOE

Daniel Defoe, best known as the author of *Robinson Crusoe* and *Moll Flanders*, was an extraordinarily prolific writer of books, essays, and pamphlets on politics, religion, and finance. He described himself with this couplet:

> No man has tasted differing fortunes more,
> And thirteen times I have been rich and poor!

Perhaps he writes as much from experience as from conviction in this 1719 polemic against London's stock-jobbers.

• • •

Proving *that* scandalous Trade, as it is now carry'd on, to be Knavish in its Private Practice, and Treason in its Publick:

The General Cry against Stock-Jobbing has been such, and People have been so long, and so justly Complaining of it as a publick Nusance, and which is still worse, have complained so long without a Remedy, that the Jobbers, harden'd in Crime, are at last come to exceed all bounds, and now, if ever, sleeping Justice will awake, and take some Notice of them, and if it should not now, yet the diligent Creatures are so steddy to themselves, that they will some time or other, make it absolutely necessary to the Government to demolish them.

I know they upon all Occasions laugh at the Suggestion, and have the Pride to think it impracticable to restrain them; and one of the top of the Function the other Day, when I casually told him, That if they went on, they wou'd make it absolutely necessary to the Legislature, to suppress them, return'd, That he believ'd it was as absolutely necessary for them to do it now, as ever it could be; But how will they do it? 'Tis

Reprinted from *The Anatomy of Exchange Alley: or, A System of Stock-Jobbing*, First Edition (London: Privately printed for E. Smith, 1719), pp. 1–6.

impossible, said he, but—if the Government takes Credit, their Funds should come to Market; and while there is a Market we will buy and sell; and there is no effectual way in the World, says he, to suppress us but this, *viz.* That the Government should first pay all the publick Debts, redeem all the Funds, and dissolve all the Charters, *viz. Bank, South-Sea,* and *East-India,* and buy nothing upon Trust, and then, indeed, says he, they need not hang the Stock-Jobbers, for they will be apt to hang themselves.

I must confess, I in part agree that this is an effectual way, but I am far from thinking it the only way to deal with a Confederation of Usurers, who having sold the whole Nation to Usury, keep the Purse-Strings of Poor and Rich in their Hands, which they open and shut as they please.

But before I come to the needful ways for restraining those People, I think 'twill be of some Service to expose their Practices to common view, that the People may see a little what kind of Dealers they are.

And first, they have this peculiar to them, and in which they out do all the particular pieces of publick Knavery that ever I met with in the World, *viz.* That they have nothing to say for it themselves; they have, indeed a particular Stock of hard Ware, as the Braziers call it, in their Faces, to bear them out in it; but if you talk to them of their Occupation, there is not a Man but will own, 'tis a compleat System of Knavery; that 'tis a Trade founded in Fraud, born of Deceit, and nourished by Trick, Cheat, Wheedle, Forgeries, Falshoods, and all sorts of Delusions; Coining false News, this way good, that way bad; whispering imaginary Terrors, Frights, Hopes, Expectations, and they preying upon the Weakness of those, whose Imaginations they have wrought upon, whom they have either elevated or depress'd. If they meet with a Cull, a young Dealer that has Money to lay out, they catch him at the Door, whisper to him, Sir, here is a great piece of News, it is not yet publick, it is worth a Thousand Guineas but to mention it: I am heartily glad I met you, but it must be as secret as the black side of your Soul, for they know nothing of it yet in the Coffee-House, if they should, Stock would rise 10 *per Cent* in a moment, and I warrant you *South-Sea* will be 130 in a Week's Time, after it is known. Well, says the weak Creature, prethee dear *Tom* what is it? Why really Sir I will *let you into the Secret,* upon your Honour to keep it till you hear it from other Hands; why 'tis this,

The Pretender is certainly taken and is carried Prisoner to the Castle of *Millan*, there they have him fast; I assure you, the Government had an Express of it from my Lord St—s within this Hour. Are you sure of it, says the Fish, who jumps eagerly into the Net? Sure of it! Why if you will take your Coach and go up to the Secretaries Office, you may be satisfied of it your self, and be down again in Two Hours, and in the mean time I will be doing something, tho' it is but a little, till you return.

Away goes the Gudgeon with his Head full of Wildfire, and a Squib in his Brain, and coming to the Place, meets a Croney at the Door, who ignorantly confirms the Report, and so sets fire to the Mine; for indeed the Cheat came too far to be baulkt at home: So that without giving himself Time to consider, he hurries back full of the Delusions, dreaming of nothing but of getting a Hundred Thousand Pounds, or purchase Two; and even this Money was to be gotten only upon the Views of his being before-hand with other People.

In this Elevation, he meets his Broker, who throws more Fire-works into the Mine, and blows him up so fierce an Inflamation, that he employs him instantly to take Guineas to accept Stock of any Kind, and almost at any Price, for the News being now publick, the Artists made their Price upon him. In a Word, having accepted them for Fifty Thousand Pounds more than he is able to pay, the Jobber has got an Estate, in the Broker 2 or 300 Guineas, the Esquire remains at Leisure to sell his Coach and Horses, his fine Seat and rich Furniture, to make good the Deficiency of his Bear-Skins, and at last, when all will not go through it, he must give them a Brush for the rest.

Part Six

Forecast, Analysis, and Performance Measurement

No Crash, But a Bull Market

ARNOLD BERNHARD

In the "lessons for the future" article excerpted here, Arnold Bernhard, the builder of Value Line, forecast a great bull market—a 100 percent rise in the Dow from 850 in 1979 to between 1,500 and 2,000 three to five years later—based on his historical analysis of dividends and book value as supports for market price.

• • •

In this year 1979, the 50th anniversary of the Great Crash of 1929, it may be appropriate to remark on what seem to be essential differences between the two periods.

Nineteen hundred twenty-nine was a year when euphoric America looked forward to a New Era in which poverty would be abolished once and for all; 1979 is a year when we soberly hope for a lesser increase of prosperity.

Nineteen hundred twenty-nine ushered in the years of pump-primed consumption; 1979 is beginning to recognize the need for saving and capital investing.

Nineteen hundred twenty-nine faced the problem of burdensome surplus; 1979, the problem of scarcity.

In 1929, the business of America, it was proudly asserted, was business; in 1979, the business of America, if it is profitable, is regarded as an obscenity.

In 1929 our money was tied to an unyielding gold standard; in 1979 it is tied to nothing but the will of the political establishment, which in turn is controlled by a thousand pressure groups, each demanding something for nothing, or at least something below cost from housing to food to energy.

Excerpted from *The Journal of Portfolio Management* 6 (Fall 1979), pp. 77–81, New York: Institutional Investor, Inc.

In 1929, the Dow Jones Industrial Average was priced at over 20 times earnings; in 1979, at 7 times.

Nineteen hundred twenty-nine, for all its bright hopes was followed by three years of devastating deflation, during which time the Dow stocks lost 90 percent of their market value; 1979, despite its black forebodings, will be followed, I think, by a 100 percent rise in the Dow to between 1500 and 2000 in the next three–five years.

This forecast of the Dow in the next three–five years is not an attempt to pinpoint the price in a particular year. Its possible usefulness is in helping to formulate investment strategy. It says in effect that stock prices will probably double some time between now and 1983. Against that prospect, the possibility of moderately lower prices in the more immediate future appears to be a risk worth taking.

Assumptions

Like any forecast over a five-year period, this one rests on certain assumptions. They are as follows:

1. Our country will not become embroiled in a major war.
2. A business recession, if one develops, will last no longer than 12 months.
3. Inflation will persist, but at no higher rate than is reflected in the current 9.25 percent Aaa bond yield; or, alternatively, inflation may decelerate, lowering the bond yield to 6 percent by 1983.
4. The American people and their followers, the politicians, will turn away from further socialization toward greater reliance upon the free market.

Although no statistical proof of the validity of these assumptions is attempted, it would probably be in order to explain briefly why they seem more realistic than alternative possibilities.

In this nuclear age, a major war would create a no-win situation for everybody. It could erupt through a series of blunders. If it did, this forecast, like everything else, would be meaningless.

The assumption that any business recession will be short-lived appears more probable than a long depression, because more is known about money and fiscal policy today than in the 1930s, and the political responsibility to prevent depression is a universally accepted imperative.

The expectation that inflation will persist simply recognizes that the market mechanism cannot cope with the unregulated monopoly power of labor unions. They control the major cost of production, and, like any other unregulated monopoly, will press for higher prices regardless of productivity. There will be little political inclination to combat such inflation both because inflation raises the revenues available to politicians for spending and because the unions have great political clout. Hence, for political reasons, money supply will be increased to accommodate the persisting rise in costs forced by wage increases that exceed productivity gains.

Still, a countervailing pressure may well build up to control inflation even if it is not likely to end it. The ordinary citizen is beginning to understand that wage increases beyond increases in productivity only take away from him at the supermarket what he has gained in his paycheck. He sees that inflation so generated promotes him into tax brackets that were originally designed for the rich only. That will make him reactionary enough to demand at least a measure of restraint.

Finally, it is assumed that the electorate will veer away from further socialization and toward greater reliance upon the free market. It has already happened in France, Italy, Britain, and Canada—and perhaps even in China. Bureaucracy and regulation are losing out in public esteem everywhere. They do not produce the goods, and the politicians are getting the message.

Is This Good News?

I must admit that I made the same 1500–2000 forecast on December 5, 1974, at the University of California, Los Angeles, Business Forecast

Conference. (The Dow price then was below 600.) I expected the 1500–2000 price target to be reached by the end of 1979, but that is obviously out of the question now. My error lay in underestimating the depressing effect inflation would have on the profit margins of corporations, on their payout ratios, and on the multiple the market would place on their dividends.

In this forecast I have tried to address myself more carefully to those factors. I see the profitability of corporations (as related to book value) recovering almost to the historical norm of 5 percentage points over the bond yield, of the payout ratio holding at 45 percent if the bond yield stays as high as 9.2 percent, but rising to 55 percent if the bond yield falls to 6 percent and, since the dividend growth in either scenario would be greater than the bond yield, I look for the dividend multiple to recover to 22.5 times or higher. That works out to be 1500–2000 on the Dow by 1983.

The picture is not as rosy for stockholders as the numbers suggest. The stockholder doubles his money, but the money is likely to be worth only half as much as today after assuming the rates of inflation. Still, the stockholder does better than the bondholder. The latter's 9.25 percent yield is reduced by income tax to about 6 percent. With inflation running at, say, 9 percent that leaves him with a negative current return, and there is very little risk that it will be any different.

The stockholder also has a negative annual return—even more negative than the bondholder on a current basis—but the stockholder doubles the number of his dollars, whatever they may be worth. The bondholder winds up with only the same number of depreciated dollars. In the end, the stockholder pays a capital gains tax on his retained earnings. But in the meantime, his retained earnings are tax deferred and compounded.

Regressing to the Mean

H. BRADLEE PERRY

The Babson Staff Letter is a favorite source of insight and perspective for many investment professionals. Brad Perry's contributions to it are particular favorites, especially for those who can imagine his New Englander's voice pronouncing the words he has written. Here, he is discussing how things seldom stay "changed" for long in investing.

• • •

Golfers and baseball players often talk about being "in the groove," having their swing following the particular pattern which has been successful for them. Different businesses also have a "groove," a mode of performance that is typical for them, and individual stocks tend to have a normal valuation "groove."

However, athletes, businesses, and stocks deviate from their typical performance from time to time, doing better or worse for a while. Such periods obviously are very significant to sports fans and investors.

Because of aging and other human frailties, golfers and ball players don't always get back into the groove. However, due primarily to competitive forces, businesses and stocks usually do. Statisticians call this "regressing to the mean." Understanding the process and observing it carefully can be very rewarding for investors.

Industry Patterns

Most types of businesses are influenced by specific factors that give them distinctive characteristics, and all the participants in those particular businesses tend to perform in somewhat similar fashion. When one

Excerpted from *The Babson Staff Letter*, August 14, 1987, by permission of David L. Babson & Co., Inc.

doesn't, history shows that eventually the "outlier" usually falls back in line with the industry pattern.

Banking is a good example. This is a very homogeneous business. All banks deal primarily with money; it is a commodity because one bank's money is just the same as another's. Through various means they all gather deposits primarily from individuals and businesses and lend those funds to other individuals and businesses.

Some banks are better managed than others so they operate a little more effectively. But in the long run there are rarely major differences in performance in such a homogeneous, competitive industry—especially within geographic areas where economic conditions are similar.

Over the years when a particular bank has been growing faster than its competitors, it has usually been more aggressive in lending. Eventually that leads to greater loan losses and in turn, a reining in of its rapid growth. Occasionally when a bank goes bonkers on profit expansion, it gets into such deep trouble that it has great difficulty regaining its position. Continental Illinois is a recent example and previously First Pennsylvania experienced the same fate (for somewhat different reasons).

However, in most instances overly aggressive banks do regress to the mean. Notable cases are Citizens & Southern many years ago and Chase Manhattan in the late 1970s.

Conversely, banks that go through a period of slower than normal growth and are tagged as "sleepy" usually wake up and get back in the groove. Wells Fargo, First Interstate, and State Street Boston are good illustrations.

The same process has occurred in just about every industry: Texaco declining from superiority in the 1970s while Exxon was moving up the scale; Union Carbide losing its position of preeminence in chemicals while Hercules rose from a subpar position to a very good one; Borden and Nabisco waking up in the food business while General Foods was sinking to mediocrity; Pfizer developing much greater strength as Upjohn slipped into the average category; Federated Department Stores sliding from its very strong position while May Department Stores was advancing from the rear of the pack; etc.

The record is clear that more often than not in a business heavily

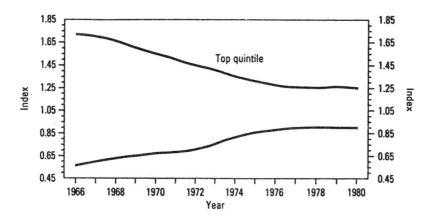

Figure 1   Convergence Tendency of Profitability: Five-Year Average Return on Equity

influenced by a few basic forces, companies rarely perform way above the industry average or way below it indefinitely. There is a constant tendency to regress toward the mean. . . .

This is illustrated in Figure 1 prepared a few years ago by Merrill Lynch. Covering a broad universe of over 1,500 corporations, it shows how those in the top quintile of profitability in 1966 gradually experienced a decline in their return on equity from way above average to moderately above average over the next 14 years—and how those at the bottom of the scale in 1966 improved to just slightly below average. . . .

Stock Market Performance

One lesson we need to remember constantly is that stock prices tend to reflect quite fully the most recent performance of companies. When a business has been going extremely well, almost invariably that fact has *already* been factored into the stock—because everyone has seen the good reports from the company. Similarly, when the recent results of a company have been poor, the stock is usually depressed.

Then when the news on the "good" companies becomes even slightly less favorable—or perhaps merely fails to get more favorable—their shares are likely to under perform the market. On the other hand, even a slight improvement in the news on a "bad" company can spark a major upswing in its stock. . . .

Conclusion

Many years ago we knew a person outside this firm who had developed a very simple—and very effective—method of selecting stocks to buy. He kept careful records of the returns on assets earned by different companies. He would only buy a stock when the firm's profitability was below its historic norm—and he would only sell the stock when profitability had risen above that norm. This gentleman was an extremely successful investor and his commonsense approach (which predates the general understanding of regression to the mean) works just as well today as it ever did.

The reason it does is that most investors take a relatively short-term view and assume that what has happened most recently will continue. They fail to recognize that economic and market forces are always working to press companies (and whole industries) back toward their respective grooves. Furthermore, there is a human element in the equation. As with athletes, it is difficult for management to play over their heads for long. Nor does any management want to continue performing badly. And if they do for very long, the directors (or an outside buyer) usually step in and replace management.

Appraising where a company is in relation to its normal pattern of performance and how its current status has affected its stock price is a very useful process. Like any other investment technique it doesn't work all the time because exceptions do occur, but clearly this type of analysis can improve one's portfolio batting average.

Likely Gains from Market Timing

WILLIAM F. SHARPE

Bill Sharpe, STANCO 25 Professor of Finance at Stanford's business school and a principal of William F. Sharpe Associates, is a winner of the Nobel Prize in financial economics who has made many important contributions to the theory and practice of investment management. Here are brief excerpts from his 1975 examination of the level of decision-making superiority necessary to implement a market timing style successfully. Readers will find considerable statistical underpinning in the complete article.

• • •

The investment manager who hopes to outperform his competitors usually expects to do so either by the selection of securities within a given class or by the allocation of assets to specific classes of securities. Potentially, one of the most productive forms of the latter strategy is to hold common stocks during bull markets and cash equivalents during bear markets ("market timing").

In a perfectly efficient market, any attempt to obtain performance superior to that of the overall "market portfolio" (taking into account both risk and return) by picking and choosing among securities would fail. Although few investment managers are ready to admit that U.S. security markets are completely efficient, there is a growing awareness that inefficiencies are few: Any divergence between the price of a security and the "intrinsic value" that would be assigned to it by well informed and highly skilled analysts is likely to be small, temporary, and difficult to identify in advance. Empirical studies of the performance of professionally managed portfolios yield results consistent with this view: Few, if any, provide better-than-average returns relative to risk year in and year out.

Excerpted from the *Financial Analyst's Journal* 31 (March/April 1975), pp. 60–69. Charlottesville, Virginia: Association for Investment Management and Research.

Some have argued that abnormal gains from selection of individual stocks or even industry groups are likely to be too small to justify the costs associated with attempts to identify and take advantage of apparent inefficiencies. Instead, it is said, the big gains are to be made by successful market timing. This approach is sufficiently popular to be recognized as one of several major "management styles." When portfolio values shrink in extended bear markets, investors increasingly regard this style as a likely cure for their ills. Thus managers committed to timing strategies with the skill or luck to have moved to cash equivalents in the bear market of 1973–1974 were able to attract money in the latter part of 1974, while their competitors suffered both decreases in the market value of assets and often actual loss of accounts. Market efficiency implies that it should be at least as difficult to predict market turns as to identify specific securities that will perform abnormally well or poorly. Moreover, attempts to take advantage of such predictions entail non-recoverable transaction costs, and expose investment funds to larger losses when errors are made. On the average, stocks outperform short-term money market instruments. Without superior predictive ability, one is likely to forego return by shifting from stocks to cash equivalents. But this is to state the obvious. How superior must one's predictions be to implement a market timing style effectively?

The conclusion is fairly clear. Attempts to time the market are not likely to produce incremental returns of more than four percent per year over the long run. Moreover, unless a manager can predict whether the market will be good or bad each year with considerable accuracy (e.g., be right at least seven times out of ten), he should probably avoid attempts to time the market altogether.

This pessimistic view will not appeal to those who feel that they can avoid the next bear market by judicious shifts of funds out of stocks and into short-term low-risk instruments. Some are now doing this, and others are actively considering it. Overall, of course, funds cannot be "shifted" beyond any changes in the market values of relevant securities outstanding. But individual investors can and do make such shifts.

It is said that the military is usually well prepared to fight the previous war. A number of investors now engaging in active market timing appear to be preparing for the previous market. Unfortunately for the military, the next war may differ from the last one. And unfortunately for investors, the next market may also differ from the last one.

You Need More Than Numbers to Measure Performance

ROBERT G. KIRBY

Bob Kirby has been one of Capital Group's lead portfolio managers for two decades, a member of the faculty at Stanford Business School for a semester, and a racer of Porsches for the better part of a lifetime. He keeps showing up in the "one-shot" sessions of our profession, easing wisdom and good humor into the fray.

• • •

It is often said in this business that there's no such thing as a free lunch. There's also no such thing as a long-term plan. That's true because most long-term plans won't survive short-term fluctuations. I think many money managers have found out over the last few years that no matter what kind of an institution you work for, it's run by people who make steel, or hamburgers, or run religious organizations, or whatever. They do not really have the experience to anticipate the fluctuations that occur in equity prices. Therefore, whether the institution is the Ford Foundation or the Topeka YMCA, when you encounter a 1973 or 1974, you're in deep grease unless you've got a plan strong enough to survive on a short-term basis. . . .

Performance measurement is one of those basically good ideas that somehow got totally out of control. In many, many cases, the intense application of performance measurement techniques has actually served to impede the purpose it is supposed to serve—namely, the achievement of a satisfactory rate of return on invested capital. Among the really negative side effects of the performance measurement movement as it has evolved over the past 10 years are:

From a paper given at a seminar sponsored by the Institute of Chartered Financial Analysts and the Financial Analysts Research Foundation, Chicago, Illinois, April 2, 1976, by permission of the author.

1. It has fostered the notion that it is possible to evaluate a money management organization over a period of two or three years—whereas money management really takes at least five and probably 10 years or more to appraise properly.
2. It has tried to quantify and to formulize, in a manner acceptable to the almighty computer, a function that is only partially susceptible to quantitative evaluation and requires a substantial subjective appraisal to arrive at a meaningful conclusion.
3. It has to take most of the blame for creating the cult of market timing.

Actually, I'm really a strong advocate of careful performance measurement. I just quarrel with some of the systems that are in use and with many of the ways in which the data are used.

One of the great weaknesses of modern performance measurement is that it often attempts to draw useful and meaningful conclusions based solely on quantitative data covering a relatively short period of time. One or two years of solely quantitative data will rarely help anyone arrive at any useful conclusion or a meaningful evaluation of a money manager. Yet, this is what performance measures often attempt to do.

At the other extreme, I will freely admit that if the time interval covered by the data is 15 or 20 years, there would be no reason to use qualitative measures at all. That observation is probably also true if the time interval is 10 years or, perhaps, even as short as five years. *Ultimately*, one has to succeed as a money manager to produce an investment return on the capital under one's supervision that is satisfactory from an absolute and a relative standpoint. Numbers alone will lead eventually to the right answer if the time interval is long enough—but it rarely is.

To gain some perspective on my complaints, let's see if we can find something that good money management organizations seem to have in common. Many qualified money managers are around. It seems to me that the outstanding characteristic the best ones all have in common is a well-defined investment philosophy that has proven to be successful over an extended period of time, such as 20 or 30 years. Most of these organizations stick closely to this investment philosophy, pretty much through thick and thin. The things that change, often violently and quickly, are the fads and fashions of the market place. These organizations know that from time to time the stock market is going to make them look a great deal smarter than they really are and at other times a great deal dumber than they really are. Most good investment managers are rational; the stock market is not.

The short-term vagaries—the excessive swings and the sudden changing fads that occur in the stock market in the short run—are primarily the product of a great many full-time, well-informed, aggressive investors all trying to outperform the investment universe on a month-to-month and quarter-to-quarter basis! The good investment management firms are not playing this game and are attempting to make long-term investment decisions consistent with a well-defined philosophy. The market itself really represents nothing more than a pendulum that swings back and forth through the median line of rationality. It spends very little time at the point of rationality and most of the time on one side or the other.

I won't state that short-term, quantitative performance data are totally useless. On the contrary, such data are often quite useful as an *inverse* indicator. If I were looking for an outside money manager to manage my company's pension or profit sharing fund, I would go through a procedure something like the following: I would first look for an organization that had been around for awhile and that had produced good, long-term performance records with a variety of portfolios. I would make sure that the individuals in the organization were experienced and talented. I would determine that the good, long-term record was the result of a consistent application of a clear investment philosophy. I would satisfy myself that the organization provided an environment in which it was rewarding to work so that good people would stay. Then, after I had identified the organizations that met all these specifications, I would hire the one who, for the past two years, had had the *worst* record. . . .

Short-term investment performance data are a far better inverse indicator of what to expect in the immediate future than anything else.

Higgledy Piggledy Growth

<hr>

I.M.D. LITTLE

**Ian M.D. Little was for many years a most successful investment bursar
or portfolio manager at Nuffield College, Oxford. He ran a very "high
turnover" portfolio based on frequent calls from his brokers in the
City and considered himself an amateur speculator. He is also a first-
rate economic observer—with an engaging good sense of humor—as
is demonstrated in the conclusions presented here of his extensive
analysis of hundreds of British companies in a pioneering 1962 study
of whether "past growth behaviour is some sort of guide to future
growth."**

· · ·

Conclusions

Mainly for Investors

1. In spite of the heavy ploughing back of profits the growth of
adjusted pre-tax earnings per share has lagged behind earned incomes,
especially in industries most concerned with exports and investment.
That the growth of dividends, except in textiles, has been fast is better
known. If the figures had been more up to date, the growth of pre-tax
earnings would undoubtedly have been much slower still. Unless there
is some fundamental change in the economy making for greater profitability of capital, the prospect for equities is worse than past performance suggests. Equity values cannot continue to ride the surf of reduced taxation and dividend relaxation. This is certainly not, however,
to say that present prices (June 1962) are too high in relation to fixed
interest investments.

Since even the smallest investor can avoid the risks attaching to a

Excerpted from *Oxford Bulletin of Economics and Statistics* 24 (1962) (extracts), pp. 387–
412. Oxford, England: Blackwell Publishers.

particular share, or small selection of shares, all that is needed to justify a reverse yield gap is the confident expectation that the sum of the dividend yield and its rate of growth should exceed the redemption yield of fixed interest investments. There is certainly nothing in the past to suggest that equity shares are over-valued, in spite of the relatively sluggish performance of earnings, and the very low apparent rate of return on money ploughed back.

2. It is useless to try to predict future earnings from any single past earnings growth ratio, or from dividend cover, or from asset size. None of these factors should influence the price of a share except insofar as a high dividend cover probably on average results in a higher than average future dividend performance. But a share's price is only loosely tied to its earnings. Mr. Scott has found a correlation between past earnings and the future share price (for up to a year after the last results). . . . This is explicable insofar as future dividends and past earnings growth *are* related: but, probably, the main reason is a naive belief that past growth tends to continue.

Mainly for Economists

1. I wrongly expected that I would be able to find some correlation of future and past growth (in relation to the average for the 'industry'), primarily on the view that some continuity of good and bad management would establish such a correlation. If a good management is one that earns a higher rate of profit on equity capital than the average for the 'industry,' and that maintains this rate on new money for a period of, say, 5–8 years or more, then good and bad management is extremely rare. Statistically speaking, Marks and Spencer does not exist. Evidently, much too high a standard was being expected. Not only may luck play so big a part that steady success or failure is more improbable, but also the forces of competition may operate to prevent above average returns being maintained.

2. It was noted that the variance of the growth distributions had greatly increased since 1955. This can be equated with an increase in

uncertainty, which may be associated with a growth in the freedom and competitiveness of markets.

3. The tentative conclusion of the lack of significant correlation between ploughback and growth is disturbing. It shows that among those firms that plough back relatively heavily, almost as many decline in relation to the average as grow. It is, of course, possible that the new investments of those that decline are just as profitable as those of the rest, the whole of their relative failure being accounted for by the declining profitability of old assets. Even so, if the heavy 'ploughers-back' contained only their fair share of declining profitability of old assets, one would still expect the group as a whole to grow faster than the average. The lack of correlation could be accounted for by the hypothesis that firms with declining profitability tend to plough back more as a kind of insurance (possibly buying mainly financial assets). But this we know to be in general false, since it is a fact that rapid growth induces a relatively high ploughback. One seems to be left with the conclusion that those that retain a relatively high proportion of profits select relatively unprofitable investments.

Futility of Stock Market Guessing

DAVID L. BABSON

Dave Babson's wonderful reputation for incisive, honest advice was earned from 50 years of blunt truth-telling. This 1951 example shows why his firm's Staff Letter is widely read by competitors, clients, and friends.

. . .

In a recent Staff Letter we discussed the futility of trying to forecast the immediate trend of stock prices. It must be apparent to intelligent investors that if anyone possessed the ability to do so consistently and accurately he would become a billionaire so quickly he would not find it necessary to sell his stock market guesses to the general public.

In many of these Letters we have attempted to point out the fundamental difference between basic value and market price. *Values can be analyzed and tested by statistical measurements.* While emotional factors and surprise news developments often temporarily upset the relationship between price and value, eventually the two become correlated.

> Consequently, we are strong advocates of basing investment decisions on thorough studies of VALUE rather than wasting time guessing whether PRICES will be higher or lower next week or next month.

If clients had the opportunity to observe the tremendous losses investors have suffered in just the post-war period by either their own guess or following someone else's guess on the immediate trend of prices and the market, they would be appalled. Almost every weekly "advisory service" that attempts to "forecast" has advocated selling stocks since 1947 and almost all are bearish today.

The market guesser pays scant attention to the fundamental mea-

Reprinted from the *Weekly Staff Letter* (August 27, 1951), by permission of David L. Babson & Co.

surements of value—the relationship of price to current and prospective earnings and dividends. He has no more adequate method of analyzing the future prospects for industrial activity than a guess. The man who is more concerned with price than value places little weight on the differing characteristics of industries and companies.

He assumes everyone interested in securities is a speculator who is concerned only with the immediate fluctuations in price. He does not understand that the real objective of the genuine investor is to conserve his living standards, not just the *number* of dollars he possesses. (If he protects his living standards, the number of dollars he owns will take care of itself.)

The price forecaster does not recognize that the responsible and intelligent man wants to buy an interest in a well-managed, financially sound business which has above-average prospects of continued growth and expansion, not to gamble on a name which is printed on the quotation page every day.

Picking "Growth" Stocks

T. ROWE PRICE, JR.

T. Rowe Price's case for viewing growth stock investing as the only way to outrun inflation's erosion of purchasing power was originally developed in a series of articles in *Barron's*. Here are several important excerpts from a reprint of those articles.

. . .

In planning an investment program, it is extremely important that the investor, before purchasing any securities, should ask himself, "What is my objective?" He must realize that except over a long period of years no common stock investment can give him safety of capital and that there may be other mediums more likely to provide him with a liberal, steady income. . . .

The three major objectives of investors are: (1) *Capital conservation*, or stability of market value of invested principal; (2) *Liberal income* at a fixed rate; and (3) *Capital growth*. While all securities involve risk, the degree varies widely in accordance with the type of security. One type, such as short-term government bonds, might well serve as a medium for safety of principal, but certainly should not be expected to produce substantial profits.

Another type, such as the common stock of an aviation company, might produce substantial profits, but certainly should not be expected to provide safety of principal. Either security may be qualified to do one job well, but no one security possesses the qualifications to accomplish all three major objectives. The individual must, therefore, determine in advance what percentage of his total fund should be invested for capital conservation, how much for liberal income and how much for

From T. Rowe Price, *Picking "Growth" Stocks* (Princeton, New Jersey, 1939), 3–18. Reprinted by permission of *Barron's*, copyright Dow Jones & Company, Inc., 1939. All Rights Reserved.

capital growth, and then select the type of security best qualified to accomplish each objective. . . .

[W]hen money is invested for capital conservation, both liberal income and opportunity for capital growth are sacrificed; when money is invested for liberal income at a fixed rate, both stability of market value and capital growth are sacrificed; and when money is invested for capital growth, the other two major objectives, capital conservation and liberal income, must be sacrificed.

The "life cycle theory of investing," which is the main subject of this study, is equally applicable to the purchase of securities for capital conservation and liberal income as it is to the selection of securities for capital growth. . . .

Earnings of most corporations pass through a life cycle that, like the human life cycle, has three important phases—growth, maturity, and decadence. Insurance companies know that a greater risk is involved in insuring the life of a man 50 years old than of a man 25, and that a much greater risk is involved in insuring a man of 75 than one of 50. They know, in other words, that risk increases as a man reaches maturity and starts to decline.

In very much the same way, common sense tells us that an investment in a business affords greater gain possibilities and involves less risk of loss while the long-term, or secular, earnings trend is still growing than after it has reached maturity and starts to decline. Once a business is well established, the greatest opportunity for gain is afforded during the period of growth in earning power. The risk factor increases when maturity is reached and decadence begins. . . .

Because the economic or business cycle runs concurrently with a company's life cycle, it is difficult to determine in advance when earning power is on the decline. Research and an understanding of social, political, and economic trends, however, should enable one to recognize the change in the long-term earnings trend of a business in time to withdraw his capital before it is seriously impaired. . . .

The best proof that it is possible to select the stocks of companies that are in the growth phase is the experience of an actual fund to which has been applied what the author calls "the life cycle theory of investing." This theory has been developed over a period of approximately 10 years. In 1934 a small experimental fund was created in order to test the soundness of the theory. Since that time the principles and methods described have been used in the management of this actual fund, with the following results:

Throughout the four-year period 1935–1938 the fund has been fully invested—no attempt was made, in other words, to catch the swings of the market. Frequent changes were made, however, in the list of growth stocks. Radical legislation and sudden and far-reaching economic developments during the period have altered the long-term earnings trends of many corporations. When stocks appeared to have reached their maximum earning power they were liquidated and the proceeds reinvested in other growth stocks. Naturally, not every selection was a successful one.

The increase in principal of this experimental fund from December 31, 1934, to December 31, 1938, amounted to 76.3 percent. During that time the gain in the *Dow-Jones* composite average, which is made up of industrials, rails, and utilities, was only 31.6 percent. The *Dow-Jones* average of 30 industrial stocks appreciated 48.7 percent during these four years. . . .

Growth of income on the experimental fund is also impressive when compared with that of the Dow-Jones averages. Income on the fund and averages is shown in the following table for each of the four years, the return being expressed as a percentage of the original principal. . . .

	1935	1936	1937	1938	4 Yr. Avg.
Growth stock portfolio	2.6%	7.8%	9.0%	6.04%	6.36%
Dow-Jones comp. avg.	4.2	6.2	7.2	4.50	5.52
Dow-Jones indl. avg.	4.3	6.7	7.8	4.80	5.90

These figures of income and capital gain, which, it should be emphasized, are based on an *actual investment experience*, and not on a theoretical investment that might involve the use of hindsight, appear to furnish convincing evidence of the soundness of restricting holdings to corporations that are still in the earnings growth phase of their life cycle. Such a policy affords the maximum gain with the minimum risk. What is also important, the figures prove *it can be done.* . . .

The two best ways of measuring the life cycle of an industry are unit volume of sales and net earnings available for stockholders. It is important to consider both, for common stock investments should be confined to industries that are growing in both volume and earnings. . . .

"Growth stocks" can be defined as shares in business enterprises that have demonstrated favorable underlying long-term growth in earnings and that, after careful research study, give indications of continued secular growth in the future.

Secular, or underlying long-term growth, should not be confused with the cyclical recovery in earnings that takes place as business activity increases from a period of depression to a period of prosperity. Secular growth extends through several business cycles, with earnings reaching new high levels at the peak of each subsequent major business cycle. . . .

The fact that a stock is considered to be a growth stock is no assurance against a decline in income or market value during the downtrend of a business cycle, as growth stocks often depreciate as much as other groups. However, the prospects for recovery are more favorable for growth stocks than for matured and decadent stocks.

There are two major types of growth stocks—"cyclical growth" stocks and "stable growth" stocks. . . .

Each of these two groups has different characteristics and qualifies for different investment purposes. A stable growth stock is more suitable for the investor requiring relatively stable income, while a cyclical growth stock is more suitable for the investor whose major objective is capital gain during a period of cyclical recovery. . . .

"Matured stocks" are shares in business enterprises that, after careful study, appear to have reached their maximum earnings. . . .

"Decadent stocks" are defined as shares in business enterprises that are experiencing a long-term, or secular, decline in earnings. . . .

Comparing the peak recovery year, 1937, with the boom year, 1929, we find the results were as follows:

	Earnings	Dividends	Market Value
Growth stocks	inc. 47.3%	inc. 148.4%	inc. 67.1%
Matured stocks	dec. 16.6%	inc. 18.3%	dec. 13.8%
Decadent stocks	dec. 56.5%	dec. 43.0%	dec. 61.0%

There are two sound reasons for investing in common stocks—growth of income and growth of principal. Many investors prefer common stocks from which a high current income can be obtained. This is a fallacious policy because in the majority of cases a common stock that affords a relatively high yield at the time of purchase possesses a greater risk of reduction of income and loss in market value in the future. . . .

Average income for the 10-year period, 1929–1938, was 4.5 percent on the matured group, 4.2 percent on the growth stocks, and 3.2 percent on the decadent stocks. The higher income on the matured stock group, taking the ten years as a whole, was the result of the fact that four of the stocks in the group continued to grow after 1929 and only reached maturity during the latter part of the decade under review. The growth stocks would compare more favorably if the comparison were limited to the past five years.

While stocks with matured and decadent earnings trends may yield more than growth stocks when purchased, over a period of several years growth stocks increase their dividends and, in the course of time, pay a better return on invested principal.

When the capital gain in the growth stocks is compared with the capital losses in the matured and decadent stocks, the results are even more convincing. One dollar invested in growth stocks in 1929 was worth, in 1938, twice as much as a dollar invested in matured stocks and five times as much as one dollar invested in decadent stocks.

Higher current income, it is evident, is obtained at the sacrifice of future income and the risk of loss of principal.

The Paradox

CHARLES D. ELLIS

The curious emphasis of investment managers on manipulating port-folios rather than on investment counseling is questioned in this es-say. If policy guidance from the client is lacking, is it not the manager's duty to either obtain it or supply it?

. . .

A Paradox Is Haunting Investment Management

The paradox is that funds with very long-term purposes are being man-aged to meet short-term objectives that may be neither feasible nor important. And they are *not* being managed to achieve long-term ob-jectives that are both feasible and worthwhile.

The unimportant and difficult task to which most investment man-agers devote most of their time with little or no success is trying to "beat the market." Realistically—without taking above-average mar-ket risk—to outperform the equity market by even one half of 1 per-cent *consistently* would be a great success that almost no sizable invest-ment managers have achieved for very long.

The truly important but not very difficult task to which investment managers and their clients could and should devote themselves involves four steps: (1) understanding the client's needs, (2) defining realistic investment objectives that can meet the client's needs, (3) establishing the right asset mix for each particular portfolio, and (4) developing well-reasoned, sensible investment policies designed to achieve the client's realistic and specified long-term investment objectives. In this work, success can be easily achieved.

For example, if the long-term average rate of return on bonds is 8 percent, and the return from investments in common stocks is 16

From Charles D. Ellis, *Investment Policy* (Homewood, Illinois, 1985), 21–28, by permission of Dow Jones-Irwin.

percent—because there must be a higher long-term rate of return on stocks to convince investors to accept the risk of equity investing—then shifting just 5 percent of the portfolio's assets from bonds to socks and keeping it there would, over time, increase the portfolio's average annual rate of return by $4/10$ of 1 percent (8×5 percent = 0.40 percent).

Shifting the asset mix of a 60 percent equity/40 percent fixed income portfolio to 65:35 is not a major proposition, but . . . consistently beating the market rate of return by 40 basis points a year through superior stock selection would be a substantial achievement.

Very few institutional investors have been able to achieve and sustain such superior results.

It is ironic that a change of even such modest magnitude in the basic asset allocation decision can capture an improvement in total return significantly greater than the elusive increment sought in the beat the market syndrome.

Clearly, if the asset mix truly appropriate to the client's objectives justified an even more substantial emphasis [on] equities—70:30, or 80:20, or 90:10, or even 100:0—the incremental rate of return, on average, over the 60:40 portfolio would be even greater: 0.8 percent annually at 70:30 increasing to 1.6 percent annually at 80:20 and 3.2 percent average annually at 100 percent. Virtually no substantial investment manager can hope to beat the market by such magnitudes.

Of course, these calculations are mechanical. They present averages ignoring the fact that actual returns in individual years come in an impressive, even intimidating, distribution around these averages.

The crucial question is not simply whether long-term returns on common stocks would exceed returns on bonds or bills *if* the investor held on through the many startling gyrations of the market.

The crucial question is whether the investor will, in fact, hold on. The problem is not in the market, but in ourselves, our perceptions, and our reactions to our perceptions. This is why it is so important for each client to develop a realistic knowledge of his own and/or his organization's tolerance for market fluctuations and his long-term investment objectives, and to develop a realistic understanding of investing and of capital markets. The more you know about yourself as an investor and the more you understand investment management and the securities markets, the more you will know what asset mix is really right for your portfolios, and the more likely you will be able to sustain your commitment for the long term.

In investment management, the real opportunity to achieve superior results is not in scrambling to outperform the market, but in establishing *and adhering to* appropriate investment policies over the long term—policies that position the portfolio to benefit from riding with the main long-term forces in the market. Investment policy, wisely formulated by realistic and well-informed clients with a long-term perspective and clearly defined objectives, is the foundation upon which portfolios should be constructed and managed over time and through market cycles.

In reality, very few investors have developed such investment policies. And because they have not, most investment managers are left to manage their clients' portfolios without knowing their clients' real objectives and without the discipline of explicit agreement on this mission as investment managers. *This is the client's fault.*

As a result of not knowing enough about the particular facts and values of their different clients, investment managers typically manage all funds in virtually the same way and with very nearly the same asset mix, even in such extraordinarily different kinds of employee benefit funds as pension funds and profit sharing funds.

The profound differences between the functions and needs of pension plans and profit sharing plans make them striking examples of a disconcertingly standardized approach to the most important investment decision: the asset mix. So far as the total sum received by each individual is concerned, profit sharing plans terminate entirely on the day he or she retires or leaves; thus the fund has a series of absolute and predictable end points.

The risk of "end period dominance" calls for an investment policy that avoids major fluctuations in market value. Pension plans, on the other hand, are virtually perpetual investment vehicles, funded to provide a stream of annuity payments to plan participants over a very long and highly predictable period; they can easily accept quite substantial market fluctuations during the long "interim" period.

That the investments of pension funds and profit sharing plans are not, in fact, differentiated on even such a powerful and basic dimension as the stock-bond ratio leads to the sobering conclusion that while investment policy conforming to the client's particular investment objectives may be honored in theory, it is little used in practice.

The differences in employees benefit plans can be substantial, but these differences will only matter if corporate executives vigorously represent the special characteristics of their company and their plan when basic investment policies are being formulated or reviewed.

It is hardly conceivable that senior corporate management would routinely delegate full operating responsibility for comparable millions of dollars to regular operating divisional executives—let alone a manager not directly supervised by top management—with only such broad guidelines or instructions as: "Try to do better than average," or "You're the experts, see what you can do for us."

The real question is not whether portfolio managers are constructing portfolios to match the goals and objectives of each specific client. (The uninspiring reality is that they do not.) The relevant question is: Who is responsible for bringing about the requisite change? The pragmatic answer is that the responsibility is not going to be fulfilled by investment managers. It will be left to the client. Clients can and should accept this responsibility.

Clients can do more for their portfolio's long-term rates of return by developing and sustaining wise long-range policies that commit the portfolio to an appropriate structure of investments than can be done by the most skillful manipulation of the individual holdings within the portfolio.

In brief, clients should subordinate portfolio operations to investment policy, and should assert their responsibility for leadership in policy formation. This is not an investment problem that should be left to portfolio managers—no matter how skilled and conscientious they are—any more than, as Clemenceau observed, war should be left to the generals. It is the client's problem, and while responsibility for it can be abdicated, it really cannot be delegated.

Only the client will know enough to speak with relevance and credibility to such important characteristics as the amount, timing, and certainty of flows *out* of the fund. Only the client knows his own or his organization's tolerance for changes in market prices—particularly at market extremes where it really matters—because it is at such stress periods when investment policies seem least certain and the pressure for change is most strong. For individual investors, only they will know their overall financial and investment situation—their earning power, their ability to save, their obligations for children's educational expenses, or how they feel about investments.

Corporate executives will know their pension plan's actuarial assumptions and how close to reality these assumptions really are; the company's tolerance for intrusions upon its quarter-to-quarter and year-to-year progression of reported earnings by a sudden need to fund a deficit in plan assets caused by an abrupt drop in market value of pension assets; the company's evolving philosophy of employee benefits and how benefit programs might be changed; the company's likeliness to increase benefits to retired plan participants to protect their purchasing power from the corrosion of inflation; and the tolerance of interim market fluctuations among staff, senior executives, and the board of directors. The "risk tolerance" of a corporate pension plan sponsor is not just the risk tolerance of the pension staff or even the senior financial officer: It is the risk tolerance of a majority of the board of directors at the moment of most severe market adversity.

Here are six important questions each client should think through, and then explain his own answers to the investment manager. (Investment managers would be wise to urge their clients to do this kind of "homework.")

First, what are the real risks of an adverse outcome, particularly in the short run? Unacceptable risks should never be taken. For example, it would not make sense to invest all of a high school senior's college tuition savings in the stock market because if the market went down, the student might not be able to pay the tuition bill. If the student's parents have been fortunate enough to win the "money game" so far, they can keep it that way simply by not continuing to play.

Second, what are the probable emotional reactions of clients to an adverse experience? As the axiom goes, some investors care about *eating* well and some care about *sleeping* well. The portfolio manager should know and stay well within the client's informed tolerance for interim fluctuations in portfolio value. The emphasis on *informed tolerance* is deliberate. Avoidance of market risk does have a real "opportunity cost," and the client should be fully informed of the opportunity cost of each level of market risk *not* taken.

Third, how knowledgeable about investments and markets are clients? Investing does not always make sense. Sometimes it seems almost perversely counterintuitive. Lack of knowledge tends to make investors too cautious during bear markets and too confident in bull markets—sometimes at considerable cost. Managers should be careful *not* to assume their clients will be more sophisticated than they really are.

Portfolio managers can help their clients by explaining the way capital markets behave—and misbehave—and clients can help educate themselves.

The client who is very well informed about the investment environment will know what to expect. This client will be able to take in stride those disruptive experiences that may cause other less informed investors to overreact to either unusually favorable or unusually adverse market experiences.

Fourth, what other capital or income resources does the client have and how important is the particular portfolio to the client's *overall* financial position? For example, pension funds sponsored by large and prosperous corporations can reasonably accept greater market risk than can a college endowment, which may have difficulty raising capital to replenish losses. A retired widow usually cannot accept as much risk as can her alma mater.

Fifth, are any legal restrictions imposed on investment policy? Many endowment funds have restrictions that can be significant, particularly when they specify how income is to be defined or spent, or both.

Sixth, are there any unanticipated consequences of interim fluctuations in portfolio value that might affect policy? A frequently cited example is the risk in a pension fund of being obliged to augment contributions if the portfolio's market value drops below a "trigger" level built into the actuaries' calculations of current contributions.

Each of these possible concerns should be rigorously examined to ascertain how much deviation from the normally optimal investment policy—broad diversification at a moderately above average market risk—is truly warranted. Understanding and using these insights into the specific realities of the particular client's situation and objectives is the basis upon which wise investment policies can be developed for each different portfolio.

The State of Long-Term Expectation

JOHN MAYNARD KEYNES

In this passage from his *General Theory of Employment Interest and Money*—full of insight, profundity, and wit—John Maynard Keynes elegantly explains the conversion from "real" investment to market-driven investment. Note in particular his concern about excessive attention to short-term market considerations rather than diligent pursuit of long-term business building—a concern others have come to share 50 years later.

· · ·

A conventional valuation that is established as the outcome of the mass psychology of a large number of ignorant individuals is liable to change violently as the result of a sudden fluctuation of opinion due to factors that do not really make much difference to the prospective yield; since there will be no strong roots of conviction to hold it steady. In abnormal times in particular, when the hypothesis of an indefinite continuance of the existing state of affairs is less plausible than usual even though there are no express grounds to anticipate a definite change, the market will be subject to waves of optimistic and pessimistic sentiment, which are unreasoning and yet in a sense legitimate where no solid basis exists for a reasonable calculation.

But there is one feature in particular that deserves our attention. It might have been supposed that competition between expert professionals, processing judgment and knowledge beyond that of the average private investor, would correct the vagaries of the ignorant individual left to himself. It happens, however, that the energies and skill of the professional investor and speculator are mainly occupied otherwise. For most of these persons are, in fact, largely concerned,

From John Maynard Keynes, *The General Theory of Employment Interest and Money*, 1936, 154–158. New York: Harcourt Brace Jovanovich, Inc.

not with making superior long-term forecasts of the probable yield of an investment over its whole life, but with foreseeing changes in the conventional basis of valuation a short time ahead of the general public. They are concerned, not with what an investment is really worth to a man who buys it "for keeps," but with what the market will value it at, under the influence of mass psychology, three months or a year hence. Moreover, this behaviour is not the outcome of a wrong-headed propensity. It is an inevitable result of an investment market organised along the lines described. For it is not sensible to pay 25 for an investment of which you believe the prospective yield to justify a value of 30, if you also believe that the market will value it at 20 three months hence.

Thus the professional investor is forced to concern himself with the anticipation of impending changes, in the news or in the atmosphere, of the kind by which experience shows that the mass psychology of the market is most influenced. This is the inevitable result of investment markets organised with a view to so-called "liquidity." Of the maxims of orthodox finance none, surely, is more anti-social than the fetish of liquidity, the doctrine that it is a positive virtue on the part of investment institutions to concentrate their resources upon the holding of "liquid" securities. It forgets that there is no such thing as liquidity of investment for the community as a whole. The social object of skilled investment should be to defeat the dark forces of time and ignorance that envelop our future. The actual, private object of the most skilled investment today is "to beat the gun," as the Americans so well express it, to outwit the crowd, and to pass the bad, or depreciating, half-crown to the other fellow.

This battle of wits to anticipate the basis of conventional valuation a few months hence, rather than the prospective yield of an investment over a long term of years, does not even require gulls amongst the public to feed the maws of the professional—it can be played by professionals amongst themselves. Nor is it necessary that anyone should keep his simple faith in the conventional basis of valuation having any genuine long-term validity. For it is, so to speak, a game of Snap, of Old Maid, of Musical Chairs—a pastime in which he is victor who says *Snap* neither too soon nor too late, who passes the Old Maid to his neighbour before the game is over, who secures a chair for himself when the music stops. These games can be played with zest and enjoyment, though all the players know that it is the Old Maid that is circulating, or that when the music stops some of the players will find themselves unseated.

Or, to change the metaphor slightly, professional investment may be likened to those newspaper competitions in which the competitors have to pick out the six prettiest faces from a hundred photographs, the prize being awarded to the competitor whose choice most nearly corresponds to the average preferences of the competitors as a whole; so that each competitor has to pick, not those faces that he himself finds prettiest, but those that he thinks likeliest to catch the fancy of the other competitors, all of whom are looking at the problem from the same point of view. It is not a case of choosing those that, to the best of one's judgment, are really the prettiest, nor even those which average opinion genuinely thinks the prettiest. We have reached the third degree where we devote our intelligences to anticipating what average opinion expects the average opinion to be. And there are some, I believe, who practice the fourth, fifth, and higher degrees.

If the reader interjects that there must surely be large profits to be gained from the other players in the long run by a skilled individual who, unperturbed by the prevailing pastime, continues to purchase investments on the best genuine long-term expectations he can frame, he must be answered, first of all, that there are, indeed, such serious-minded individuals and that it makes a vast difference to an investment market whether or not they predominate in their influence over the game-players. But we must also add that there are several factors that jeopardise the predominance of such individuals in modern investment markets. Investment based on genuine long-term expectation is so difficult to-day as to be scarcely practicable. He who attempts it must surely lead much more laborious days and run greater risks than he who tries to guess better than the crowd how the crowd will behave; and, given equal intelligence, he may make more disastrous mistakes. . . . It needs *more* intelligence to defeat the forces of time and our ignorance of the future than to beat the gun. Moreover, life is not long enough—human nature desires quick results, there is a peculiar zest in making money quickly, and remoter gains are discounted by the average man at a very high rate. The game of professional investment is intolerably boring and overexacting to anyone who is entirely exempt from the gambling instinct; whilst he who has it must pay to this propensity the appropriate toll. Furthermore, an investor who proposes to ignore near-term market fluctuations needs greater resources for safety and must not operate on so large a scale, if at all, with borrowed money—a further reason for the higher return from the pastime to a given stock of intelligence and resources. Finally it is the long-term investor, he who most promotes the public interest, who will in practice come in for most criticism, wherever investment funds are managed by committees or boards or banks. For it is in the essence of his behaviour that he should be eccentric, unconventional, and rash in the eyes of average opinion. If he is successful, that will only confirm the general belief in his rashness; and if in the short run he is unsuccessful, which is very likely, he will not receive much mercy. Worldly wisdom teaches that it is better for reputation to fail conventionally than to succeed unconventionally. . . .

Keynes as an Instructor

As the result of . . . experience, I am clear that the idea of wholesale shifts is, for various reasons, impracticable and indeed undesirable. Most of those who attempt it sell too late and buy too late, and do both too often, incurring heavy expenses and developing too unsettled and speculative a state of mind, that, if it is widespread, has besides the grave social disadvantage of aggravating the scale of the fluctuations. I believe now that successful investment depends on three principles:

1. A careful selection of a few investments (or a few types of investment) having regard to their cheapness in relation to their probable actual and potential *intrinsic* value over a period of years ahead and in relation to alternative investments at the time;

2. A steadfast holding of these in fairly large units through thick and thin, perhaps for several years, until either they have fulfilled their promise or it is evident that they were purchased on a mistake;

3. A *balanced* investment position, i.e., a variety of risks in spite of individual holdings being large, and if possible opposed risks (e.g., a holding of gold shares amongst other equities, since they are likely to move in opposite directions when there are general fluctuations).

On the other hand, it is a mistake to sell a £1 note for 15s. in the hope of buying it back for 12s. 6d., and a mistake to refuse to buy a £1 note for 15s. on the ground that it cannot really be a £1 note (for there is abundant experience that £1 notes *can* be bought for 15s. at a time when they are expected by many people to fall to 12s. 6d.).

Another important rule is the avoidance of second-class safe investments, none of which can go up and a few of which are sure to go down. This is the main cause of the defeat of the average investor. The ideal investment portfolio is divided between the purchase of really secure future income (where future appreciation or depreciation will depend on the rate of interest) and equities that one believes to be capable of a *large* improvement to offset the fairly numerous cases that with the best skill in the world, will go wrong.

Part Seven

Tips, Rules, and Commandments

Barnum's Rules for Success in Business

PHINAEUS T. BARNUM

Phinaeus T. Barnum is best known for producing the world's first three-ring circus. He also wrote four books (including *The Life of P.T. Barnum*, from which these rules are taken), organized a model industrial community in East Bridgeport, Connecticut, and brought New York City its first hippopotamus.

· · ·

1. *Select the kind of business that suits your natural inclination and temperament.*   Some men are naturally mechanics; others have a strong aversion to any thing like machinery, and so on; one man has a natural taste for one occupation, and another for another. "I am glad that we do not all feel and think alike," said Dick Homespun, "for if we did, every body would think my gal, Sukey Snipes, the sweetest creature in all creation, and they would all be trying to court her at once."

I never could succeed as a merchant. I have tried it unsuccessfully several times. I never could be content with a fixed salary, for mine is a purely speculative disposition, while others are just the reverse; and therefore all should be careful to select those occupations that suit them best.

2. *Let your pledged word ever be sacred.*   Never promise to do a thing without performing it with the most rigid promptness. Nothing is more valuable to a man in business than the name of always doing as he agrees, and that to the moment. A strict adherence to this rule, gives a man the command of half the spare funds within the range of his acquaintance, and always encircles him with a host of friends who may be depended upon in almost any conceivable emergency.

3. *Whatever you do, do with all your might.*   Work at it if necessary early and late, in season and out of season, not leaving a stone unturned,

Reprinted from *The Life of P.T. Barnum* (New York: Redfield, 1885), Chapter 14, pp. 394–399.

and never deferring for a single hour that which can be done just as well *now*. The old proverb is full of truth and meaning, "Whatever is worth doing at all, is worth doing well." Many a man acquires a fortune by doing his business *thoroughly* while his neighbor remains poor for life because he only *half* does his business. Ambition, energy, industry, perseverance, are indispensable requisites for success in business.

4.   *Sobriety.*   Use no description of intoxicating drinks. As no man can succeed in business unless he has a *brain* to enable him to lay his plans, and *reason* to guide him in their execution, so, no matter how bountifully a man may be blessed with intelligence, if his brain is muddled, and his judgment warped by intoxicating drinks, it is impossible for him to carry on business successfully. How many good opportunities have passed never to return, while a man was sipping a "social glass" with his friend! How many foolish bargains have been made under the influence of the *nervine*, which temporarily makes its victim so *rich*! How many important chances have been put off until to-morrow, and thence for ever, because the wine-cup has thrown the system into a state of lassitude, neutralizing the energies so essential to success in business. The use of intoxicating drinks as a beverage is as much an infatuation as is the smoking of opium by the Chinese, and the former is quite as destructive to the success of the business man as the latter.

5.   *Let hope predominate, but be not too visionary.* Many persons are always kept poor, because they are too *visionary*. Every project looks to them like certain success, and therefore they keep changing from one business to another, always in hot water, always "under the harrow." The plan of "counting the chickens before they are hatched" is an error of ancient date, but it does not seem to improve by age.

6.   *Do not scatter your powers.*   Engage in one kind of business only, and stick to it faithfully until you succeed, or until you conclude to abandon it. A constant hammering on one nail, will generally drive it home at last, so that it can be clinched. When a man's undivided attention is centered on one object, his mind will constantly be suggesting improvements of value, which would escape him if his brain were occupied by a dozen different subjects at once. Many a fortune

has slipped through men's fingers by engaging in too many occupations at once.

7. *Engage proper employees.*   Never employ a man of bad habits, when one whose habits are good can be found to fill his situation. I have generally been extremely fortunate in having faithful and competent persons to fill the responsible situations in my business, and a man can scarcely be too grateful for such a blessing. When you find a man unfit to fill his station, either from incapacity or peculiarity of character or disposition, dispense with his services and do not drag out a miserable existence in the vain attempt to change his nature. It is utterly impossible to do so. "You cannot make a silk purse," etc. He was created for some other sphere. Let him find and fill it.

8. *Advertise your business. Do not hide your light under a bushel.* Whatever your occupation or calling may be, if it needs support from the public, *advertise* it thoroughly and efficiently, in some shape or other, that will arrest public attention. I freely confess that what success I have had in my life may fairly be attributed more to the public press than to nearly all other causes combined. There may possibly be occupations that do not require advertising, but I cannot well conceive what they are.

Men in business will sometimes tell you that they have tried advertising, and that it did not pay. This is only when advertising is done sparingly and grudgingly. Homoeopathic [sic] doses of advertising will not pay perhaps—it is like half a potion of physic, making the patient sick, but effecting nothing. Administer liberally, and the cure will be sure and permanent.

Some say, "they cannot afford to advertise"; they mistake—they cannot afford *not* to advertise. In this country, where everybody reads the newspapers, the man must have a thick skull who does not see that these are the cheapest and best medium through which he can speak to the public, where he is to find his customers. Put on the *appearance* of business, and generally the *reality* will follow. The farmer plants his seed, and while he is sleeping, his corn and potatoes are growing. So with advertising. While you are sleeping, or eating, or conversing with one set of customers, your advertisement is being read by hundreds and thousands of persons who never saw you, nor heard of your business, and never would, had it not been for your advertisement appearing in the newspapers.

9. *Avoid extravagance; and always live considerably within your income, if you can do so without absolute starvation!*   It needs no prophet to tell us that those who live fully up to their means, without any thought of a reverse in life, can never attain to a pecuniary independence.

Men and women accustomed to gratify every whim and caprice, will find it hard at first to cut down their various unnecessary expenses, and will feel it a great self-denial to live in a smaller house than they have been accustomed to, with less expensive furniture, less company, less costly clothing, a less number of balls, parties, theatre-goings, carriage ridings, pleasure excursions, cigar smokings, liquor-drinkings, etc., etc., etc.; but, after all, if they will try the plan of laying by a "nest-egg," or in other words, a small sum of money, after paying all expenses, they will be surprised at the pleasure to be derived from constantly adding to their little "pile," as well as from all the economical habits which follow in the pursuit of this peculiar pleasure.

The old suit of clothes, and the old bonnet and dress, will answer for another season; the Croton or spring water will taste better than champagne; a brisk walk will prove more exhilarating than a ride in the finest coach; a social family chat, an evening's reading in the family circle, or an hour's play of "hunt the slipper" and "blind man's buff," will be far more pleasant than a fifty or a five hundred dollar party, when the reflection on the *difference in cost* is indulged in by those who begin to know the *pleasures of saving.*

Thousands of men are kept poor, and tens of thousands are made so after they have acquired quite sufficient to support them well through life, in consequence of laying their plans of living on too expensive a platform. Some families in this country expend twenty thousand dollars per annum, and some much more, and would scarcely know how to live on a less sum.

Prosperity is a more severe ordeal than adversity, especially sudden prosperity. "Easy come easy go," is an old and true proverb. *Pride,* when permitted full sway, is the great undying cankerworm which gnaws the very vitals of a man's worldly possessions, let them be small or great, hundreds or millions. Many persons, as they begin to prosper, immediately commence expending for luxuries, until in a short time their expenses swallow up their income, and they become ruined in their ridiculous attempts to keep up appearances, and make a "sensation."

10. *Do not depend upon others.* Your success must depend upon your own individual exertions. Trust not to the assistance of friends; but learn that every man must be the architect of his own fortune.

With proper attention to the foregoing rules, and such observation as a man of sense will pick up in his own experience, the road to competence will not, I think, usually be found a difficult one.

The Time-Tested Maxims
of the Templeton Touch

WILLIAM PROCTOR

John Templeton—with deep faith, a drive for excellence, and a habit of goal setting—has achieved a remarkable record in investment management. Here are his maxims for investors.

• • •

These are the twenty-two key guiding principles that Templeton says have enabled him to become one of the world's greatest living investors. These points are expressed in his own words, and they serve as a kind of summary statement of the Templeton Touch. Some of these have been discussed in depth in previous pages; others are relatively new nuggets of wisdom; all are maxims that the savviest investors should keep in mind as they decide where to place their money.

1. For all long-term investors, there is only one objective—"maximum total real return after taxes."
2. Achieving a good record takes much study and work, and is a lot harder than most people think.
3. It is impossible to produce a superior performance unless you do something different from the majority.
4. The time of maximum pessimism is the best time to buy, and the time of maximum optimism is the best time to sell.
5. To put "Maxim 4" in somewhat different terms, in the stock market the only way to get a bargain is to buy what most investors are selling.
6. To buy when others are despondently selling and to sell when

others are greedily buying requires the greatest fortitude, even while offering the greatest reward.

7. Bear markets have always been temporary. Share prices turn upward from one to twelve months before the bottom of the business cycle.

8. If a particular industry or type of security becomes popular with investors, that popularity will always prove temporary and, when lost, won't return for many years.

9. In the long run, the stock market indexes fluctuate around the long-term upward trend of earnings per share.

10. In free-enterprise nations, the earnings on stock market indexes fluctuate around the replacement book value of the shares of the index.

11. If you buy the same securities as other people, you will have the same results as other people.

12. The time to buy a stock is when the short-term owners have finished their selling, and the time to a sell a stock is often when short-term owners have finished their buying.

13. Share prices fluctuate much more widely than values. Therefore, index funds will never produce the best total return performance.

14. Too many investors focus on "outlook" and "trend." Therefore, more profit is made by focusing on value.

15. If you search worldwide, you will find more bargains and better bargains than by studying only one nation. Also, you gain the safety of diversification.

16. The fluctuation of share prices is roughly proportional to the square root of the price.

17. The time to sell an asset is when you have found a much better bargain to replace it.

18. When any method for selecting stocks becomes popular, then switch to unpopular methods. As has been suggested in "Maxim 3," too many investors can spoil any share-selection method or any market-timing formula.

19. Never adopt permanently any type of asset or any selection method. Try to stay flexible, open-minded, and skeptical. Long-

term top results are achieved only by changing from popular to unpopular the types of securities you favor and your methods of selection.

20. The skill factor in selection is largest for the common-stock part of your investments.
21. The best performance is produced by a person, not a committee.
22. If you begin with prayer, you can think more clearly and make fewer stupid mistakes.

If you own one stock and are considering switching to a second, the second stock should be at least 50 percent more valuable than the first one for the switch to be worthwhile.

On Speculating Successfully

PHILIP L. CARRET

Phil Carret is still investing—successfully—an amazing 65 years after he wrote The Art of Speculation, from which these rules are taken. He will soon celebrate his 100th birthday; he continues to work actively as an investment manager.

. . .

Twelve Commandments for Speculators

As in any business there are standards of management that cannot be disregarded by the business man, so in speculative investment it is possible to formulate certain rules that must be followed intelligently if success is to be attained. The speculator will never be a suc-cess if he attempts to follow any set of rules blindly. There will always be exceptions, he must apply his intelligence keenly in any given situation. . . .

Twelve precepts for the speculative investor may be stated as follows:

1. Never hold fewer than ten different securities covering five different fields of business.
2. At least once in six months reappraise every security held.
3. Keep at least half the total fund in income-producing securities.
4. Consider yield the least important factor in analyzing any stock.
5. Be quick to take losses, reluctant to take profits.
6. Never put more than 25% of a given fund into securities about which detailed information is not readily and regularly available.

Excerpted from *The Art of Speculation* (Burlington, Vermont, 1979; originally published 1930).

7. Avoid "inside information" as you would the plague.
8. Seek facts diligently, advice never.
9. Ignore mechanical formulas for valuing securities.
10. When stocks are high, money rates rising, business prosperous, at least half a given fund should be placed in short-term bonds.
11. Borrow money sparingly and only when stocks are low, money rates low or falling, and business depressed.
12. Set aside a moderate proportion of available funds for the purchase of long-term options on stocks of promising companies whenever available.

Minimizing Chance

The first rule given suggests a minimum standard of diversification. It is just as important in speculation as in investment that a given fund be divided among several baskets. Diversification accomplishes three important results for the speculator. It minimizes the factor of chance, allows for an occasional error of judgment, and minimizes the importance of the unknown factor. As in every other field of human activity, chance plays its part in speculation. An earthquake or some other unforeseeable "act of God" may make a mockery of the best-laid plans. No such accident will affect all securities equally, however, and diversification affords the best possible protection against the effect of accidental factors. Errors of judgment are likewise inescapable. Even the most astute speculator is likely to arrive at wrong conclusions from the data in hand 20 percent to 25 percent of the time. If he stakes his entire fund on one security about which his conclusions are wrong, he will suffer heavy loss. On the other hand, a 25 percent margin of error in judgment will not seriously affect the speculator who has scattered his commitments among ten different securities.

The most important factor affecting the value of any single security at any given moment is the unknown factor. Not even the president of a company knows all the facts affecting the intrinsic value of its securities. The speculator must allow a considerable margin for the unknown, even in the case of companies that make frequent reports of their condition and make an honest attempt to keep their stockholders and the public fully informed regarding their affairs. By sufficient diversification these unknown factors affecting individual securities cancel each other. The loss that is due to the unknown factor in one case will be counterbalanced by an unexpectedly large profit in another.

A Psychological Difficulty

It is conventional advice to the investor that he should go over his holdings in search of weak spots at least annually. The speculator will naturally watch his holdings much more closely. The second rule means something more than a mere scanning of his list of commitments and calculation of the paper profit or loss that they show. It means that the speculator should seek so far as possible to reanalyze each commitment from a detached standpoint. Psychologically this is a very difficult thing to do, to consider dispassionately a venture in which he has already risked his funds. Nevertheless, the speculator should make a determined effort to do just this. If he has 100 shares of a given stock, for example, which is selling at 90, he should disregard entirely the price that he paid for it and ask himself this question: "If I had $9,000 cash today and wished to purchase some security, would I choose that stock in preference to every one of the thousands of other securities available to me?" If the answer is strongly in the negative, he should sell the stock. It should make not the slightest difference in this connection whether the stock cost 50 or 130. That is a fact which is entirely beside the point, though the average individual will give it considerable weight.

Patience Essential

It is not suggested that the speculator undertake this process of reanalysis much more frequently than once in six months. If he tries to do it oftener, he is likely to fall into the evil and usually fatal habit of frequently switching his commitments. One of the essential qualifications of the successful speculator is patience. It may take years for the market in a given stock to reflect in any large degree the values that are being accumulated behind it. Twenty years of plowing earnings back into property were followed in the case of the Southern Railway by an advance in its common stock from 25 to 120 within two years. Careful analysis may detect values far in excess of market price behind a given stock. The market may not reflect these values until the combination of a bull market and a change in dividend policy supplies the necessary impetus. Even in a bull market a sound stock may lag behind the procession in a discouraging manner for weeks or months. The trader who is always looking for "action" in the market will usually jump from one stock to another during the course of a bull movement only to find at the end that he has made far less money than he would have made by putting his money in 10 or 12 carefully chosen issues at the beginning and holding them.

What I Learned from the Depression

DEAN MATHEY

Dean Mathey was a partner in Dillon Read, headed the Empire Trust Company, and from the 1920s to the 1940s was the remarkably successful chairman of the investment committee at Princeton. In 1966, he privately printed *Fifty Years of Wall Street*, from which these lessons are excerpted.

. . .

1.   That once in about every 7 to 10 years there is a period of excessive general speculation culminating in a severe panic or depression when the man that is borrowing money is at a great disadvantage and he who has ready cash stands like a tower, four square to the ill winds that blow.

2.   Extreme situations do not last, no matter what the apparent justification. No ladder is high enough to reach to Heaven. While we may have "new eras," old laws will still operate.

3.   Avoid commitments, particularly of the delayed variety, they are more insidious. These birds may be depended upon to come home to roost when they are least welcome. Also, be definite about commitments made to you by others. When the storm comes, misunderstandings are so easy and so natural. What a joy a good clear record is in such a predicament!

4.   Both in 1920 and 1929 the so-called "big fellows" in general said everything was o.k. But if the big fellows in general thought otherwise the stage could not be set for the unexpected. Panics occur because the leaders themselves have lost the way. And panics on Wall Street are notoriously periodic.

Excerpted from *Fifty Years of Wall Street* (Princeton, New Jersey, 1966), pp. 67–68, by permission of Dean Mathey, Jr., David Mathey, and Macdonald Mathey.

5.   Never borrow money, without continuously reviewing and questioning your ability to pay it back under the worst conditions. Never borrow short-term money on unmarketable collateral.

6.   It's right to be an optimist, but be prepared for the worst.

7.   Make a practice of not giving GRATUITOUS ADVICE ABOUT THE PURCHASE OF SECURITIES.

8.   People borrow money in good times and pay it back in bad times—just the opposite of what they should do.

9.   The public are just as blind to recognizing the bottom of a depression as they are in recognizing the top of the boom. While there is no ladder that reaches to Heaven, the ladder that reaches all the way down to Hell in a country like America is just as fantastic.

Footnote to 1966 Printing

This memorandum was made around 1934 and 1935 after the storm was over. It was a soul-searching review on my part of what my thoughts were on the agonizing experiences I had been through during the depression. It is published just as it was written, without amendments or explanations I might make today.

The Roy Neuberger Almanac

ROY R. NEUBERGER

Roy Neuberger has been successfully—and enthusiastically—investing and trading for two or three times as many years as some of the profession's current leaders have been in business. Here are some of his beliefs and observations.

．．．

I have set down in random fashion on the pages that follow a variety of thoughts, ideas, and loose principles that have served me well. In my last forty-four years of buying and selling securities, I have used these tools to my advantage. If you gain useful knowledge in the pursuit of profit as well as enjoyment from these comments, I shall be more than content.

Rule #1: *Be flexible.* My philosophy has necessarily changed from time to time because of events and because of mistakes. My views change as economic, political, and technological changes occur both on and now off our planet. It is imperative that you be willing to change your thoughts to meet new conditions.

Rule #2: *Take your temperament into account.* Recognize whether you are by nature very speculative or just the opposite: Fearful—timid of taking risks. But in any event—

Rule #3: *Be broad gauged.* Diversify your investments, make sure that some of your principal is kept safe, and try to increase your income as well as your capital.

Rule #4: *Always remember there are many ways to skin a cat!* Ben Graham did it by understanding basic values, Ben Smith did it by knowing when and how to sell short, T. Rowe Price appreciated the

importance of the growth of new industries (like mobile homes); each was successful in his own way. But to be successful, remember to
    Rule #5: *Be skeptical.*   To repeat a few well-worn useful phrases:
        A. Dig For Yourself.
        B. Be From Missouri.
        C. There's a sucker born every minute. (Compliments of
           P.T. Barnum). . . .

Psychology

Don't underrate the importance of psychology in the stock market. When people buy they are more anxious to buy than the seller, and vice versa. So many things go into the buy or sell decision besides economic statistics or security analysis. A bad (or good) buy or sell decision may be made merely because of a headache.

Some people try to guess what the crowd will do, believing they can be swept along in a favorable current. But this is dangerous. The crowd may be very late in acting. Suppose it's an institutional crowd. Sometimes they over-influence each other and are the victims of their own habits.

Personally, I like to be contrary. When things look awful, I become optimistic. When the crowd and the world looks most rosy, I like to be a seller, perhaps prematurely, but usually profitably. . . .

Fads

There seem always to have been fads in Wall Street. For some reason or other the move in Stutz Bearcat autos was a fad in the 1920s. Conglomerates were a fad in the 1960s when reported earnings were often helped by some athletic bookkeeping. In any case, the criteria for purchase of any substantial amount of stock should remain on solid grounds: 1—good products, 2—a necessary product, 3—an honest management, 4—honest reporting. The investment can always be helped by a bit of luck, but fads come and go. Beware.

Falling in Love

One should fall in love with ideas, with people, or with idealism based on the possibilities that exist in this adventuresome world. In my book, the last thing to fall in love with is a particular security. It is after all just a sheet of paper indicating a part ownership in a corporation and its use is purely mercenary. The fact that a number of people have been extremely fortunate in the past by falling in love with something that went their way is not necessarily the proof it will always be that way. Stay in love with a security until the security gets overvalued, then let somebody else fall in love.

Characteristics for Success as Aggressive Investors

DOUGLAS H. BELLEMORE

Douglas Bellemore taught investment for 40 years at New York University's night school. After 50 years of investing savings from Navy pay and teaching—and investment counseling—he put his money where his mouth was, investing all he had in General Motors at $32–$34 (on a scale) because it met all of his tests for a superior investment. It then more than doubled. Here, he identifies the characteristics required for success as an aggressive investor.

• • •

Not all investors have the innate or acquired personal characteristics that are mandatory to succeed in building a portfolio of common stocks that will significantly outperform the market over the years.

What are these traits required for success as aggressive investors? Basically they are five:

1. Patience.   The aggressive investor should not expect quick results although occasionally this occurs. Success depends, in large measure, on the ability to select undervalued situations not presently recognized by the majority of investors and to wait for expected developments to provide capital gains that may only come after several years. After the investment commitment has been made, he must calmly hold common stocks, perhaps five to eight years. Individual investment in this sense is not unlike corporate investment, in which management must wait in order to reap benefits of new investment programs. Results cannot be expected to come quickly. In fact, many of the personal qualities for successful business management are the same as those for an aggressive investor.

From Douglas H. Bellemore, *The Strategic Investor* (Omaha, Nebraska, 1963), 23–25, by permission of Simmons-Boardman Publishing Corp.

2. Courage. The investor must have solid convictions and the courage and confidence emanating from them—that is, courage, at times, to ignore those who disagree. Resembling the courage displayed by top corporate management, it is tantamount to willingness to make and to accept responsibility for difficult decisions. Decision-making ability, which is the key to success in business, is vital to success in investing. Although not all decisions will be correct, a high majority must be.

Decisions should be made only after careful analysis of facts and consideration of recommendations of others. The final decision may be at variance with such recommendations. But it is this willingness to differ and to accept responsibility that distinguishes the top executive and the top investor, assuming, of course, judgments are right more often than wrong.

3. Intelligence. To realize success, the aggressive investor must possess average intelligence, but by no means does he need to be a genius. Intelligence alone, however, is by no means the only requisite for success. Common sense—impossible to test except by experience— is equally important in judgment decisions. Many highly intelligent investors have had poor investment records because they lacked common sense; i.e., the down-to-earth, practical ability to evaluate a situation.

4. Emotional stability. Although akin to patience this trait is broader in scope. Initially, it is needed to prevent the investor from being engulfed in waves of optimism and pessimism that periodically sweep over Wall Street. Moreover, it is required to separate the facts from the entangled web of human emotions. Bernard Baruch said once that most facts reach Wall Street through "a curtain of human emotions," and even sophisticated professionals in Wall Street find difficulty in distinguishing fact from emotion.

5. Hard work. To be successful an aggressive investor must do thorough research which requires considerable time and effort. He must be knowledgeable about the company in which he considers making an investment, the industry, the position of the company in the industry, and the place and future of that industry in the economy as a whole. Furthermore, he must do considerable financial analysis for which he

must have some general knowledge of statements. Although not on the advanced level of a professional security analyst, he must adequately determine relative financial strength and earning power and project future earnings. The fundamentals of accounting and corporation finance can readily be self-taught for these purposes.

Brokers, of course, through the services of their research departments are a great help in stock analysis and will do much of the work of ferreting out facts; nevertheless, the investor can never escape judging the facts himself, and this takes knowledge.

6. **Willingness to sacrifice the investment protection of diversification.** Diversification based on the insurance principle can considerably reduce investment risks, although it cannot be achieved haphazardly. Nor can diversification be substituted for a certain amount of investment judgment, although a portfolio large enough to be distributed rather evenly among New York Stock Exchange stocks or all major industrial stocks would, for all practical purposes, reduce risk to that inherent in common stocks as a group. But diversification, say, among 20 or 30 stocks, cannot substitute for investment judgment.

While the conservative investor relies extensively upon diversification to minimize risks, his aggressive counterpart must sacrifice wide diversification if his portfolio is significantly to outperform the general market. Although wide diversification reduces risks by offsetting mediocre selections with good ones, it also reduces substantially the profit or capital gain potential of a portfolio. Just as no speculator ever amassed a fortune while following the principle of diversification, no investor who expects his portfolio to outperform the averages significantly and to provide major capital gains can practice broad diversification.

Finally, each investor must ask himself whether he meets all the qualifications that have been discussed for successful investing. Failure to meet any of these makes it probable that by following an aggressive approach to investment, the investor will have a poorer record than if he adhered to the tenets held by the conservative investor. Should the investor decide to become conservative, he will at least have the satisfaction of knowing he should do considerably better than the unqualified investor who attempts to pursue aggressive tactics.

There are no short cuts to successful investment for aggressive investors. To earn really sizable capital gains requires substantially more effort, patience, courage, and intelligence than that required of the conservative investor.

It requires much more on all of these counts. As in other fields, the investor cannot get something for nothing. Once the investor has selected his own investment classification, he must pursue adamantly the principles of his particular group.

Name Index

Subject Index